A TEACHER'S

Excellence IN EVERY Classroom

Creating Support Systems *for* Student Success

JOHN R. WINK

Solution Tree | Press

555 North Morton Street
Bloomington, IN 47404
800.733.6786 (toll free) / 812.336.7700
FAX: 812.336.7790

email: info@SolutionTree.com
SolutionTree.com

Visit **go.SolutionTree.com/instruction** to download the free reproducibles in this book.

Printed in the United States of America

Library of Congress Cataloging-in-Publication Data

Names: Wink, John R., author.
Title: A teacher's guide to excellence in every classroom : creating support systems for student success / John R. Wink.
Description: Bloomington, IN : Solution Tree Press, [2019] | Includes bibliographical references and index.
Identifiers: LCCN 2019023396 (print) | LCCN 2019023397 (ebook) | ISBN 9781947604797 (paperback) | ISBN 9781947604803 (ebook)
Subjects: LCSH: Teacher effectiveness. | Teacher-student relationships. | Academic achievement. | School improvement programs.
Classification: LCC LB1025.3 W565 2019 (print) | LCC LB1025.3 (ebook) | DDC 371.14/4--dc23
LC record available at https://lccn.loc.gov/2019023396
LC ebook record available at https://lccn.loc.gov/2019023397

Solution Tree
Jeffrey C. Jones, CEO
Edmund M. Ackerman, President

Solution Tree Press
President and Publisher: Douglas M. Rife
Associate Publisher: Sarah Payne-Mills
Art Director: Rian Anderson
Managing Production Editor: Kendra Slayton
Senior Production Editor: Christine Hood
Content Development Specialist: Amy Rubenstein
Copy Editor: Jessi Finn
Proofreader: Kate St. Ives
Editorial Assistant: Sarah Ludwig

Acknowledgments

This book wouldn't have been possible without the support of so many people. First and foremost, I want to express my deepest appreciation and love to my wonderful wife, Carolyn, for her love and constant support throughout this process. For twenty-six years, she has continuously pushed me to excel as a husband, father, and leader, and for that I am eternally grateful and blessed beyond measure. I love you! Next, I want to thank my children, Hunter, Hannah, Holly, and Haley. You inspire me to become a better father every day, and watching your journey into the young adults you are today has been the greatest gift in my life.

Professionally, I am most thankful for the amazing educators and leaders that have helped me become a better leader along my journey. First, I would like to thank the board of trustees, leaders, teachers, and staff members of Carthage Independent School District. Your love of children and dedication to making every student a champion is inspiring. I would also like to thank the amazing educators and board members of Blue Ridge Independent School District, who transformed an ordinary district into a school of excellence. Specifically, I can't thank Matthew Todd, Shawn Harris, Dr. Chris Miller, and Phillip Lentz enough for the strong leadership, friendship, and trust they gave me during my time there.

Finally, I would like to thank the powerful educators I have had the pleasure to learn from over my life in Tatum, Gilmer, Hallsville, and Longview Independent School Districts. Throughout my career, countless educators showed me the way, gave selflessly of themselves for the benefit for all students, and served as a catalyst for positive change. I thank you for your influence on my life.

Solution Tree Press would like to thank the following reviewers:

Jennifer Evans
Principal
Burnham School
Cicero, Illinois

Amanda Mahr
Instructional Coach
Pleasant Hill, Iowa

Adrienne Paone
Instructional Coach and English Teacher
Pedro Menendez High School
St. Augustine, Florida

Regan Porter
Core Teacher
Pioneer Middle School
Tustin, California

Brad Randmark
Assistant Principal
Burnham School
Cicero, Illinois

Visit **go.SolutionTree.com/instruction** to download the free reproducibles in this book.

Table of Contents

Reproducible pages are in italics.

About the Author

John R. Wink serves as the superintendent of Carthage Independent School District in Carthage, Texas. From 2016 to2019, John served as superintendent of Blue Ridge Independent School District, where in just three years the successful strategies in this book transformed a small district with average academic performance into a highly successful district that earned the highest ratings in state accountability. From 2014 to 2016, John served as the assistant superintendent of curriculum, instruction, and assessment for the Tatum Independent School District in Tatum, Texas. During his time in Tatum, students and teachers grew tremendously in their performance on standardized testing and in college and career preparation. Prior to that, John served as principal at Gilmer Elementary School (2011–2014), where he led the school through improvement status to academic distinction. As principal of Hallsville Middle School (2002–2008), he led the school from acceptable to exemplary status in four years; and as principal of Hallsville High School (2008–2011), he led the school to become one of the top academic high schools in Texas.

John earned a bachelor of music in vocal performance from Stephen F. Austin State University, a master of education administration from Texas A&M University–Texarkana, and his superintendent's certificate from Texas A&M University–Commerce. Prior to his work as an administrator, John was the choir director at Longview High School in Longview, Texas, from 1996 to 2002, where numerous students earned membership into the Texas All-State Choir. His choirs earned numerous first-division and sweepstakes honors. John and his wife, Carolyn, have four children: Hunter, Hannah, Holly, and Haley.

To learn more about John's work, visit LeadLearning With John Wink (http://leadlearner2012.blogspot.com), www.johnwink.com, and www.facebook.com/leadlearner2012, or follow him @johnwink90 on Twitter and Instagram.

To book John R. Wink for professional development, contact pd@SolutionTree.com.

Introduction

The best thing about being a teacher is that it matters. The hardest thing about being a teacher is that it matters every day.

—Todd Whitaker

Teachers are the backbone of democracy. Without their influence, students would not develop the knowledge and skills necessary to realize their right to become productive contributors to society. If you consider the history of the United States, it seems each generation has experienced a better life than the generations before. Advancing technologies, automation, and the simplifications to virtually every aspect of life have made many people's lives more comfortable and enjoyable, and I can't help but think that this is, in part, due to the constantly improving education that students receive from amazing teachers each and every year.

With that said, the future of the United States is sitting in our classrooms, and we possess an immense responsibility to meet students' ever-changing and increasing needs. Make no mistake, each year, educators find new and innovative ways to become more effective at creating a more prepared workforce, but each generation of students needs teachers more than the generation that preceded it. Students depend on teachers more than ever to guarantee their future success. While our citizenry becomes wealthier, more students come to school each each year lacking adequate financial supports. From 2010 to 2013, the number of American students on free and reduced lunch increased from 38 percent to 48 percent (National Center for Education Statistics, 2016). That means almost half our students are experiencing financial hardships that have the potential to impede learning.

Today's teachers no longer just deliver content. They counsel and console students who have difficulties at home. They mentor students who lack the proper training, manners, and etiquette to succeed as model citizens. They provide a shoulder to cry on and celebrate big and small wins for students each day in unique and innovate ways. They buy food and school supplies for students with money out of their own pocket, and they do this because they know students need all these supports before they can begin the arduous task of learning. Yes, teachers do a whole lot more than teach.

They know that what they do matters, and that what they do makes a difference for students now and in the future. What matters most is not the recognition teachers receive for their hard work and heavy workload but the impact that teachers make on every student, every day. They are changing our country for the better one student at a time, one day at a time.

Overview of the Book

I wrote this book with the explicit intent not to add one more thing to teachers' already-maximized workload, but to help all teachers reduce the redundant, mundane, and unnecessary actions that can at times overwhelm even the most seasoned veteran. While some of the information may not be new to readers, I have packaged it in a way that will help them prioritize the essential steps to systemically and thoughtfully design the classroom so it meets the unique and diverse needs of all students. To support this approach to classroom design, I have included research and best practices from the field's leading education researchers.

While the intended audience is teachers, this book also gives instructional coaches, mentors, and administrators the necessary tools and information to support every teacher in his or her quest for professional growth. My hope is that all teachers (and those who support them) can find inspiration in this book to remove low-impact and ineffective practices from their routines. Furthermore, I hope this book renews teachers' faith in their power to change the world one student at a time, because I know that teachers do that every single day for an awful lot of students.

I believe all students can learn at high levels, and if you believe the same, then this book is for you. We must remember that how much every student learns depends on our abilities as educators to meet all students where they are and create meaningful learning experiences that guide them to discover their potential. To help every student achieve excellence, we must realize that the conditions and supports for learning that we create are just as important as, if not more important than, the art of teaching.

Chapter 1 establishes the groundwork for these supports. It outlines the research that shows why highly effective teachers have the biggest impact on student achievement using the research of Robert Marzano, John Hattie, and Eric Jensen. This chapter introduces the graduated series of steps teachers take to create a classroom of excellence, the Hierarchy of Student Excellence. Modeled after Abraham Maslow's Hierarchy of Needs, the Hierarchy of Student Excellence graphically represents the levels of academic skills students must master, in order, to achieve success (see figure I.1).

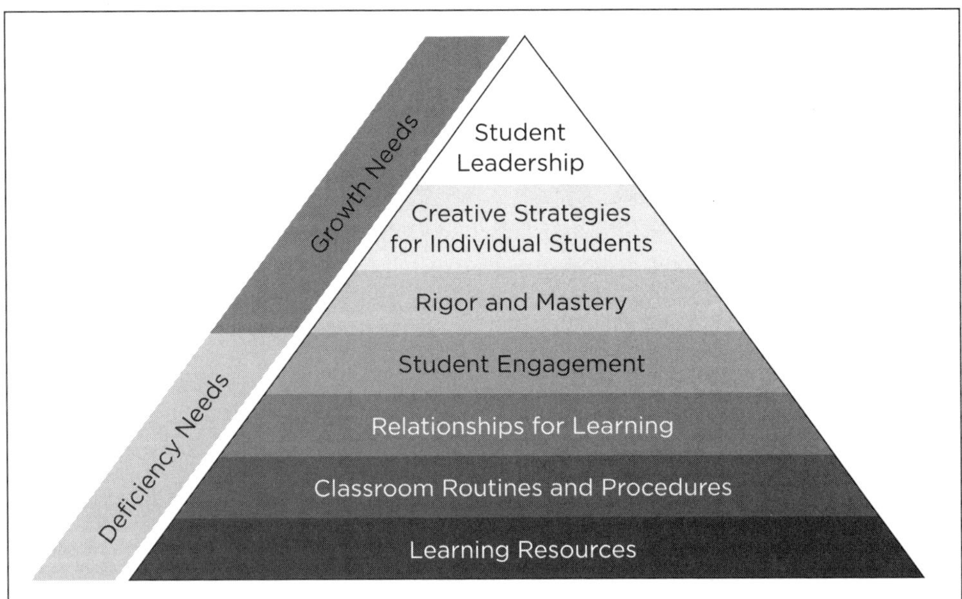

Figure I.1: Hierarchy of Student Excellence.

To support students in their quest to find excellence at each level, chapter 1 provides readers with an overview of the Student Excellence Support System, which summarizes how teachers can anticipate and respond to student failure. This three-step system—teacher collaboration, classwide supports, and individualized student supports—mirrors response to intervention (RTI), a multitiered approach to student support in which teachers provide Tier 1 support for all students, Tier 2 support for smaller groups of students who need additional support, and Tier 3 support for individual students who don't respond well to Tier 1 and Tier 2.

Each of the remaining chapters (2–8) focuses specifically on each level within the Hierarchy of Student Excellence, beginning with the first level, learning resources, and concluding the with uppermost level, student leadership. Each chapter follows a similar structure, opening with a brief scenario about a student who is experiencing a hypothetical struggle in that level. The chapter then describes what student excellence looks like at that level and how great teachers prepare for, deliver, and reflect on instruction related to that level of growth.

As previously noted, the Student Excellence Support System leverages the power of professional learning communities (PLCs) through the responsive nature of response to intervention. Combined, these two structures give teachers the tools they require to identify the expectations that all students need in order to learn. These structures will help you determine where students struggle in their learning, and they will guide you to create a targeted plan for ensuring *all* students overcome the barriers that inhibit their learning. The following three levels of support help teachers ensure they are reaching every student.

1. **Teacher team collaboration:** Teacher team collaboration helps teachers who share students or curriculum to create aligned expectations for student success in each hierarchy level. This allows expectations for student learning behaviors and teacher responses to students to be high, tight, and consistent in every classroom.
2. **Classwide supports:** Once teachers have collaborated to develop consistency across classrooms, individual teachers can take the team's expectations and personalize them to meet the the needs of students through supports they can implement with all students in their individual classrooms.
3. **Individualized student supports:** This step is reserved for students who fail to respond to classwide supports. In this step, teachers create a targeted and prescriptive plan to address the student's individual needs at the hierarchy level that presents the greatest difficulty.

I support this structure with research as well as strategies I have seen implemented in schools that I have led and schools that have generated outstanding results in student achievement. My work with Blue Ridge Independent School District is a testament to the success of these strategies. In 2019, it earned the highest state rating in student achievement because every teacher designed his or her classroom to align with the Hierarchy of Student Excellence and to the other teachers they worked with. The teachers spoke a common language about what they expected from their students, their instruction, and their colleagues. As a result, students grew socially, behaviorally, and academically in a school environment where all teachers were deeply committed to each other's and their students' success.

This book provides proven strategies to help you prepare for, deliver, and reflect on your effectiveness as a teacher and on how to build a collaborative culture among your peers that will yield a strong, consistent, and aligned learning environment in every classroom for your team's students.

Conclusion

In a school's quest for learning and growth in every student, teachers possess an ever-increasing responsibility to guarantee every student's success. Sometimes teachers can get overwhelmed with waves of multiplying expectations and demands. The effectiveness of teacher responses to student failure are the keys to substantial growth in student achievement. If teachers can hone their skills in order to grow each and every day in their craft, work with peers as a unified team, and support one another to ensure that every student learns, excellence in every classroom is within their reach.

I encourage readers to view this book as a guide. No matter your level of experience, you will have students who experience failure for a variety of reasons. I hope that as you discover struggling students in your classes, you will see this book as a resource to not only diagnose problems but also find viable solutions and ideas that can motivate students to overcome their obstacles through targeted and specific supports.

I am honored that you have chosen this book. I hope that you find lots of great ideas to meet the needs of all students, especially those who challenge you the most. The work you do may be overwhelming at times, but I know you can help every student learn, grow, and excel. You were born to become an excellence maker and a game changer for students. I believe this book can bring forth your confidence, your excellence, and your amazing abilities to inspire and empower every student to believe in his or her excellence as well.

CHAPTER 1

Teachers: Our Most Powerful Resource

When professionals know better, they have an obligation to do better.

—Richard DuFour, Rebecca DuFour, Robert Eaker, Thomas Many, & Mike Mattos

Education and the educators who serve students have shaped the United States in accomplishing goals that the country's forefathers couldn't even fathom. Progress and advancements in every industry would not exist without an education system that reaches every student and supports their academic success and growth.

U.S. leaders continue to believe that education was and still is the central mechanism for success and advancement, and presidents from the United States' infancy to the present have gone to great lengths to prioritize education. Following are just a few quotes about education from U.S. presidents, which education blogger Aric Mitchell (n.d.) has gathered.

- "The best means of forming a . . . virtuous, and happy people will be found in the right education of youth. Without this foundation, every other means, in my opinion, must fail." —George Washington, first U.S. president
- "There are two educations. One should teach us how to make a living and the other how to live." —John Adams, second U.S. president
- "Learned institutions ought to be favorite objects with every free people. They throw that light over the public mind which is the best security against crafty and dangerous encroachments on the public liberty." —James Madison, fourth U.S. president

- "Upon the subject of education, not presuming to dictate any plan or system respecting it, I can only say that I view it as the most important subject which we as a people may be engaged in. That everyone may receive at least a moderate education appears to be an objective of vital importance." —Abraham Lincoln, sixteenth U.S. president
- "Knowledge—that is, education in its true sense—is our best protection against unreasoning prejudice and panic-making fear, whether engendered by special interest, illiberal minorities, or panic-stricken leaders." —Franklin D. Roosevelt, thirty-second U.S. president
- "Let us think of education as the means of developing our greatest abilities, because in each of us there is a private hope and dream which, fulfilled, can be translated into benefit for everyone and greater strength for our nation." —John F. Kennedy, thirty-fifth U.S. president
- "Think about every problem, every challenge, we face. The solution to each starts with education." —George H. W. Bush, forty-first U.S. president

It's evident that education has been a priority, but as we prepare to enter the third decade of the 21st century, extraordinary debate continues about the role that education and the teachers in the trenches now play. With debates about public versus private education, the need for standardized testing, and the case for standards-based grading, educators are caught in the middle, and therefore, the profession's collective future holds in the balance while arguments get more divisive.

To define the vision of education in the 21st century, let's look to the thoughts of Barack Obama, forty-fourth president of the United States:

> When it comes to developing the high standards we need, it's time to stop working against our teachers and start working with them. Teachers don't go into education to get rich. They don't go into education because they don't believe in their children. They want their children to succeed, but we've got to give them the tools. Invest in early childhood education. Invest in our teachers and our children will succeed. (Mitchell, n.d.)

In the 21st century, educators still believe that they hold the future in the palms of their hands each and every day, and they will be the deciding factor in whether the United States continues to lead on the world stage. Educators are a precious resource, and we, as educators, must own our moral imperative and mission to guarantee every student learns at high levels and graduates from high school with not one foot but both feet firmly planted on the college and career pathway.

This chapter takes a closer look at the critical evidence that supports the power teachers have to influence the trajectory of a student's life. It begins by examining research regarding teachers' impact on student learning based on evidence of their effectiveness. It then offers teachers a clear roadmap for a system that supports students at every stage of their learning with the Hierarchy of Student Excellence. Finally, the chapter outlines the Student Excellence Support System. This framework provides teachers with collaborative structures, systems of classwide supports, and individualized student supports to help all students learn.

A Teacher's Powerful Influence

As teachers, we must ask ourselves the question, "How much can students learn?" Robert Marzano's (2003) research indicates that the answer to this question depends on one variable—teacher effectiveness. Marzano's (2003) book *Classroom Management That Works* illustrates the powerful influence on student success that teachers possess. Marzano's meta-analysis of teacher influence on student achievement in grades K–12 (see figure 1.1) concludes that all students can learn without any adult support. In fact, they can mature 6 percentile points in one calendar year, simply through the daily experiences with effective instruction.

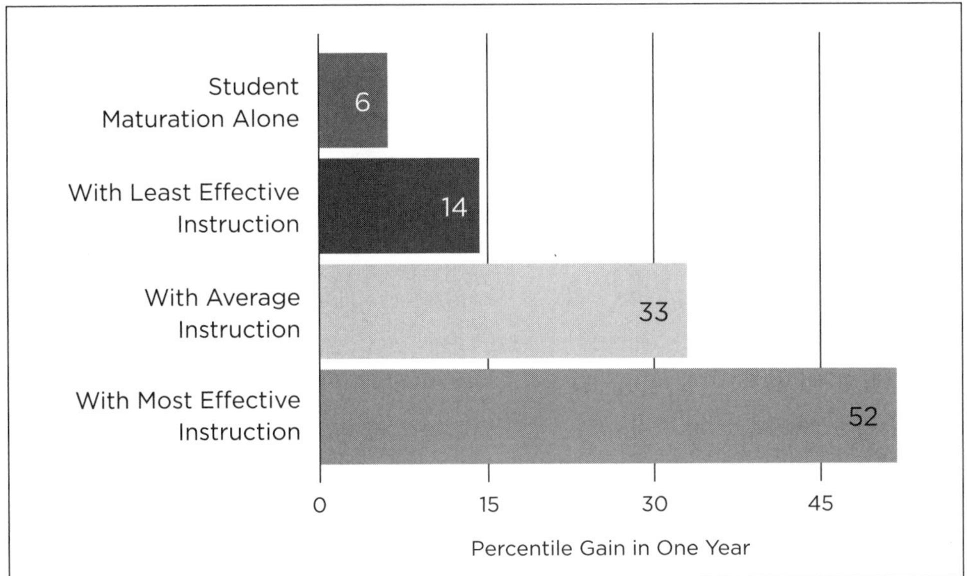

Source: Adapted from Marzano, 2003, p. 2.

Figure 1.1: Teacher impact on student achievement.

The research shows that if a student had access to the least effective instruction, the student would only mature 14 percentile points in one year. To put it in perspective, ineffective instruction would cause the student to regress greatly in one calendar year by not making a year's growth in learning. Conversely, if the student were guaranteed the most effective instruction, he or she would mature a whopping 52 percentile points in one year. In other words, the student would gain well over one year's growth simply because of highly effective instruction.

That leaves average instruction. While there is no exact research noted, if you averaged least effective and most effective instruction, an average student would mature approximately 33 percentile points, which equates to making roughly one year's growth in one year. That might seem good enough if all students were average, but that is not the case.

Figure 1.2 illustrates a possible scenario of what might happen to students after one year of instruction based on the previous research—they are all over the spectrum of learning proficiency. With ineffective instruction, above average students (80th percentile) fail to stay above average, average students (50th percentile) are no longer average, and struggling students (20th percentile) regress. With average instruction, students stay where they are, and that means low students stay low. But with the most effective instruction, all students increase in achievement, and that's what we're here for—to help students grow, not to merely teach them.

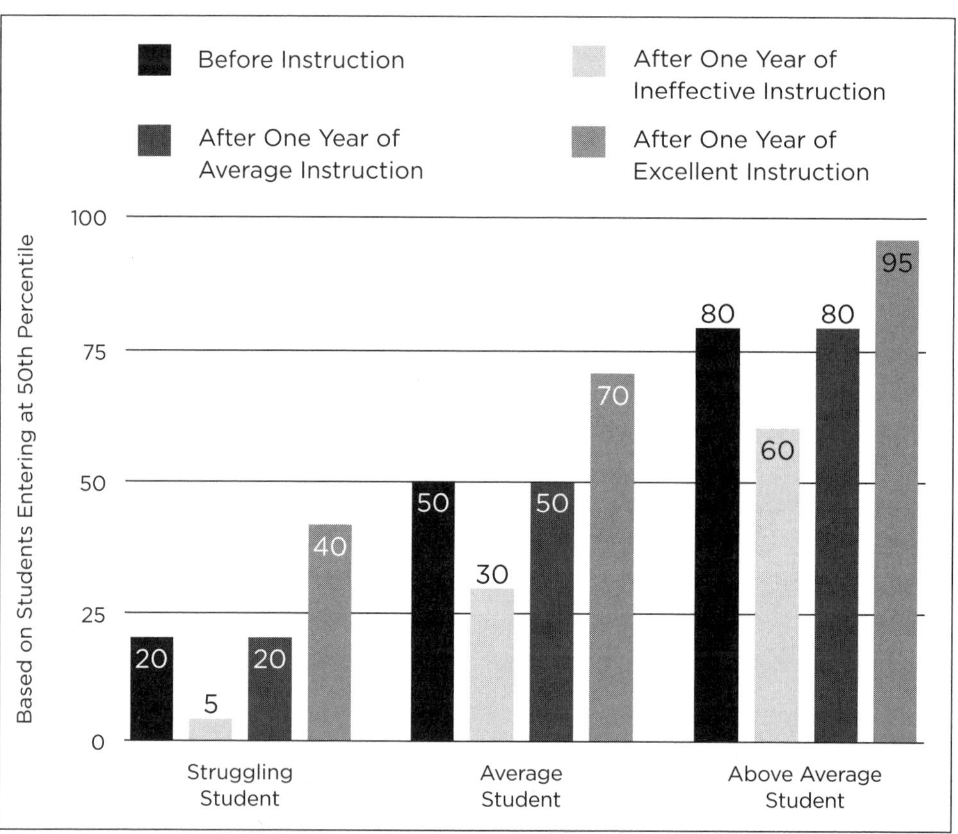

Figure 1.2: Student learning proficiency after one year.

Students come to us on grade level, above grade level, and below grade level. If our goal is to guarantee that *all* students graduate with a firm foundation for college and career success, then what do they need to get there? Obviously, the least effective instruction is not the answer, and average instruction only maintains every student's current level of performance. There's only one answer: we as professionals must become highly effective in the work we do with all students.

If we choose to own our moral imperative, then we must determine whether our teaching is, for example, ineffective, effective for some students, or highly effective for every student, regardless of level or label. We should ask ourselves, "What does *effective* really mean?" In its most fundamental definition, *effective* means "adequate to accomplish a purpose; producing the intended or expected result" (Dictionary.com, n.d.). So in order to be most effective, what we do must work for all students all the time. If we are honest with ourselves, we will admit that we have more growing to do, because *all students all the time* is quite a lofty goal. Therefore, it's important that we address this question: "How do we become the most effective at meeting the learning needs of all students all the time?" To do this, teachers must focus on two rules of teacher excellence that serve as a platform for creating excellence in every student.

1. If we focus on everything, we focus on nothing.
2. Before we focus on Bloom's taxonomy, we must address student deficits in Maslow's hierarchy.

If We Focus on Everything, We Focus on Nothing

Teaching is a very complex profession. We have a massive goal—to have instruction work for all students all the time—but twenty to thirty variables affect this goal throughout the day. Those variables are our students, and with all these variables, we have a myriad of instructional strategies, resources, products, and nuances to choose from that could impact each situation that we encounter in the course of a day. So it's no surprise that teachers can become overwhelmed. They simply have too many things to address and not enough time to implement them all.

But that's not all that teachers have to consider. They must couple their ideas with those they get from their teams, along with campus and district initiatives designed to make teachers' lives more efficient and effective. Before students even enter the classroom on the first day of school, teachers' plates are overflowing to the point that they can't even begin the arduous journey toward excellence in every student.

In order to end the insanity of *too much to do*, we should rethink how we can reach this goal of the most effective instruction. This goal of bringing out the excellence in every student begins with adopting the first rule of excellence: if we focus on everything, we focus on nothing.

To adopt this, we must let go of practices we know are nothing more than going through the motions. We need to evaluate and identify practices that do not lead to the goal, and we must redirect our focus to actions, practices, and behaviors that help students grow.

To help you adopt this rule, following are five reflective questions to help you determine how to remove unproductive practices.

1. List each practice or action that you employ in your work.
2. Is this practice or action required by U.S. or state law? If yes, continue or ask for assistance to complete the practice more efficiently. If no, evaluate whether or not to continue.
3. Is this practice or action required by the district or my school? If yes, continue or ask for assistance in making the practice more efficient or simplified. If no, evaluate whether or not to continue.
4. Does this practice help make students successful? If yes, continue or ask for assistance to simplify the practice. If no or unsure, consider abandoning the practice.
5. Does this practice have a large time investment that yields little impact on your work with students? If yes, abandon the practice. If no or unsure, continue or investigate other ways to be make the practice more time efficient.

If our practices don't help students grow, we shouldn't be using those practices in the first place. Sometimes we are required to use certain practices, so we can't abandon them. However, we can ask leaders and colleagues for assistance to make those practices less time-consuming. Sometimes we do things simply out of comfort or automaticity without determining if they really help students learn.

Before We Focus on Bloom's Taxonomy, We Must Address Student Deficits in Maslow's Hierarchy

In 1943, psychologist Abraham Maslow created a theory about the prioritization of human needs. This hierarchy of human needs (see figure 1.3) has evolved over time, from having five levels to including seven or eight. For the purposes of this book, I will discuss Maslow's Hierarchy of Needs that includes seven levels. This hierarchy sorts human needs from the most basic (food, shelter, and water) to the most complex (transcendence or self-actualization). Maslow (1954) then categorizes these levels into two basic groups—(1) deficiency needs and (2) growth needs.

Before we delve into the deficiency needs, it's important that we review *growth needs*, the top-three levels of the hierarchy. The growth needs represent our ultimate goal for students—to learn at high levels. Growth needs focus on a person's quest to gain knowledge, learn new things, experiment with creativity, and offer his or her best for the greater good. There is no threshold for how much a person can grow, as these levels have limitless capacity and potential. However, growth needs cannot be met unless the lower-level needs—the deficiency needs—are at least partially met first.

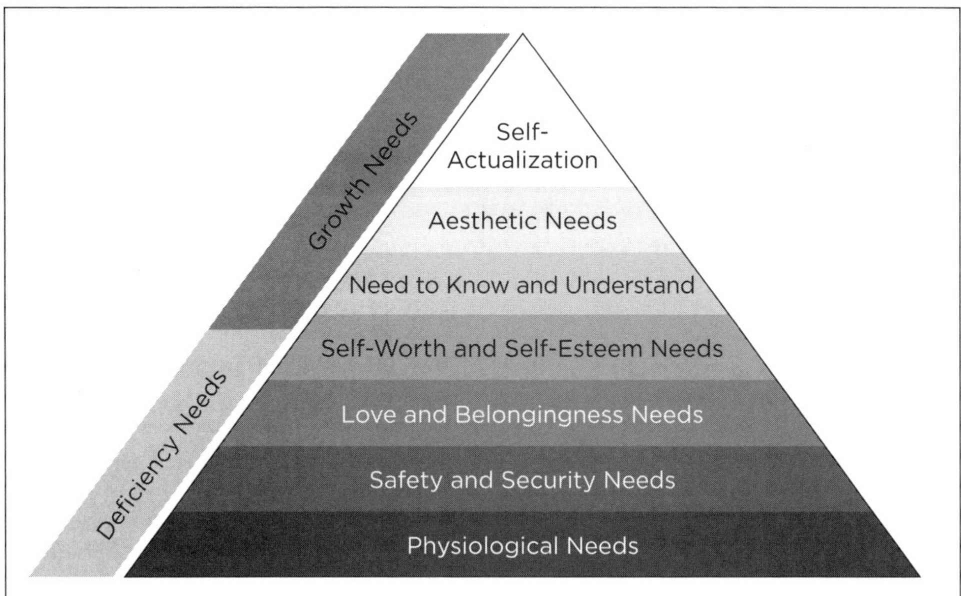

Source: Adapted from Martin & Loomis, 2007, pp. 72–75; Maslow, 1954.

Figure 1.3: Maslow's Hierarchy of Needs.

The first four levels of Maslow's hierarchy are called *deficiency needs* because they "arise due to deprivation and are said to motivate people when they are unmet. Also, the motivation to fulfill such needs will become stronger the longer the duration they are denied" (McLeod, 2018). Maslow (1943) initially asserted that people must completely satisfy lower-level deficit needs before progressing to meet higher-level growth needs (McLeod, 2018), but his later research clarifies that not all deficiency needs must be 100 percent met in order to pursue growth needs (McLeod, 2018). That's good news for educators who work with large populations of students who continuously struggle with one or more deficiency needs.

Maslow's theory suggests that as our deficiency needs are met or partially met, our interests transition toward satisfying needs at higher levels in the hierarchy. In short, motivation in a particular deficiency level decreases as those deficiency needs are met. For example, if you're extremely hungry, after you eat, you will eventually become full and no longer need food or feel motivated to fulfill that physiological deficit; therefore, your motivation would move to a higher level in the hierarchy, such as safety and security or love and belongingness. Every person is genetically wired to pursue his or her needs all the way to the top of the hierarchy pyramid; however, deficits in the bottom four levels cause many people to be unable to fulfill their growth needs.

According to Emelina Minero (2017), assistant editor at Edutopia:

> Data show that more than half of all U.S. children have experienced some kind of trauma in the form of abuse, neglect, violence, or

challenging household circumstances—and 35 percent of children have experienced more than one type of traumatic event, according to the Centers for Disease Control and Prevention (CDC).

More specifically, six in ten students have one or more adverse childhood experiences that negatively impact their learning (CDC, 2019), as figure 1.4 illustrates. Adverse childhood experiences might include all types of abuse, neglect, and other potentially traumatic experiences that occur in the lives of people under the age of eighteen.

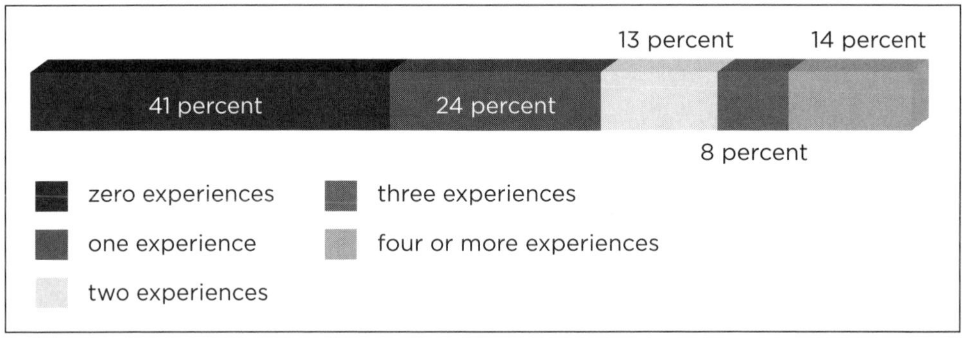

Source: CDC, 2019.

Figure 1.4: Number of adverse childhood experiences among U.S. students upon entry to school.

Sadly, almost one-fourth of U.S students have three or more adverse childhood experiences (CDC, 2019), which means teachers need to equip themselves to help students overcome multiple deficiencies in their hierarchy of needs.

The National Center for Education Statistics (2016) reports that 51.8 percent of U.S. students received free and reduced lunch in 2014–2015. The states with the highest percentage of students receiving free and reduced lunch were southern states. Among them, Mississippi had the highest percentage; 73.7 percent of its students received this vital assistance during lunch. This evidence supports the theory that more than half of U.S. students enter school every day with one or more of Maslow's deficiency needs unmet since they require school assistance for the most basic human need—food.

This begs the question, What were schools designed to do? The prevailing belief is that they were designed to start with and build on growth needs (learning), not to address the deficiency needs many students now lack. But as time goes on, schools have to realize that in order to help students develop their growth needs, teachers need to address students' deficiency needs first. If left unchecked, gaps in a student's deficiency needs could possibly widen the achievement gap in learning.

Therefore, it is incumbent on educators to remember the second rule of excellence: before we focus on Bloom's taxonomy, we must address student deficits in

Maslow's hierarchy. We can no longer presume that these deficits are beyond our control. Furthermore, we must remember that all learning has a list of prerequisites, which include students' physiological, social, and emotional needs. Obviously, students are impacted by their home environment and the adults who influence that environment, but great teachers possess a distinct ability to help students overcome the obstacles that their deficiency needs create so they can learn at high levels. Great teachers know that they have to motivate all students to reach Maslow's fifth level—learning.

If we align Bloom's taxonomy with Maslow's Hierarchy of Needs (see figure 1.5), we see that the most basic level of learning in Bloom's taxonomy, knowledge, corresponds with Maslow's fifth level, the desire to know and understand. This means that many students often arrive at school unprepared to begin learning, not because they are unintelligent or apathetic but because so many needs and barriers prevent them from focusing on learning.

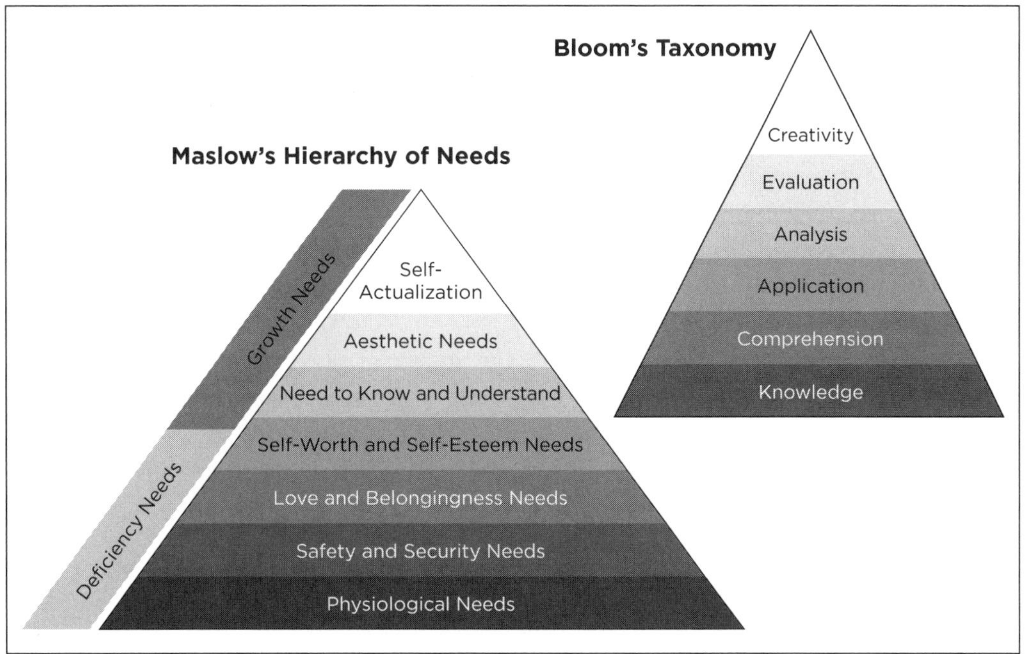

Source: Adapted from Armstrong, n.d.; Bloom, 1956; Martin & Loomis, 2007, pp. 72–75; Maslow, 1954.

Figure 1.5: The Maslow-Bloom connection.

In order for teachers to help all students learn at high levels, they must be equipped with the knowledge and skills to meet students where they are and lead them to where they need to be. This requires us to redefine classrooms as homes for learning where teachers intentionally define the learning space with Maslow's deficiency needs in mind. This means that we need to reimagine learning in a way that considers students first and content second. After all, deficiency needs are about students, not content, and growth needs help all students learn, grow, and excel through the content.

So, if the two rules of excellence require us to address Maslow first and Bloom second, then we need a hierarchy that will help us prioritize learning for all students, with the most basic needs for learning first and then developmental needs that inspire students to chase excellence through the content.

In order to help students grow in their learning, we can only address one deficit at a time; therefore, we should consider where each student's most basic need lies in this hierarchy and begin our work there. Once we satisfy or fill that gap, we can move on to the next gap until the student is learning at or above grade level.

In the next section, we will explore the Hierarchy of Student Excellence to gain knowledge and skills about building a prioritized structure of excellence that has the potential to meet all students where they are and lead them to unleash their full learning potential.

The Hierarchy of Student Excellence

Excellent teachers know that most students cannot learn if their deficiency needs are not met. With Maslow's hierarchy in mind, we must consider how we can create a culture of learning in our classrooms that prioritizes human needs first and leads to each student pursuing learning beyond the learning target. To help teachers with that process, I developed a model called the Hierarchy of Student Excellence, as shown in figure 1.6.

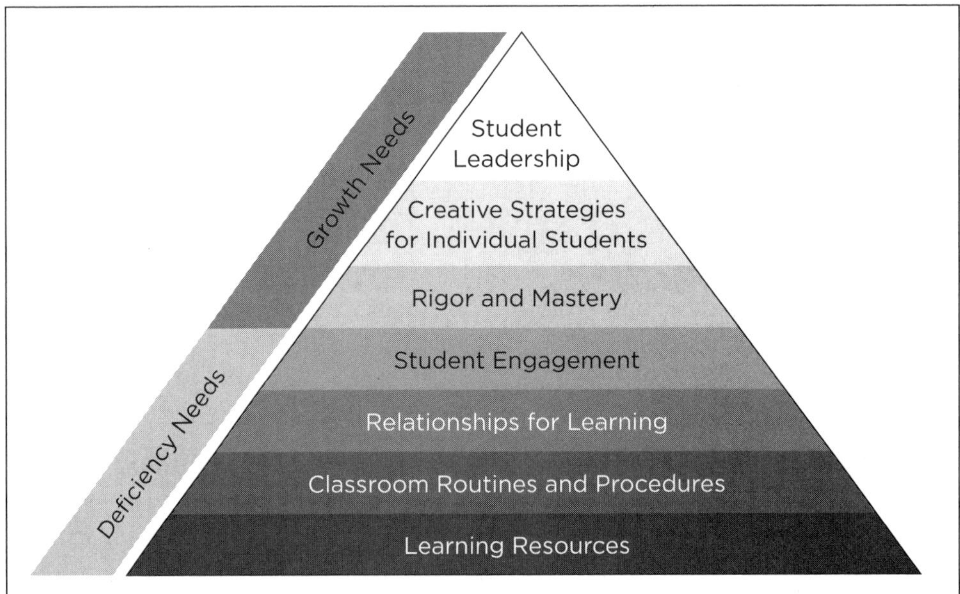

Source: Wink, 2017, p. 7.

Figure 1.6: Hierarchy of Student Excellence.

As previously noted, this model presents student growth as levels of progress, each of which rests on the one beneath it. These levels possess both the skills that teachers need to master to become truly excellent instructors and the structures that students must receive in order to achieve academic, behavioral, and social-emotional success.

Teachers must recognize that students come to them with learning deficiencies that also align to the Hierarchy of Student Excellence. Understanding how these levels relate to the levels in Maslow's Hierarchy of Needs can help teachers and leaders collaboratively recognize the critical role we play in leading every student to excellence.

While the following paragraphs give you a glimpse into each level, the remaining chapters in this book delve much deeper into the seven levels of the Hierarchy of Student Excellence. In chapters 2–8, we'll examine specific strategies that teachers can leverage to help ensure all students first have equitable access and then can advance through the levels to discover their unique excellence.

Level 1: Learning Resources

According to Maslow, the most basic human needs are biological requirements for human survival, such as air, food and drink, shelter, clothing, warmth, and sleep. "If these needs are not satisfied, the human body cannot function optimally. Maslow considered physiological needs the most important as all the other needs become secondary until these needs are met" (McLeod, 2018). The first level in Maslow's hierarchy represents these physiological needs. Until our physiological needs are met, we can't actively work to fulfill any other need. We must recognize that students who have physiological deficiencies, because they either are hungry or exhausted, have no place to stay, or lack basic clothing to stay warm, cannot focus on learning. Simply put, students cannot learn if their physiological needs are not met.

Similarly, in the Hierarchy of Student Excellence, students need equitable access to appropriate learning resources and the confidence to use those resources to pursue learning. If a teacher does not have the resources necessary to teach or, even worse, lacks the skills for using those resources, students can't grow in their learning or skillfully use learning resources; as a result, students cannot leverage any subsequent learning experience to advance toward their own success. Meeting students' need for access to learning resources and the skills to use those resources effectively is our most fundamental responsibility in guaranteeing student excellence.

Level 2: Classroom Routines and Procedures

The second level of Maslow's Hierarchy of Needs is the need for safety and security. When people feel safe and secure, they don't fear that physical, mental, or emotional harm will come to them. Students who feel their security is threatened are likely to find it difficult to focus on learning.

The second level of progress in the Hierarchy of Student Excellence correlates safety and security needs with classroom routines and procedures. Creating a safe and secure learning environment requires structure, consistency, routines, and procedures that facilitate learning, especially for students who lack a safe and secure environment at home. Teachers also benefit from systems, routines, and procedures that help them manage their own learning processes as well as those of their students. Only with these routines and procedures will students be engaged, inspired, and positively challenged to take risks in their learning.

Level 3: Relationships for Learning

The third level in Maslow's hierarchy addresses our need for a sense of love and belonging. The desire to be accepted by others is the key motivation driving this need. In the Hierarchy of Student Excellence, the third level of progress, relationships for learning, addresses a teacher's skill in fulfilling this human need. Meaningful relationships are essential to both our personal and our professional development. After all, the failure to belong often exacerbates the failure to learn. As such, fulfilling needs at this level is critical for teachers as well as students. In order for students to take reasonable risks, they must feel that they belong in the classroom and that the teacher and their classmates accept them. We mustn't forget that each classroom has its own unique culture of learning.

In the classroom, fostering strong relationships with and among students is a critical responsibility for teachers. Achieving excellence in this area demands more than merely basking in the warm fuzzies of positive teacher-student relationships. Instead, educators also must be skilled at leveraging these relationships to inspire learners toward a college- and career-ready future. This leverage is most effective when teachers facilitate strong relationships among students and the class as a whole.

Level 4: Student Engagement

The fourth level of Maslow's hierarchy is devoted to the need for self-worth and self-esteem. Once people feel safe and secure and possess a sense of acceptance and belonging, they can begin to develop positive feelings about themselves. Deficiencies in self-worth and self-esteem can interfere with student progress.

In the Hierarchy of Student Excellence, this level—the last of the four fundamental or deficiency levels—addresses skills for fostering student engagement that leads to empowerment. At any age, when people work in a learning environment that excites their interest and challenges their intellect, and in which they are actively involved in driving progress, they have opportunities to explore their capacity for ideas and innovation and to participate in the learning process. That kind of engagement forces students out of the comfortable and mind-numbing role of passive observer, gives them more autonomy and ownership over their work, and, as a result, helps them build self-esteem and self-worth.

In an article reviewing techniques for improving student engagement, authors and educators Leah Taylor and Jim Parsons (2011) cite research finding that students who received opportunities to work on a technology-rich project that dramatically improved their engagement "developed a genuine passion for learning and a solid set of learning and research skills" (p. 16). The findings all indicate "improved pupil self-esteem and self-confidence" (Doppelt & Barak, 2002, p. 27, as quoted in Taylor & Parsons, 2011). In describing another group of students involved in a technology-based education project, Taylor and Parsons (2011) also note that "students were engaged, staying after school and during lunch hours to work on projects together" (p. 16).

That kind of bell-to-bell focus on learning is significant for students. When students are more actively involved in their work, they are less actively involved in acting out with distracting or disruptive behavior. That enables teachers to devote more of their time and attention to student learning and less time to crowd control and enforcement, which results in more successes for everyone.

Level 5: Rigor and Mastery

In Maslow's Hierarchy of Needs, the fifth level is the need to know and understand, which represents the first of the three higher levels—growth needs. Human beings spend their lives in a perpetual state of growth, so learning and development within these levels never stops. The same is true for the areas of growth represented in the top three levels of the Hierarchy of Student Excellence. The fifth level, and the first of the growth levels in that hierarchy, is rigor and mastery. It represents the student's growth in the skills necessary to pursue rigorous learning and master high-leverage skills in the content.

At this level, teachers actively engage in learning how to design more effective learning for students. While students must be engaged in the learning process to feel motivated to tackle learning challenges and master their content, instructional skills in this level go beyond those required to develop student engagement.

Level 6: Creative Strategies for Individual Students

Maslow's sixth level encompasses our aesthetic needs, which are needs associated with developing appreciation for and expression of creativity. People who are focused on growth in their aesthetic needs apply what they have learned in creative ways. In the Hierarchy of Student Excellence, this need for developing the appreciation and command of aesthetics correlates to students developing their unique creativity and gifts in the learning process.

In an excellent classroom, instruction requires and promotes creativity and innovation by encouraging individual students to express themselves in meaningful ways through their artistic abilities and creative cognition. Additionally, students deserve targeted and prescriptive interventions based on the content and skills that they have yet to master. At this level, teachers plan and deliver interventions for struggling students while personalizing meaningful enrichment opportunities for students once they master the content. This level of growth is where the magic happens, as the phrase *learning for all* takes on a whole new meaning.

Level 7: Student Leadership

In Maslow's hierarchy, self-actualization or transcendence is the highest order of human need and the pinnacle of human growth. Self-actualized people discover and employ all their mental, physical, emotional, and social faculties and talents in the desire to define and achieve their full potential. Maslow (1943) defines the need for self-actualization, in part, as the need to "become everything that one is capable of becoming" (p. 383). That's a goal few of us will ever meet. Like other growth levels in Maslow's hierarchy, this one involves continually building on capabilities that never truly stop expanding. In fact, Maslow estimates that "less than two percent of [adults] achieve self-actualization" (as cited in McLeod, 2018). But most of us have taught or had the pleasure of meeting students who possess a distinct ability to positively influence other students and educators throughout their school by unleashing their potential. Basically, these students are leaders.

Our goal and moral imperative as educators must include promoting the narrative that students are the leaders of the next generation, and we must diligently work to empower teachers to become leaders so they can build the leadership capacity in every student, not just those who are the brightest and most obvious leaders. Leadership is not a title or position. It is each person's innate ability to make this world a better place.

The Student Excellence Support System

In *A Leader's Guide to Excellence in Every Classroom* (Wink, 2017), I articulated how leaders must create a pyramid of interventions for teachers in the same way teachers create interventions for students. I called this intervention system the Excellence Support System. For the purposes of this book, teachers must have a support system to help students, and I will call this the Student Excellence Support System. This system works within each level of the Hierarchy of Student Excellence to provide a stepped process for providing student supports at three levels of engagement.

1. Teacher team collaboration
2. Classwide supports
3. Individualized student supports

Step 1: Teacher Team Collaboration

The very first step teachers should take to ensure that they provide the very best instruction and supports for all students is to collaborate with their team. Step 1 in the Student Excellence Support System leverages the power of the PLC process (DuFour, DuFour, Eaker, Many, & Mattos, 2016) to ensure that all students receive the very best instruction and supports for learning. Education researchers Richard DuFour, Rebecca DuFour, Robert Eaker, Thomas Many, and Mike Mattos (2016) describe a PLC as:

> An ongoing process in which educators work collaboratively in recurring cycles of collective inquiry and action research to achieve better results for the students they serve. Professional learning communities operate under the assumption that the key to improved learning for students is continuous job-embedded learning for educators. (p. 10)

To help build excellence in every student, teachers should refer to the four critical questions of a PLC (DuFour et al., 2016):

1. What do students need to know and be able to do?
2. How will we know when they have learned it?
3. What will we do when they haven't learned it?
4. What will we do when they already know it? (p. 251)

These four questions are critical to help schools, teachers, and individual students grow and thrive. While question 4 does not apply to struggling students who need supports from the Student Excellence Support System, teacher teams should give thoughtful consideration to how they will enrich students who are successful.

Team-level supports guide struggling teachers and teams toward proficiency with content and knowledge in classroom strategies that support delivery of instruction. Team-level supports only work, however, when we empower teams to personalize schoolwide ideas to meet the needs of all team members.

Teachers form collaborative teams so they leverage collective efficacy in creating instructional norms that they all can agree to provide to students in their instruction. *Norms* are guidelines for how team members will behave and contribute in their collaborative work, and they are helpful in ensuring that the teacher team functions well. However, teacher teams can go beyond how they will act and interact with one another by creating instructional norms for their classrooms. For example, a fifth-grade team could establish norms for routines and procedures inside all the team members' classrooms. A high school mathematics department could create norms for student engagement and how they will optimize instructional time to foster high levels of learning. When teams create norms for the consistent and aligned learning conditions that all students will experience, students stand a greater chance of success because teachers are consistent in how they support students learning.

The goal of collaboration at step 1 is for teachers to create consistency from classroom to classroom and among teachers who share students or content. Collaboration with this purpose should set the stage for all students to find higher levels of learning success.

Step 2: Classwide Supports

Once teacher teams create norms they all agree on, they can use these norms to build classwide supports. These supports manifest through either strategies or expectations to help all students succeed. Classwide supports are fundamental to helping all students discover their excellence because they provide general accommodations that each student can access independently before he or she needs individualized support from the teacher. While teachers work with other teachers to lay the foundation for classwide supports, they can also solicit advice and guidance from instructional coaches, mentors, and even administrators to build and strengthen these supports.

Step 3: Individualized Student Supports

Teachers create individualized student supports after they've developed and revisited team norms and classwide supports but some students have not yet succeeded. Step 1 and step 2 usually benefit the majority of students in the classroom, but some students may not have made individual gains in learning. Basically, this plan is the beginning stages of the RTI process. The RTI Action Network (2019) defines RTI as a "a multi-tier approach to the early identification and support of students with learning and behavior needs." The RTI process begins by identifying the student's greatest area of need that inhibits learning. Next, the teacher determines the causal factors for the deficiency and develops a personalized learning plan for remediation. Individualized student supports exemplify what great teachers do; they focus on the individual student to first find his or her strengths and then find the underlying reasons why he or she is not succeeding in the classroom.

In the following chapters, the individualized student supports offer ideas and guiding questions to help teachers deconstruct the student's challenges so they can create a personalized plan for his or her growth. Excellent teachers don't leave excellence to chance, and they don't leave a single student behind. They demonstrate their unwavering belief in learning for all by doing the right work—what needs to be done to ensure every student succeeds at high levels.

Conclusion

The great equalizer in student achievement is the effectiveness of the classroom teacher. When teachers are able to move their effectiveness to the highest levels, students can expect to grow nine times the amount that they could by themselves, four times more than they could grow with ineffective instruction, and nearly double what average instruction could provide (Marzano, 2003).

To fulfill their power, teachers must each create vibrant learning environments that inspire all students, regardless of ability and background, to unleash their potential.

Teaching must move from the 20th century concept of presenting information to a new mindset of creating a culture of learning that meets students where they are and takes them where they need to be. In order to do this, we have to regard students as leaders of the next generation and create classroom cultures and learning experiences that will inspire and challenge them to lead their own learning. The goal of leading every student to excellence will become a reality when we stop thinking of excellence as a destination but rather a journey that continues for the rest of students' lives.

CHAPTER 2

Teaching for Excellence: Learning Resources

Creating meaningful learning spaces for today's students depends on something more than your willingness and/or ability to sprinkle shiny iGadgets everywhere.

—Bill Ferriter

Imagine walking into a classroom as a student and finding no resources to help you learn. There are no books, no technology, and no procedural texts telling you what to do, and no furniture other than the teacher's desk, students' desks, and a chalkboard. What would you think? How would you know what to do? How would you drive your learning? Basically, you would be rendered helpless to learn until the teacher arrives to give instruction, and from that point forward, you would be completely dependent on the teacher as your sole resource for learning.

Many classrooms have an abundance of resources, in many cases more than anyone could possibly use. However, the number of resources doesn't necessarily transform a classroom into a home for learning. This chapter is not about gathering abundant resources. It's about teaching students how to be *resourceful* in their learning with the resources provided. In other words, students are filled with optimal learning only when they have—and know how to use—tools in their learning environment that feed their learning needs (the metaphorical food, shelter, and water of learning).

This chapter discusses what great teachers do to get the very best out of their students with the resources at their disposal. We will consider how teachers can prepare for excellence with resources in mind and reflect on and revise how they optimize resources to deliver the most effective instruction. To support students in the use of resources, the Student Excellence Support System unleashes the power of collaborative teacher teams to help students utilize the most essential resources, creates classwide supports to ensure students learn how to use resources independently, and creates individualized excellence plans for students who need resource supports beyond what classwide supports provide.

The following story illustrates how a teacher identified a need at this level and developed a plan to overcome the issue. Teachers should aim not to have multitudes of resources but to teach students how to be resourceful. Great teachers can instantly identify resources that fail to make students resourceful, and they know how to help students develop the skills to find success through various tools for learning.

Meeting Students' Basic Needs for Using Learning Resources

Hunter returned to his school the summer after a great second year of teaching social studies. His students had grown by leaps and bounds, and he felt good about his efficacy as a teacher. However, once back at school, he received notice that the school had adopted a new textbook and instructional software, so he could no longer use the textbook he used last year, and he would need to familiarize himself with the new resources. Not being part of the textbook adoption process, Hunter was unfamiliar with the new textbook and the brand-new digital software that accompanied it, but he still felt he would be prepared for when the students began school.

As students entered the classroom on the first day of school, Hunter rolled out the new textbook and briefly explained how students would use the digital resource to complete assignments for each day's lessons. As expected, instruction was slow at first, due to students' need to get familiar with the tool. But as the weeks rolled on, more and more students began to reject the resource. They would moan when Hunter made assignments, and his students who struggled the most basically shut down the minute it was time for them to get to work.

Mateo, one of Hunter's English learners, started out the year like everyone else in the class, eager and hopeful to learn but also became quickly frustrated with the course, the overwhelming language in the textbook, and the complexity of the digital software. By the end of the third week, he joined the ranks of the apathetic learners, dejected due to the difficulty of the resources and disconnected from the learning. Whenever Hunter asked him to get to work, Mateo smiled, politely refused, and just sat there as Hunter's frustration continued to build.

After six weeks of painstaking and unsuccessful efforts to engage Mateo in learning, Hunter finally asked Mateo why he didn't like his class or the work he gave him. Mateo replied, "It's just too hard. There are too many big words in that book, and I hate the computer work. I tried to do the work at first, but I got so far behind, I just gave up."

Blindsided by Mateo's statement, Hunter didn't know how to respond, so he thanked Mateo for his answer and affirmed that he would figure out a plan to make the resource work. Later that evening, Hunter reflected on Mateo's response and his own lack of one. The more he thought about it, the more he realized that Mateo's learning was deeply impacted by language. After all, he had immigrated to the United States from Guatemala three years earlier. Hunter knew that Mateo's language was developing, but he had failed to prepare for the fact that the text in this resource was above grade level for the students, and he had given Mateo no supports to help him navigate the difficult text. Even worse, Hunter had provided no supports for all the others who were also rejecting his instruction due to the resource.

Before he went to bed that night, Hunter made a plan to meet with his fellow teachers the next day so they could collaborate on the difficulties his students were having and he could seek their advice and input on how to solve the problem associated with this resource. He had isolated the root cause of the problem, and now, he was determined to solve it.

All too often, we assume if we have good resources, students will learn. But that's not always the case. As educators, we must remember that having resources is not the goal of this level in the Hierarchy of Student Excellence (see figure 2.1). It is to create a resourceful learning environment where all students can access resources and become resourceful learners. Learning resources are the metaphorical food, shelter, clothing and water from the first level in Maslow's Hierarchy of Needs. If we fail to provide students with the structures, supports, and guidance to leverage the learning resources, that will create problems for students in all of the other levels in the hierarchy.

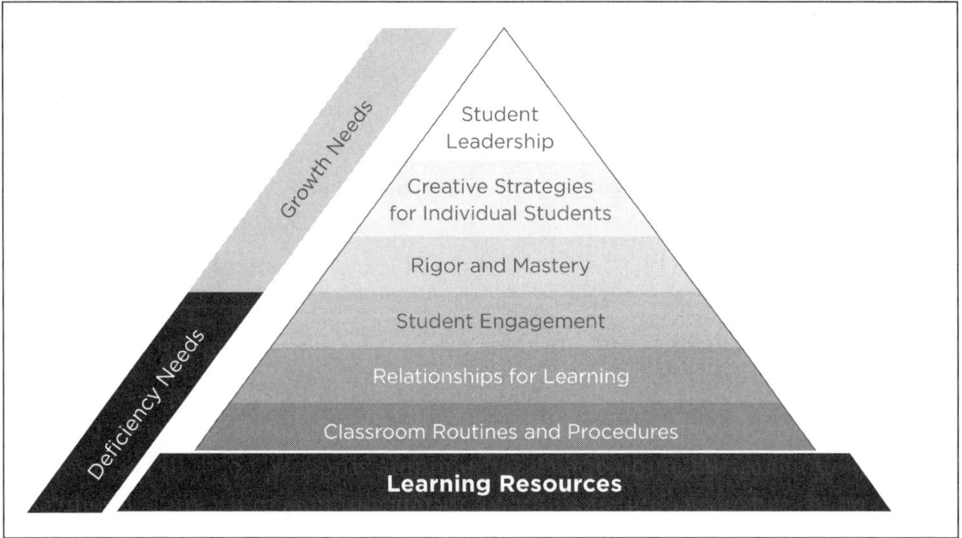

Figure 2.1: Hierarchy of Student Excellence—learning resources.

The following sections of this chapter offer strategies for creating a resourceful classroom that meets the needs of every student. Additionally, you will explore how teachers can work together to create a Student Excellence Support System to ensure all students become resourceful learners.

Leveraging Learning Resources

It might appear to some that to have success in this level of the Hierarchy of Student Excellence, teachers merely need resources for students to learn; however, as we learned from Hunter's story, that is not the case. Simply having learning resources would be enough if the purpose of education were to have students consume content by casually or passively observing instruction. But we know that the ultimate purpose of education is to inspire all students to own their learning; therefore, students' competence with resources, not the teacher's, is ultimately what matters most. When students can competently use learning resources, it makes the classroom feel like home for learning for all students.

Don't get me wrong; teacher competence matters, and it matters a lot. In fact, teachers must have a solid understanding of every resource, and they must have the expertise to strategically employ every resource to support student learning. "If all teachers have a thorough knowledge of the school's resources, then there is a strong likelihood that teachers will be equipped to skillfully use those resources to help students learn" (Wink, 2017, p. 29). Charlotte Danielson (2013), who has written extensively on the importance of a teacher's knowledge of resources, states, "Student learning is enhanced by a teacher's skillful use of resources" (Danielson, 2013, p. 15). A teacher's ability to identify and leverage all the learning resources available is as important as the resources themselves in promoting a student's academic success (Wink, 2017). This includes creating a classroom environment or arrangement that invites students to engage in the learning process. As Danielson (2013) writes:

> Both the physical arrangement of a classroom and the available resources provide opportunities for teachers to advance learning; when these resources are used skillfully, students can engage with the content in a productive manner. At the highest levels of performance, the students themselves contribute to the use or adaptation of the physical environment. (p. 37)

Excellent teachers want students to feel welcome into their classrooms because at their core, teachers care about their students. Excellent teachers also want students to feel as though the classroom is designed specifically for them because they know that is essential in connecting students to the content. Further, excellent teachers understand that they must sell the learning environment to students as a great resource that will drive their learning experience.

We have resources in our classrooms for one reason—so students can become resourceful learners. Resourceful learners know how to use the resources at their disposal. Seymour Papert (1998) states that being resourceful is a critical life skill. In fact, he identifies this skill as the most competitive skill all students need to succeed in work and life (Ferriter, 2017; Hattie, 2012).

In order for students to drive their learning, they must know how to act in situations for which they are not specifically prepared, which depends on their ability to gather and interpret information, identify clear goals worth pursuing, accurately describe headway (or the lack thereof) made toward reaching those goals, and successfully develop cogent plans for additional progress. In other words, the most successful students know what to do when they don't know what to do. We must teach students how to respond with confidence, instead of shutting down and waiting for the teacher to recognize that they have disconnected from learning altogether. When they encounter a problem and don't know what to do, excellent learners tap into all the resources within the room to find the solution. If we want students to own the learning, then they must also own resources that inspire them to take ownership of the problems to find solutions to those problems. Great teachers create a resourceful learning environment that teaches all students how to be independent and resourceful learners.

Great teachers can empower students to find success with learning resources by implementing the following three components of excellence: (1) preparation, (2) delivery, and (3) reflection (see figure 2.2).

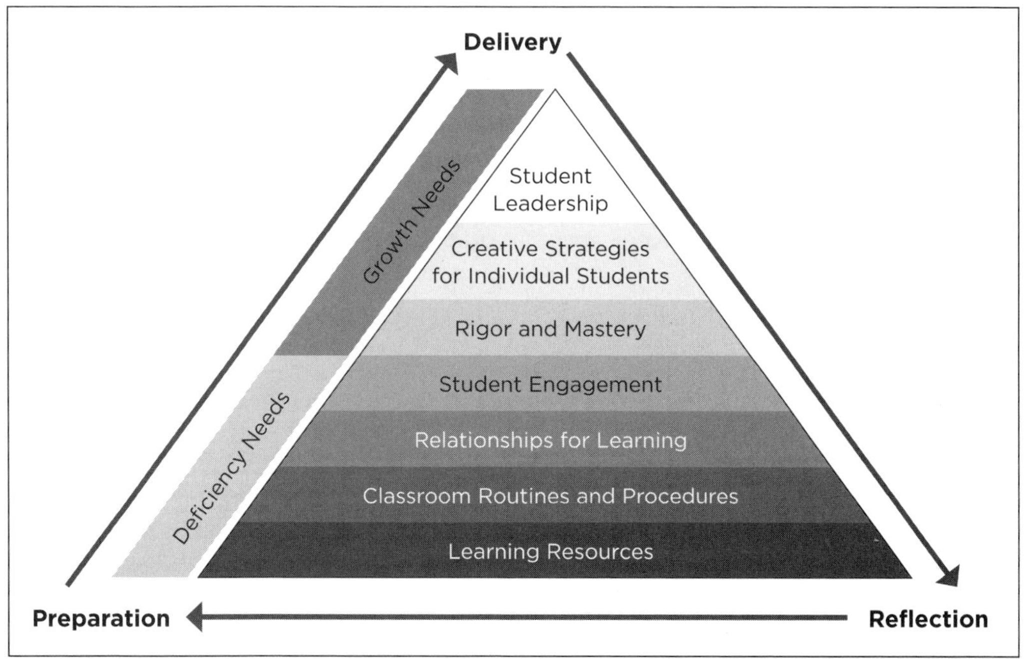

Source: Martin & Loomis, 2007, pp. 72-75.

Figure 2.2: The Student Excellence cycle.

Preparation is the planning necessary to ensure that students have every support necessary to learn at high levels. *Delivery* is the actual instruction students receive that is based on the preparation, and *reflection* is the evaluation needed to determine how successfully the plan impacted student outcomes. These components are interdependent and can make or break the success of each student.

Preparation is essential to effective delivery, and delivery improves when teachers reflect on it. When done well, reflection leads to improvements in preparation, which, in turn, lead to improvements in delivery and, finally, deeper reflection—a cycle of continuous improvement. In the following sections, I discuss how great teachers prepare, deliver, and reflect on how they empower students to take full ownership of those resources.

Preparation

Excellence starts with preparation. The very best teachers understand that in order to create a culture of learning, they must first consider the classroom and how they design, present, and explicitly teach every resource in the room so every student knows what resources are available and how to use those resources to pursue learning. Additionally, teachers understand that instruction can come to a screeching halt if students believe that the only resource that can help them is the teacher.

The currency of learning is time, and teachers should spend time setting up the classroom so students can learn how to use the resources without help from the teacher. And when students still don't know what to do, they have a strategy called See 4 Before Me (C4B4Me), that helps them figure it out before they go to the teacher. With this strategy, teachers create four structured and sequential expectations for students to seek assistance from someone or something other than the teacher when they don't know what to do.

1. The brain and student-created resources
2. The classroom and teacher-provided resources
3. Student collaboration
4. Technology and social media

After students have exhausted these resources, they can move to step 5.

5. The teacher

The Brain and Student-Created Resources

The very first resource students must use in learning any subject is their brain. If we believe that all students can learn, then we must also believe that they can and should rely on their learning muscle as the first resource to solve problems without the teacher's help. Helping students without making them use their brain first does them a great injustice.

Once a teacher has introduced information or exposed students to a resource, he or she should consider the power of allowing students to tinker with the information, figure out how the information or resource works, and use it to persevere through a problem and find a solution. Sometimes, we want students to succeed so badly that we prematurely come to their rescue without allowing students to use their brains to solve problems on their own. Great teachers believe that it maximizes true learning when students struggle first, persevere second, and find success in the end.

Step 1 of C4B4Me also includes student-created resources. If we believe that student brains are important, then we must believe that the resources students create with their brains are equally important. Examples of student-created resources include class notes, summaries, drawings representing their knowledge and understanding, graphic organizers, and so on. Marzano has identified summarizing and note taking as a high-yield instructional strategy that results in large gains in learning; this strategy has an effect size of 1.00, or nearly two years of growth (Marzano, Pickering, & Pollock, 2001). The student-led activity of note taking allows students to process information as they hear or see it modeled or presented to them and then create their own representation showing their understanding of that information. Although teachers sometimes ask students to keep notes brief, the more notes students take, the more information they tend to remember later. The quantity of notes is directly related to how much information students retain (Nye, Crooks, Powley, & Tripp, 1984, as cited in Gonzalez, 2018). When students take notes frequently, they have a written resource that they believe in, no matter if it is in paper or digital form.

Students as young as prekindergarten have the ability to take notes even if they do not possess a command of the alphabet; they simply represent their learning through pictorial representations or drawings. Students who do have a command of the alphabet but who have an affinity for art or are visual learners can enhance their learning through visual note taking, which involves drawing or doodling their learning in their notes.

Finally, success on the first step of C4B4Me involves expecting students to use their brain or notes when they don't know what to do. Teachers should reach a basic understanding with students that when students don't know what to do, they should rely on their brains and the resources they create as the first step to solving the problem. Many times, they'll find the answer to their question in their head or in their notes; if not, they should move on to step 2, classroom and teacher-provided resources.

The Classroom and Teacher-Provided Resources

Close your eyes and picture your classroom and everything inside it. Now picture your students in that classroom. Do they see the room as a resource for learning with many helpful resources inside, or do they see a classroom with a bunch of stuff that they tepidly avoid? Do they readily access resources on their own initiative, or do they wait for you to tell them it's ok to use them? In order for students to know what to do when they don't know what to do, they should confidently and independently take ownership of step 2 of C4B4Me—the classroom and every teacher-provided resource within the room.

If students are to become resourceful learners, they must view the classroom as an abundance of learning resources thoughtfully structured in a way that invites every student into the learning process. "A classroom's physical arrangement can influence a student's desire to learn, and it can reflect the teacher's ability to engage students" (Wink, 2017, p. 31). Teacher and educational journalist Mark Phillips (2014) says, "The physical structure of a classroom is a critical variable in affecting student morale and learning." Traditional thinking may lead educators to believe that orderliness, cleanliness, and aesthetic design are the most critical aspects of setting up the room, but in order to create a resourceful classroom, teachers must ensure that every surface of the classroom provides learning supports and learning opportunities for students.

In a resourceful classroom, everything in the classroom is a resource for learning. That means everything from the pencils and paper to the walls, to the books, and even the furniture is leveraged as a resource for learning. Teachers ensure that they provide adequate quantities of textbooks and technology for students. Textbooks are accessible and at an appropriate reading level for diverse learners. Technology is accompanied by procedural text that guides students on how to troubleshoot when log-in issues or Wi-Fi difficulties arise. Teachers replace cute motivational posters with anchor charts that remind students of the steps to use when solving a problem or when writing a paper. They strategically post signs for students to use when they encounter the most common problems in the classroom. The intent of step 2 is simple: when students encounter a problem they can't solve with their brain or their notes, they immediately look around the room for tools or procedural text that can help them stay focused on their learning tasks and, more importantly, help them solve their problems.

Student Collaboration

If students don't know what to do, they should think about it and consult their student-created resources or notes. If they are still stumped, they can use classroom resources to solve the problem. However, if they are still unsuccessful, students should remember that they are in a home for learning and they can rely on their classmates to help find solutions. Teachers employ student collaboration as a powerful method to keep the learning momentum going. Often, a student has already solved the problem; and with the proper structure, he or she can help another student solve it.

Remember, students are learning resources for each other, and they can learn from each other when they collaborate effectively. This includes how students phrase requests for help from one another, such as: "Can you help me with . . . ?," "Can you show me how to . . . ?," and "Where do I find . . . ?" These question stems give struggling students a mental model of how to collaborate in a productive way. Without structure, collaboration can lead to off-task discussions and unproductive work. Additionally, without structure, the students who are struggling the most can take advantage of collaboration to avoid work. In these situations, teachers should limit how many peers students can seek help from and structure the conversations so they don't dissolve into unproductive time. You can find more ideas for student collaboration in chapter 5 (page 101).

Technology and Social Media

As a last resort, students must learn to tap into the power of technology to find solutions and guidance. Adults commonly use technology when they want to know something, so we must teach students how to leverage technology to help them with their learning. Technology is not just a resource to *find* information; it's also a resource to *share* information. Students possess the ability to create and share their own content and learning, and they have the ability to curate the resources they find.

Following are a few tools teachers can use to integrate technology that simultaneously teaches and reinforces critical thinking skills in instruction. Note that it is important to follow your district's policy regarding access to technology and ensure that you obtain permission from students' parents or guardians if needed.

- **Google (www.google.com):** When students don't know the answer to a question or need to find more information about a given topic, they can do a simple Google search.
- **Twitter (https://twitter.com):** Using hashtags and keyword searches, students can find a lot of content that they can use to drive their learning. Furthermore, using a hashtag structure, students can tweet out resources they have found or resources they have made to help other students throughout the school.
- **YouTube (www.youtube.com):** Students are turning to YouTube to learn how to, for example, do origami and get better at popular video games. Great teachers encourage and guide students to safely find instructional videos about classroom content by teaching them how to conduct a proper search, filter information to find the best video for learning, and report videos that are inappropriate. Additionally, teachers use YouTube to share short screencasts and instructional videos with their students in the flipped-instruction format. (Chapter 4, page 73, will discuss flipped instruction in more detail.)
- **Vocaroo (https://vocaroo.com):** This powerful web tool is great for students who need high-level text read to them aloud. Teachers can record themselves reading the text aloud using this site and share these audio recordings through a unique URL or QR code. Students can play, replay,

rewind, and fast-forward the audio so they are in charge of the pace of their work.

- **Flipgrid (https://flipgrid.com):** Accessing this powerful tool from their personal device or a school device through a URL or QR code, teachers can post a question or share important information on their grid. They can then invite students to share their thoughts by recording a video of their thoughts and their learning. Then for fun, they can add stickers to their face as they would on Instagram or Snapchat.
- **Instagram (www.instagram.com) and Snapchat (www.snapchat.com):** These social media tools remain greatly underutilized for learning. Students can use them to share pictures of their learning or record a video of themselves explaining how they solved a problem and post it on their story or feed so other students can find more ways to think about learning.

Technology is a powerful tool that can accelerate learning, and we mustn't be afraid to leverage it in our instruction. We must teach students how to responsibly and effectively use technology to research and find the answers to any questions they might have. This 21st century tool is essential for students to master in order to succeed at school and beyond.

The Teacher

If students use steps 1–4 to find out what to do when they don't know what to do, there is a strong chance that they will not need you, the teacher, as much as they would without this structure for learning. Students need to hear you loudly and clearly say that when successful learners (or scholars) don't know what to do, they don't quit until they find the answer. In classrooms of excellence, teachers expect students to work hard at their learning and use steps 1–4 as a support system. When that fails, students must then come to the teacher for help. This structure of resourcefulness puts the students in the driver's seat and preserves the teacher's time to work with students who need his or her help the most.

Delivery

In a classroom of excellence, the teacher rolls out the resources in a way that ensures they meet students where they are. Great teachers don't roll out a new resource without explicit instructions. They make sure students understand the purpose of the resource and how to use it. In the first days of school, teachers need to show students how to use the resource, how to troubleshoot when difficulties with the resource arise, and how to accelerate their learning using the resource. A tool won't work properly unless students believe in the value of the tool and understand how using it properly can help them learn.

Great teachers also anticipate the needs of diverse or nontraditional learners and ensure that a resource doesn't turn into a roadblock that stalls learning. For example, the teacher should ensure that a student with a reading disability would not just have access to a resource three or four grade levels above the student's reading level. The resource should have reading supports or accommodations. The teacher should make sure that a student who doesn't speak English would have access to resources with linguistic accommodations that help the student learn without him or her having to depend solely on the English language. In order for tools to work, students must *want* to use them, so teachers should make sure they have resources that are appropriate for and meet the diverse needs of the students whom they expect to use the resources.

Finally, when teachers are rolling out tools and resources, the most important part of delivery is monitoring and adjustment. Monitoring requires teachers to observe students as they use resources so they help students develop competence and confidence. That is the only way students will find resources relevant to their learning.

Great teachers are always adjusting during delivery. Delivery is all about letting students' responses to the resource influence your instruction as much as your instruction influences their learning.

Reflection

Reflection is critically important for teachers, but with so many demands that steal their time, reflection is often the first thing they neglect. Through reflection, great teachers find their areas for growth. When it comes to meaningful reflection, the best teachers go beyond determining the good and bad of instruction. They seek adjustments that will make the classroom more effective for all students, especially those who are reluctant to chase learning.

In order to reflect on resources, great teachers constantly scan the room to determine which resources accelerate learning and which resources stifle learning or turn students off of learning altogether. From there, they determine if the resource difficulty applies to the class as a whole, a group of students, or specific students. Next, they determine if the root cause for resource rejection is the complexity of the resource, boredom from use of the resource, or lack of interest. Finally, the teachers use that information to make a plan of action to reteach use of the resource or help students discover the value the resource provides.

Figure 2.3 (pagse 36–37) helps teachers reflect on their effectiveness at providing learning resources. By answering the questions in this reflection tool and using the Student Excellence Support System, teachers can begin closing instructional or learning gaps for students who struggle at this level. Teachers need to reflect on all components related to learning resources and determine where student learning needs the most improvement. Furthermore, teachers need to prioritize reflection by progressing through the C4B4Me steps to ascertain where students are struggling with the resources. Last, reflection is not just about difficulties. Great teachers reflect on their learning resources often to determine where they are successful as well as where they need improvement.

Resource	Reflection
The Brain and Student-Created Resources	How well do students use their brains to solve problems independently? How well do students take notes to synthesize their learning and make a representation of it? How well have my expectations for using the brain and student notes impacted the learning of my students who struggle the most? How well do students use their notes as a resource when they come to a problem for which they can't find a solution? What opportunities am I missing to optimize student thinking and note taking to drive student learning?
The Classroom and Teacher-Provided Resources	How well do students respond to the physical layout of the room to drive their learning? How much confidence do students have in the capability of instructional resources, such as textbooks, to drive their learning? How well do my classroom resources impact the learning of my students who struggle the most? How well do students respond to anchor charts and other procedural text in the classroom? What opportunities am I missing to optimize classroom resources to help students stay engaged in their learning?
Student Collaboration	How well do students see each other as learning partners in my class? Do I provide students with structures to help guide them in collaboration? How well does collaboration impact the learning of my students who struggle the most? How well do students take responsibility for collaboration so they don't allow the other students to do the work for them? What opportunities do I need to create so students more readily and more effectively communicate and collaborate with one another?

Technology and Social Media	Which technologies do students rely on the most to help them know what to do when they don't know what to do? How well do students stay engaged with technology and not engage in off-task technology behaviors (surfing or scrolling)? How well does technology impact the learning of my students who struggle the most? What technologies do I need to introduce to provide variety in student learning? How well have I created a culture where students use technology to develop their own resources and share their resources with classmates? What opportunities have I missed to better integrate technology into every student's learning?
Teacher	How consistent am I at verifying that students have used C4B4Me before I begin to help them? If students have not used one of the steps, how well do I determine why they didn't use it and respond to their lack of use? How targeted is my response to students' needs? What changes or modifications do I make to C4B4Me to better help every student's learning?

Figure 2.3: Learning resources reflection tool.

Visit ***go.SolutionTree.com/instruction*** *for a free reproducible version of this figure.*

With reflection, teachers learn what kinds of adjustments they should make within each step of the process to increase student engagement as a whole class to direct more targeted and prescriptive support to struggling students. Excellent teachers understand that when students master the tools at their disposal, it establishes the foundation for learning for every student. The more we understand how to leverage resources to drive student learning, the more successfully we will help all students pursue learning far beyond the learning target, because we will have created a support system that empowers all students to use resources to become resourceful learners.

Building a Student Excellence Support System: Learning Resources

In order for every student to discover his or her excellence, teachers must prepare a support system. That support system is not isolated but rather collaborative in nature. As explained in chapter 1 (page 7), the first step to supporting all students involves creating consistency with colleagues who share students or content. The second step leverages the teacher team norms that establish classwide expectations and supports for learning. The final step to supporting every student is creating individualized student supports that teachers strategically target for specific students who fail to respond to classwide supports.

Teachers should create a support system that better addresses student difficulties with classroom resources they are expected to use to drive learning. These supports should build students' confidence and competence in how to use these resources by focusing on increasing automaticity and building students' belief in the resources; as a result, students will be more willing to stick with learning. Remember that the learning resources level is similar to Maslow's level on physiological resources. Just as physiological resources are essential to life, being able to leverage the learning resources is essential to learning.

Step 1: Teacher Team Collaboration

While student learning depends on our effectiveness as educators, the biggest barrier to ensuring all students learn is the consistency of teachers within the school. Educators must come together and collaborate on how they plan to design the classroom as a home for learning. Collaborative teacher teams build shared knowledge of learning resources and best practices for using those resources to support learning. Team members must understand the purpose of all the resources and develop competence and expertise with those resources so students can have equitable access.

As a best practice, collaborative teacher teams should establish norms for working and learning together. These norms should include when the team will meet and the role each team member will play to support one another. For each learning resource, teams should identify one person as the expert for the resource, so he or she can commit to teaching the rest of the team how to become proficient in driving student learning with that resource. In order for the team to work interdependently, it should clearly set the expectation that all teachers must lead in their area of expertise, helping others along the way. The essence of collaboration is sharing your best while also seeking the best from every team member. For teams to work interdependently, the leader for each resource is essentially a resource for his or her teammates. The leader is responsible for providing supports and updates about the resource as he or she develops knowledge and expertise. Furthermore, leaders regularly communicate new findings about best practices in using the resources and engage colleagues in meaningful discussion to strengthen each teacher's competence of the resource and language of instruction.

Step 2: Classwide Supports

Once collaborative teams develop a common framework and language for the use of all learning resources, teachers should prepare to personalize their classrooms in a way that maintains consistency with their teammates' classrooms but also individualizes their own classrooms for their students, making it a power space for learning.

Look at your classroom, and ask yourself how the room's design promotes the steps in C4B4Me. Are there structures in place that encourage students to use their brain and to create their own resources, such as notes? Is technology set up so that students can easily make their own resources? Are paper and pencils available for students when they forget those resources? If students don't have access to these basic resources in the classroom, your classroom does not have the first step of resourcefulness in place.

Look at your classroom furniture and walls. Is the furniture set up so that students can easily see the front of the room? Are the walls full of informational and procedural texts that guide student learning when they encounter a problem? Do the textbooks and other instructional resources present themselves as a support or a stumbling block for students? Great teachers are always thinking about their classroom and whether it burdens students who struggle in learning or offers a variety of supports to all.

For example, students might become frustrated if they can't remember the order of steps for completing a task. Great teachers anticipate this problem by posting anchor charts around the room that remind students of steps for tasks so they can stay engaged in learning. Technology should always have some type of procedural text nearby that reminds students how to log in and how to access instructional software. Furthermore, teachers should post the agenda for the day's lesson or the lesson plan itself somewhere in the room so students know what to expect that day. Great teachers don't just teach—they inform students of what they can expect to learn that day.

How are students arranged in the classroom? Great teachers strategically arrange students in the room so they can easily collaborate with one another. If you do not allow students to collaborate, they might disengage from the lesson or engage in off-task behavior. Great teachers understand the importance of student conversation and create structures so students can easily work together.

Technology isn't useful until students can actually access it to accelerate their learning. Great teachers explicitly teach students about the technologies they can use to seek out information as well as share information with peers. What technology do you want students to use to find an answer when they don't know it? Should they do a Google search? Should they use YouTube? You can say no to those options, but be prepared to provide students with a technological resource that they can employ to help them find the answer.

For example, you might decide to use Google Docs (www.google.com/docs). This resource allows you to create a digital document for students to use as the fourth step in C4B4Me when they are lost. The digital document provides students with a multitude of hyperlinks that lead them to specific sites, screencasts, or videos that support the day's instruction. Some teachers might choose to prerecord their lesson or lecture using Swivl (www.swivl.com) and upload a video of themselves teaching the lesson so students can review it as many times as they like. For students who struggle with reading, some teachers use Vocaroo (https://vocaroo.com) to prerecord an oral reading of the text. No matter what technological resources we provide for students, it is imperative to give students explicit instructions on how to use them efficiently and effectively to drive learning.

Step 3: Individualized Student Supports

When students fail to learn with the learning resources, the teacher must first determine if the competence issue is due to student deficits or a lack of explicit instruction. If the student failure is due to a lack of structure or explicit instructions, the teacher should collaborate with his or her colleagues to find strategies to resolve the problem. If the student failure is due to individual student deficits, the teacher should move to step 3 in the Student Excellence Support System—individualized student supports.

This step embraces the spirit of response to intervention (RTI; Buffum, Mattos, & Weber, 2009; Buffum, Mattos, & Malone, 2018) and serves as a Tier 1 intervention support in the general classroom that differentiates learning for struggling learners during regular instruction. For learning resources, student supports must consider learning styles, reading levels, disabilities, and other variables, because many times, these issues are the barriers that prevent students from using the resources or cause them to reject the resources altogether. Therefore, great teachers find creative ways to ensure that they transform those stumbling blocks into stepping stones.

Providing individualized student supports includes three steps: (1) isolate the root cause of the problem, (2) prescribe one or two supports to address the root cause with frequency for several days, and (3) gauge improvement. After taking these steps, if you are unsuccessful helping the student, you must keep trying. If you are still unsuccessful, then you should reach out to colleagues, or teammates, to get their support in helping the student succeed.

Figure 2.4 provides a flowchart that illustrates the process teachers can use to help students who fail to make progress in their competence using learning resources. First, teachers should determine whether the student is succeeding. If the student is not successful, the teachers would simplify the problem by isolating the its root cause. From there, the teacher develops possible solutions or interventions to address the student's deficiency.

In order for an intervention to work, teachers must provide adequate time for it to take effect and then gauge student growth. If the intervention works, then the teacher continues providing the support with the same frequency and duration until the deficit is sufficiently addressed. If the intervention is unsuccessful, the teacher returns to simplifying the problem and then determines whether the intervention needs more time or he or she should try a new intervention. If the new or retried intervention is unsuccessful, the teacher should then reach out to his or her team to develop a new or more strategic intervention for the student.

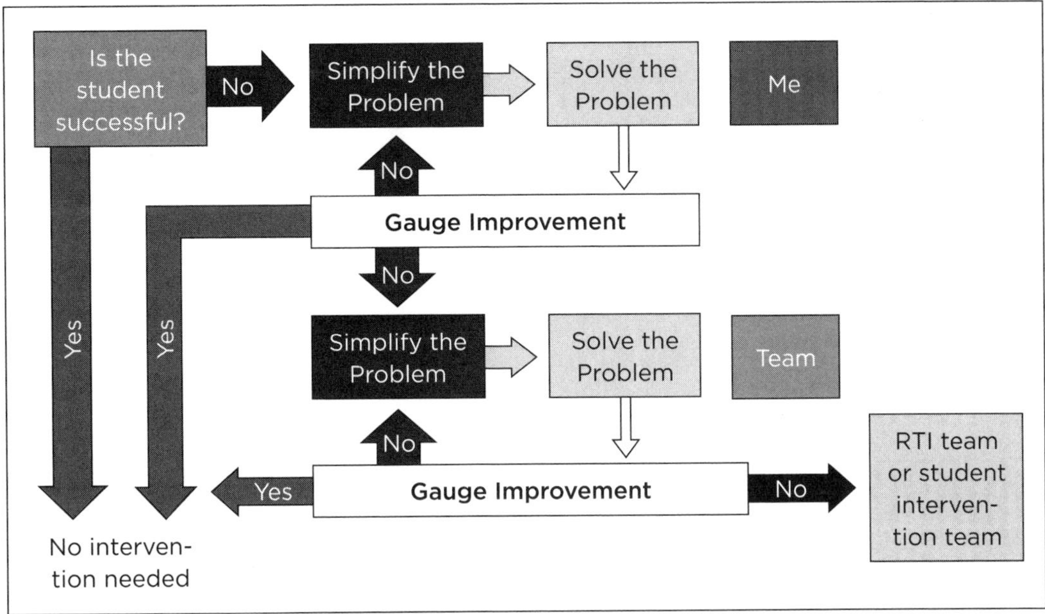

Figure 2.4: Problem-solving flowchart.

Teachers can use figure 2.5 to isolate the problem with learning resources, prescribe a support, and finally determine the effectiveness of that support. With this tool, teachers can more efficiently develop potential solutions to close the gaps with learning resources.

Individualized Student Support Problem-Solving Tool: Learning Resources	
Question 1: Has the teacher team created common expectations and supports for all students at this level? (Circle yes or no.) (If your answer is yes, continue. If your answer is no, stop and correct this area.)	Yes No
Question 2: Based on the team's work, has the teacher implemented his or her classwide C4B4Me structure? (Circle yes or no.) (If your answer is yes, continue. If your answer is no, stop and correct this area.)	Yes No
Question 3: Are the majority of students successfully using the classwide C4B4Me structure? (Circle yes or no.) (If your answer is yes, continue. If your answer is no, stop and correct this area.)	Yes No

Figure 2.5: Individualized student support problem-solving tool—learning resources.

continued →

Individualized Student Support Problem-Solving Tool: Learning Resources
Question 4: Which student is struggling with learning resources? Student: ______________________ Check the boxes next to the items for which the student is proficient, and place an X next to items for which the student is not yet proficient. Beginning with the first step (the brain), identify the area for which the student needs more support. This would be your targeted are of growth. ☐ The brain and student-created resources ☐ Note taking ☐ Specific classroom resources ☐ Collaboration ☐ Technology and social media List the student's strengths and difficulties with each component at this level.
Question 5: What learning barriers prevent the student from using the most important resource? (Check all that apply.) ☐ Reading disability ☐ Language barrier ☐ Writing disability ☐ Technology deficit ☐ Other: ______________ ☐ Other: ______________ ☐ Other: ______________
Question 6: What potential supports will help this student be successful with the resource? ☐ Reading supports ☐ Oral administration ☐ A Vocaroo recording of how to use the resource ☐ Procedural text with specific instructions ☐ Pictorial instructions ☐ Verbal instructions ☐ A study buddy ☐ Frequent reminders by the teacher ☐ Video instructions or screencast instructions ☐ Other: ______________

<table>
<tr><td colspan="2">Question 7: What are the goal and the deadline for the student to successfully use the resource?
Goal:

Deadline:</td></tr>
<tr><td>Question 8: Did the student meet the goal by the deadline? (Circle yes or no.)
(If your answer is yes, continue the support. If your answer is no, return to question 4.)</td><td>Yes No</td></tr>
<tr><td colspan="2">Notes:</td></tr>
</table>

Visit ***go.SolutionTree.com/instruction*** *for a free reproducible version of this figure.*

Conclusion

The first level in the Hierarchy of Student Excellence is the most basic level of helping all students learn, grow, and excel. At this level, teachers have the important job to create a learning environment that is a home for learning and shows students how to be resourceful learners. Great teachers don't just decorate their classrooms; they design them so that every student feels like he or she can use all the tools in the classroom to grow both in confidence as a scholar and in competence with the content. If students do not know how to competently use resources, they will likely experience difficulty learning at high levels. It is critical that teachers fill the gaps for these students.

This chapter concludes with a reflection tool (pages 44–45) that teachers can use to evaluate their understanding of the challenges they face when identifying and making the most effective use of learning resources. As you consider the questions and your responses to them, explore possibilities for improving those systems, including teacher team collaboration, classwide supports, and individualized student supports based on the information and ideas in this chapter.

Reflection Tool: Learning Resources

Answer the following questions to help you create a more engaging classroom where students have access to learning resources that will help them succeed.

Teacher Team Collaboration

- Has our team identified the resources and leaders to help each team member become more competent with all the learning resources?
- How well do team members lead one another in developing skillful use of the resources?
- How well do team members focus on building student efficacy in the use of essential learning resources?
- When a teacher experiences difficulty with a resource, what steps does he or she take to seek help from the team?

Classwide Supports

- How well have I taken knowledge of resources from my team and applied that knowledge to my classroom environment?
- What evidence do I collect to gauge student effectiveness and comfort with the learning resources?
- How well do I gauge students' acceptance of or desire to use the resource to drive learning?
- Of the four steps in C4B4Me, which ones are strengths for my students, and which ones do students resist or avoid altogether when they don't know what to do?

Individualized Student Supports

- What do I do to determine if a student is struggling due to lack of competence with the learning resources?
- Once I determine that a student is struggling with a resource, what do I do to verify that the failure is not due to my classroom supports?
- Before I help the student, what do I do to isolate his or her area of greatest difficulty in using the learning resource?

- When I prescribe an intervention, how committed am I to providing the intervention with frequency and consistency?
- How do I gauge student growth with the learning resource to determine if my intervention was effective?
- If the student is still unsuccessful, how do I reflect and refine the intervention to better help the student?
- When my efforts to help the student continue to fail, how do I reach out to my team members to help me better respond to the student?

CHAPTER 3

Teaching for Excellence: Classroom Routines and Procedures

If the classroom feels safe, students will drop their guard, become less oppositional, and take learning risks.

—Eric Jensen

A great barrier and great accelerant of learning lies in the effectiveness of classroom routines and procedures that teachers provide for students. A *routine* is a commonplace task or duty that teachers implement at regularly or specified intervals every day, while a *procedure* is the manner in which student would complete the task. A routine tells students what to do, while a procedure describes *how* they will do it.

Hattie (2009) states that "having high expectations for behavior and learning has an effect size of 0.43, a full year's growth" (p. 121). Expectations are powerful, and when they are clear and accompanied by supports to ensure that every student reaches them, student growth is certain. Conversely, when routines and procedures are ambiguous or not coupled with supports, only some students will meet the teacher's expectations. "By providing clear learning targets and communicating them, we can help students become our partners in reaching the rigor demanded. Clarity precedes competence" (Hansen, 2014).

Sometimes, it's not content or student behavior that impedes learning. Sometimes, a lack of clarity in the routines and procedures for working and learning prevents students from realizing their true potential as scholars. Teachers must consider the power of routines and procedures to fulfill Maslow's second deficiency need—safety and security. Routines and procedures make students feel safe in the classroom, and they can create an environment where students feel inspired to pursue learning at high levels.

In this chapter, we will explore the idea of transforming the traditional rules and consequences into routines and procedures that foster student independence in learning. Also, we will examine how the four critical PLC questions can help create consistent and aligned routines and procedures so all students understand the common expectations for behavior and learning. Finally, we will discuss how to respond to individual students who fail to succeed with routines and procedures by using an RTI approach to behavior.

To begin learning about routines and procedures that support excellence, read about Martina, a third-year teacher in a new school. You will discover how her belief system about classroom management is negatively impacted by the dichotomy of rules and consequences. But through working with her colleagues and students, she creates a positive learning environment with strong routines and procedures that not only yield good behavior but also strong *learning* behaviors.

Developing a Student Behavior Plan

Martina started her third year of teaching with a big wish—for all her classes to walk through her door on the first day of school instantly knowing what to do and how to do it, and successfully doing it with little help from her. After two years at a school where she had perpetually felt frustrated with students and their behavior, and even more frustrated with the administration's lack of behavior enforcement, she thought that working in a high-performing school with a reputation for students with good behavior would allow her to focus more on teaching and learning than correcting bad behavior. Prior to the first day of school, Martina was hoping that students would come to her class from the previous grade determined to behave well and work hard. Additionally, she had high hopes that their parents would quickly get behind her, instill in their children the importance of hard work, and respect her expectations for behavior and learning.

Sadly, her wish failed to come to fruition. After the first week of school, she realized that no matter how much she responded to misbehavior by enforcing the rules or how much she communicated with parents, there were always groups of students whose behavior would disrupt her lessons. With each passing day, she positively communicated her behavioral expectations and followed through with consequences to make her most challenging students comply with her expectations. With her classroom management in reaction mode, each day saw her expectations, rules, and consequences do little more than make both her and the students more frustrated. Because she had only hoped for good student behavior and didn't instead unleash a plan to ensure it, Martina was feeling upset and resentful.

As the weeks went on, Martina became more and more cynical when the bell rang at the end of first period because she knew her most difficult class, second period, was on its way to challenge her once again. Her frustration grew every day, and she didn't like the way she felt, so one day, she reached out to her teacher team colleagues.

As Martina shared her disappointment with her peers, she realized that the real problem with those classes and her most difficult students was not with the students but with her ability to reach them. Her reflection on students' behaviors revealed that she was more concerned about her teaching than their learning, and her approach to student behavior reflected that. Although she communicated her rules and consequences from the onset, she didn't budge from her rigid system and held firm to her way of doing things. The expectation was simple: follow my rules and don't deviate from that plan.

One day during her conference period, she walked by a fellow teacher's classroom and saw some of her most difficult students. She stopped and watched through the window and was amazed by what she saw. The students were smiling. They were working, and most surprising to her, they were doing it without misbehaving at all.

She thought to herself, "Now why don't they do that for me?" She then turned her attention to the teacher. The teacher was smiling; she stated her expectations in specific terms without the threat of consequences. The teacher praised students, including her most challenging students, for meeting her expectations. She also moved about the room ensuring all students stayed on task without having to correct them. As Martina watched her students succeeding, she knew what the real problem was—herself.

After watching her students thrive in that classroom, Martina spent some time reflecting on her own performance, and then she turned her reflection into resolve. She wanted all her students to be successful, and she knew that she would have to start wishing less and planning more to make this happen. Her team members became her resources for learning, and she made efforts to better align her expectations with the team's. She committed to meeting her students where they were and taking them to where they needed to be. She defined the level of independence she wanted all students to exhibit, and she built expectations, accountability protocols, clear communication, and—most importantly—student supports to ensure that all her students not only learned in her class but did so in a way that would make them successful in the future.

Martina realized that she needed to change the possessive pronoun in her thinking from *my* to *our*. *Her* routines and procedures quickly became the *class's* routines and procedures, and ultimately, students became excited about learning and transformed into independent learners who committed to her expectations for not only behavior but also learning.

The lesson that Martina learned is that rules focus on student compliance, while routines inspire student commitment to learning. As educators, we must remember to set high expectations for ourselves in developing routines and procedures that will set the stage for high levels of student learning. We must also reflect on the conditions we create for students and determine whether demanding compliance with rules inspires commitment to learning.

The second level of Maslow's Hierarchy of Needs includes those needs that foster safety and security. Maslow defines this level as demanding "protection from elements, security, order, law, stability, [and] freedom from fear" (McLeod, 2018). If you think about the students in your school, many of them most likely possess one if not many deficits in this area, which causes insecurity in many forms, such as choosing whether to engage in learning. This level in Maslow's hierarchy aligns with the second level of the Hierarchy of Student Excellence—classroom routines and procedures (see figure 3.1).

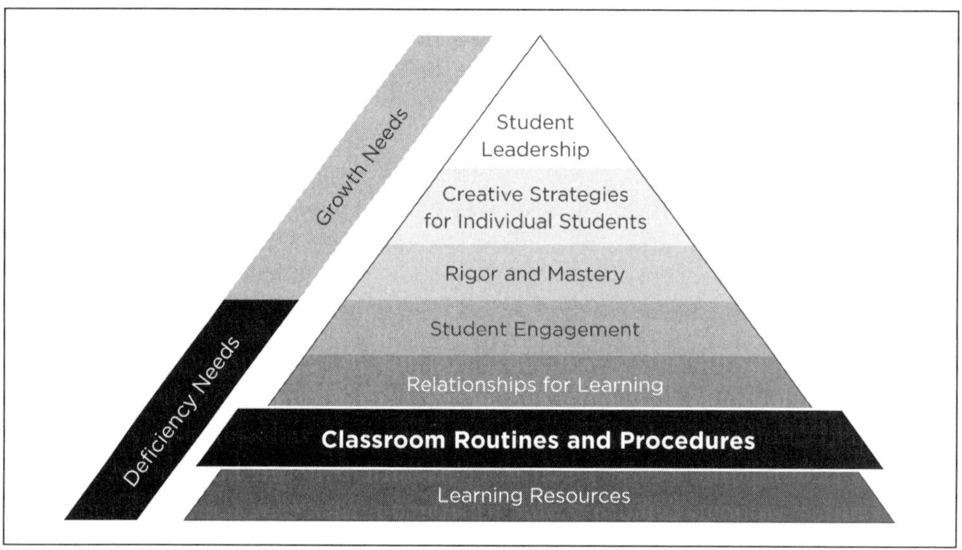

Figure 3.1: Hierarchy of Student Excellence—classroom routines and procedures.

At any point in their school career, students can enter your classroom with a deficit in safety and security needs. As teachers, we must be prepared to recognize this deficit and create routines and procedures that foster safety and security so students can learn at high levels in the classroom.

Managing Classroom Routines and Procedures

While the goal of Maslow's second level is fulfilling safety and security needs, the goal of the Hierarchy of Student Excellence's second level is creating classrooms with secure and predictable routines and procedures so all students feel safe to learn. If students are to feel safe and secure in the classroom, they need to feel some level of ownership of the room and the routines and procedures within it. Teachers should establish routines and procedures that develop and eventually unleash student confidence, which leads to independence and ownership of learning. We should create routines and procedures that inspire students to independently manage their behavior while the teacher focuses his or her efforts on monitoring and responding to behaviors that move students away from independence.

In the following sections, we will explore what great teachers do to prepare routines and procedures that focus on students doing the work instead of the teacher. We will then discuss how great teachers turn their plans for great routines and procedures into action, and finally, we will cover how teachers can reflect on their efforts to help students succeed.

Preparation

The first step to excellent classroom management is planning around the active nature of students, making sure to consider how to develop routines and procedures focused on students' desire to be independent and in charge of how they move about the room, talk with other students, and engage in various activities. This begins with setting goals for student behavior that prepare them to succeed.

From there, teachers determine the most common routines that students will perform in the classroom and then specify the procedures for accomplishing the routine in a way that yields automaticity in both student work and behavior. This way, the chances of misbehavior decrease due to the clarity within the routine and procedure. For example, when students enter the classroom each day, you may specify how to enter the room, how to get materials ready, and how to get started on the first learning task.

Classes are not homogenous. They are composed of students of different races, genders, economic challenges, and cultures, and each student enters the room with his or her own hardwiring for what appropriate behavior looks and sounds like. Furthermore, they have a wide variety of ways to negotiate their problems with learning or with a classmate. With all these variables in mind, we must have a constant. If we want routines and procedures to have success, we should collaborate with team members to ensure they are consistent.

The success of a student behavior plan partly relies on its power to steer students away from misbehavior. In my experience as both a teacher and leader, many behavior infractions occur because students are unsure of what the expectations for behavior and learning look and sound like. To that end, teachers should work collaboratively to create routines and procedures that let students know what the teachers expect and how to meet those expectations.

Common routines that students will experience in the classroom include routines for the following.

- Entering the room
- Leaving the room
- Transitioning in the room
- Going to the restroom, office, counselor, or nurse
- Accessing classroom resources independently
- Responding to visitors

Common learning procedures that students will experience in the classroom include the following.

- Whole-group instruction
- Small-group instruction
- Partner work
- Independent work
- Technology use
- Testing

Once teachers identify and define common routines and procedures, the next step is to consider seven questions that will flesh out the expectations and how to carry them out.

1. What are my expectations for students?
2. How will I communicate the expectations?
3. How will I teach the expectations?
4. How will I reinforce positive behaviors when I see them?
5. How will I anticipate off-task behaviors so I can intercept them before they disrupt learning?
6. What must I stop doing so I can expect students to be independent in this routine or procedure?
7. How will I empower or build student leadership in this routine or procedure?

Beyond planning expectations for routine behaviors, great teachers also plan lessons for teaching the procedures to students and giving them an opportunity to practice. As part of planning, teachers anticipate and intercept student misbehaviors and develop and practice how they will give feedback to correct mistakes when students fail to meet behavioral expectations. Finally, teachers must prepare and practice how they will respond positively when students meet expectations.

Figure 3.2 (page 54) offers a chart to help teacher teams collaboratively develop common expectations for common classroom routines. For every routine or procedure, teachers answer the previous seven questions to help them develop their plan to make each routine or procedure student led, not teacher managed. The reason for this is simple: if we want to focus on learning, we must first ensure that our routines and procedures do not create student dependency on the teacher.

Figure 3.3 (page 55) helps teacher teams collaboratively develop common expectations for common learning procedures.

Preparation for high levels of learning begins with preparing for the learning behaviors we want students to display. Engagement in learning is more or less a behavior, and how we design what we expect (routines) and how we expect it to look and sound like (procedures) will be the deciding factor in whether we will be able to engage students while they are in our classrooms.

Delivery

Once teachers have their plan in place, it's time to deliver. After they've welcomed students into the room, the best teachers immediately engage students in bell-ringer or warm-up activities that warm up students and their brains to begin the learning process. It is critical to note that the first day of school's lesson should have a heavy emphasis on routines and procedures, and great teachers explicitly teach, model, and practice with their students. From that point on, the teacher regularly teaches routines and procedures through direct instruction based on student needs and consistently reinforces them every day. When a teacher introduces a routine and procedure for the first time, he or she shows students what is expected through modeling. Once the teacher has taught routines and procedures, he or she should post them in the classroom as a reminder of classroom expectations. Posting routines and procedures serves as visual reminder so the teacher can refer to them often throughout the year.

To ensure that routines and procedures are student led instead of teacher driven, teachers focus their efforts on monitoring behaviors, reinforcing positive behaviors, and intercepting misbehaviors before they require redirection. This can only happen when students do the work, not the teacher. Great teachers are constantly scanning the room, actively monitoring student behavior and learning. They find students who are doing well and publicly praise their behavior for two reasons: (1) to affirm the student and (2) to reinforce the expectation to the rest of the class.

Teachers know which students have the highest propensity for getting off task, and they make concerted efforts to monitor those students and intercept their antecedents of misbehavior before they have to stop class to redirect these students' disruptive behavior. They intercept the beginning signs of misbehavior and encourage the student to stick with the task by using proximity to the student, vocally reminding the student to stay on task, and occasionally stating the student's name. In order to find

	Entering the Room	**Leaving the Room**	**Transitioning in the Room**	**Going to the Restroom, Office, Counselor, or Nurse**	**Accessing Classroom Resources Independently**	**Responding to Visitors**
Establish Expectations						
Communicate Expectations						
Teach Expectations						
Reinforce Positive Behaviors Subtly						
Intercept Misbehaviors Fluidly						
Expect Student Independence						
Expect Student Leadership						

Figure 3.2: Expectations and responses for classroom routines.

Visit ***go.SolutionTree.com/instruction*** *for a free reproducible version of this figure.*

	Whole-Group Instruction	Small-Group Instruction	Partner Work	Independent Work	Technology Use	Testing
Establish Expectations						
Communicate Expectations						
Teach Expectations						
Reinforce Positive Behaviors Subtly						
Intercept Misbehaviors Fluidly						
Expect Student Independence						
Expect Student Leadership						

Figure 3.3: Expectations and responses for learning procedures.

Visit ***go.SolutionTree.com/instruction*** *for a free reproducible version of this figure.*

excellence in routines and procedures, great teachers remember that their primary responsibilities are to monitor, praise, and intercept behaviors. Those three actions will accelerate both learning and positive behavior.

In summarizing Robert Marzano's (2003) recommendations for solidifying routines and procedures, the Association for Supervision and Curriculum Development (ASCD) lists involving students as a valuable part of the process, noting that "effective management includes getting input, feedback, and suggestions from the students" (p. 2). Student involvement in developing procedures helps students gain ownership of and commitment to the routines that guide their behavior.

To further encourage student ownership over classroom routines and procedures, and to maximize instructional time, teachers can also empower students to "take initiative in the management of instructional groups and transitions, and/or the handling of materials and supplies" (Danielson, 2013, p. 33). This means that they assign students jobs within the routine. Some of those jobs could involve managing materials, leading a procedure, or managing the time clock during transitions. Student ownership can't occur if the teacher manages all the tasks.

Throughout the year, effective teachers take time to teach, practice, and provide feedback on routines and procedures that fall out of automaticity. They recognize that students aren't perfect and neither are the routines, and it's natural for students to reject rules that promote order and organization. And they also know that the teacher's first job is not to teach content but to teach and reinforce routines and procedures because they actually build behavioral skills that help students become productive employees, parents, and members of society.

When great teachers notice that they are repeatedly responding to the same misbehaviors, they recognize that students are acting out of compliance, not commitment. In this case, teachers should stop the lesson and lead students in a conversation about the significance of expectations, how expectations support the learning goals of the class, and how failing to meet expectations undermines those goals. Teaching and reteaching expectations with consistency ultimately makes highly effective teachers most successful in delivering classroom routines and procedures.

Delivery is about executing the plan, adapting to ever-changing student needs, and understanding that students will need reteaching whenever they make mistakes. These aren't just good ideas for teaching students to behave; they're also effective for inspiring students to chase content mastery.

Reflection

Sometimes, teachers get frustrated when student behavior keeps missing the mark. Typically, student misbehavior occurs repeatedly because little details in the routine or procedure slipped day by day, and when not addressed over time, they compounded. It's important to remember that great teachers build excellence one step at a time by planning for it, delivering it consistently every day, and then reflecting on their effectiveness.

Figure 3.4 helps teachers reflect on and analyze their planning and delivery of routines and procedures in the classroom. Teachers ask themselves eight specific questions for every classroom routine and procedure to assess the following.

- Clarity of expectations
- Effectiveness of teacher communication
- Teacher instruction of expectations
- Reinforcement of behaviors that successfully meet expectations
- Interception of students before misbehaviors require redirection
- Student independence
- Student leadership

Routine	Reflection
Entering the Room	How clear and specific are the expectations of this routine for students?
	How frequently and consistently do I communicate my expectations for this routine?
	How effectively do I teach, reteach, and model my expectations for this routine to students?
	How well do I monitor students in this routine?
	How effective am I at positively reinforcing students' behavior when I see them successfully execute this routine?
	How well do I anticipate student misbehaviors and intercept them before I have to stop instruction to redirect students?
	Do students complete this routine independently, or do they depend on me to successfully complete this routine?
	Which student leaders can help all students complete this routine?

Figure 3.4: Classroom routines and procedures reflection tool. continued →

Routine	Reflection
Leaving the Room	How clear and specific are the expectations of this routine for students? How frequently and consistently do I communicate my expectations for this routine? How effectively do I teach, reteach, and model my expectations for this routine to students? How well do I monitor students in this routine? How effective am I at positively reinforcing students' behavior when I see them successfully execute this routine? How well do I anticipate student misbehaviors and intercept them before I have to stop instruction to redirect students? Do students complete this routine independently, or do they depend on me to successfully complete this routine? Which student leaders can help all students complete this routine?
Transitioning in the Room	How clear and specific are the expectations of this routine for students? How frequently and consistently do I communicate my expectations for this routine? How effectively do I teach, reteach, and model my expectations for this routine to students? How well do I monitor students in this routine? How effective am I at positively reinforcing students' behavior when I see them successfully execute this routine? How well do I anticipate student misbehaviors and intercept them before I have to stop instruction to redirect students? Do students complete this routine independently, or do they depend on me to successfully complete this routine? Which student leaders can help all students complete this routine?
Going to the Restroom, Office, Counselor, or Nurse	How clear and specific are the expectations of this routine for students? How frequently and consistently do I communicate my expectations for this routine? How effectively do I teach, reteach, and model my expectations for this routine to students? How well do I monitor students in this routine? How effective am I at positively reinforcing students' behavior when I see them successfully execute this routine?

	How well do I anticipate student misbehaviors and intercept them before I have to stop instruction to redirect students? Do students complete this routine independently, or do they depend on me to successfully complete this routine? Which student leaders can help all students complete this routine?
Accessing Classroom Resources Independently	How clear and specific are the expectations of this routine for students? How frequently and consistently do I communicate my expectations for this routine? How effectively do I teach, reteach, and model my expectations for this routine to students? How well do I monitor students in this routine? How effective am I at positively reinforcing students' behavior when I see them successfully execute this routine? How well do I anticipate student misbehaviors and intercept them before I have to stop instruction to redirect students? Do students complete this routine independently, or do they depend on me to successfully complete this routine? Which student leaders can help all students complete this routine?
Responding to Visitors	How clear and specific are the expectations of this routine for students? How frequently and consistently do I communicate my expectations for this routine? How effectively do I teach, reteach, and model my expectations for this routine to students? How well do I monitor students in this routine? How effective am I at positively reinforcing students' behavior when I see them successfully execute this routine? How well do I anticipate student misbehaviors and intercept them before I have to stop instruction to redirect students? Do students complete this routine independently, or do they depend on me to successfully complete this routine? Which student leaders can help all students complete this routine?

continued →

Routine	Reflection
Whole-Group Instruction	How clear and specific are the expectations of this procedure for students? How frequently and consistently do I communicate my expectations for this procedure? How effectively do I teach, reteach, and model my expectations for this procedure to students? How well do I monitor students in this procedure? How effective am I at positively reinforcing students' behavior when I see them successfully execute this procedure? How well do I anticipate student misbehaviors and intercept them before I have to stop instruction to redirect students? Do students complete this procedure independently, or do they depend on me to successfully complete this procedure? Which student leaders can help all students complete this procedure?
Small-Group Instruction	How clear and specific are the expectations of this procedure for students? How frequently and consistently do I communicate my expectations for this procedure? How effectively do I teach, reteach, and model my expectations for this procedure to students? How well do I monitor students in this procedure? How effective am I at positively reinforcing students' behavior when I see them successfully execute this procedure? How well do I anticipate student misbehaviors and intercept them before I have to stop instruction to redirect students? Do students complete this procedure independently, or do they depend on me to successfully complete this procedure? Which student leaders can help all students complete this procedure?
Partner Work	How clear and specific are the expectations of this procedure for students? How frequently and consistently do I communicate my expectations for this procedure? How effectively do I teach, reteach, and model my expectations for this procedure to students? How well do I monitor students in this procedure? How effective am I at positively reinforcing students' behavior when I see them successfully execute this procedure?

	How well do I anticipate student misbehaviors and intercept them before I have to stop instruction to redirect students? Do students complete this procedure independently, or do they depend on me to successfully complete this procedure? Which student leaders can help all students complete this procedure?
Independent Work	How clear and specific are the expectations of this procedure for students? How frequently and consistently do I communicate my expectations for this procedure? How effectively do I teach, reteach, and model my expectations for this procedure to students? How well do I monitor students in this procedure? How effective am I at positively reinforcing students' behavior when I see them successfully execute this procedure? How well do I anticipate student misbehaviors and intercept them before I have to stop instruction to redirect students? Do students complete this procedure independently, or do they depend on me to successfully complete this procedure? Which student leaders can help all students complete this procedure?
Technology Use	How clear and specific are the expectations of this procedure for students? How frequently and consistently do I communicate my expectations for this procedure? How effectively do I teach, reteach, and model my expectations for this procedure to students? How well do I monitor students in this procedure? How effective am I at positively reinforcing students' behavior when I see them successfully execute this procedure? How well do I anticipate student misbehaviors and intercept them before I have to stop instruction to redirect students? Do students complete this procedure independently, or do they depend on me to successfully complete this procedure? Which student leaders can help all students complete this procedure?

continued →

Routine	Reflection
Testing	How clear and specific are the expectations of this procedure for students? How frequently and consistently do I communicate my expectations for this procedure? How effectively do I teach, reteach, and model my expectations for this procedure to students? How well do I monitor students in this procedure? How effective am I at positively reinforcing students' behavior when I see them successfully execute this procedure? How well do I anticipate student misbehaviors and intercept them before I have to stop instruction to redirect students? Do students complete this procedure independently, or do they depend on me to successfully complete this procedure? Which student leaders can help all students complete this procedure?

Visit ***go.SolutionTree.com/instruction*** *for a free reproducible version of this figure.*

As you ponder the questions in figure 3.4 (pages 57–62), remind yourself that you want students to do the work, not you. When students are leading routines and procedures, and teachers are monitoring them, learning is the focus.

Building a Student Excellence Support System: Classroom Routines and Procedures

Now that we have defined excellence in routines and procedures, it is time that we define the support system that teachers can create to guarantee every student's success with those routines and procedures. To reach the goal of student independence, teachers and schools should employ a consistent support system.

Let's consider the goal of positive behavioral interventions and supports (PBIS). According to the PBIS website's home page (www.pbis.org), "The broad purpose of PBIS is to improve the effectiveness, efficiency and equity of schools and other agencies. PBIS improves social, emotional and academic outcomes for all students, including students with disabilities and students from underrepresented groups." Effectiveness, efficiency, and equity in school can improve only if teachers work interdependently in collaborative teams to achieve the common goal—learning for all.

In the following sections, we will discuss how to build a Student Excellence Support System. The first step is teacher team collaboration to establish consistency so all students have common expectations from classroom to classroom. Next, teachers create classwide supports that personalize routines for teachers, while also maintaining consistency across the team. Finally, teachers need to anticipate how they will respond when students struggle with expectations; they must be prepared to create individualized student supports, which embody the RTI structure, for students who have behavioral deficiencies.

Step 1: Teacher Team Collaboration

Schoolwide rules are critical for student success and succeed only when teachers collectively and consistently enforce these rules. Furthermore, teachers best support these rules when grade-level or department-level teams personalize their adherence to and enforcement of schoolwide rules and expectations within their classrooms.

Throughout the year, teams must periodically take time to review and refine how schoolwide expectations should look and sound within their teams. The best teams make time to create norms for how they will work together, as well as norms for what they expect from students inside and outside the classroom. Additionally, teacher teams should establish norms for their collective response to students who violate classroom or school rules.

Teams work together to create team-specific positive behavior supports and incentives that motivate students to make smart choices in their behavior and learning. High-performing teams ensure that every member responds in roughly the same way when students commit minor infractions, regardless of which teacher is responding or which student is exhibiting the behavior. In other words, high-performing teams take ownership for the success of *all* students, and behavior is a big part of that success.

Creating teacher team norms for responding to student misbehavior is essential for two reasons.

1. New teachers and teachers who struggle with classroom management benefit from others' expertise.
2. Students rarely interact with just one teacher, especially at the secondary level. Instead, they typically encounter several teachers. When they know that all teachers are on the same page with disciplinary expectations and behavioral responses, students are more inclined to respond positively, regardless of which teacher is addressing them.

Even as teacher teams align their classroom expectations for behavior with schoolwide expectations, they also must ensure that their efforts do not take away flexibility or autonomy from individual teachers. Figures 3.3 (page 55) and 3.4 (pages 57–62) illustrate some routines and learning procedures students experience in most classrooms. When teachers can create commonalities in these procedures, students stand a greater chance of following them. Those commonalities, however, don't have to represent exact duplications of procedures. Teacher teams must support their members in aligning common procedures and, at the same time, promote each teacher's individual teaching style, student population, and coursework. For example, teachers across the school might establish the same expectation for entering the classroom, but how students accomplish that routine (the procedure) can vary from room to room.

To guide their alignment of their basic expectations for these common routines and procedures while allowing for flexibility, teacher teams should ask themselves adapted versions of the four critical questions of a PLC (DuFour, DuFour, Eaker, Many, & Mattos, 2016). These questions allow for customization for individual teachers and classrooms (DuFour et al., 2016).

1. What do we expect all students to do in following each of these routines and procedures?
2. How will we know whether they are exhibiting the behaviors correctly and independently?
3. How will we respond when students are not meeting expectations, without negatively impacting student learning?
4. How will we reinforce and empower students who are meeting our expectations?

When teachers can agree on their basic expectations for and responses to behavior, they level the playing field for all students. Having this conversation is critical for teachers who share students as well as teachers in secondary schools. Students have to adjust to a new teacher and different procedures each time they change classes, and when teachers can lessen that adjustment, they have more time to invest in teaching students as opposed to responding to misbehavior. Finally, aligning expectations from class to class helps struggling teachers develop their skill set in effectively providing classroom routines and procedures.

Step 2: Classwide Supports

Once teams establish consistent routines and procedures, they then take those plans and integrate them into their classrooms. Teachers personalize routines and procedures so they fit both the teacher's and students' personalities. Furthermore, the routines and procedures must support the content and more specifically the learning targets for that content.

Before implementing routines and procedures, teachers should follow these seven steps and ask the corresponding questions about communicating and establishing expectations with students.

1. **Establish expectations:** How will I use the room to communicate my expectations? Where should I post procedural text and organizational charts so the expectations are available to students?
2. **Communicate expectations:** How will I verbally communicate expectations to students in a concrete and specific way so I will be aligned with my team and consistent in my implementation?

3. **Teach expectations:** What will I say while I explicitly teach and reteach routines and procedures to students?
4. **Reinforce excellence:** What phrases or celebration statements will I specifically say to reinforce students who are meeting my expectations with routines?
5. **Intercept misbehavior:** What specific phrases will I use to intercept students who show early warning signs of misbehavior or off-task behavior?
6. **Expect independence:** What will I say to students to encourage them to be independent learners?
7. **Empower leadership:** What affirmative statements can I make to build leadership in students, and what questions can I ask to challenge students to take leadership roles in the classroom?

Not only should teachers consider the communication strategies they will use, but they should also anticipate the types of behaviors that will challenge them when students are apathetic, apprehensive, or even defiant. Great teachers consider these kinds of behaviors and prepare for how they will respond to students in a way that encourages them to get back into learning, instead of possibly escalating behavior. Crisis Prevention Institute (CPI, n.d.) has developed a program called Nonviolent Crisis Intervention that focuses on preventing students with behavior issues from escalating their behaviors to severe behavior incidents. The program teaches educators the following skills:

- How to identify behaviors that could lead to a crisis
- How to most effectively respond to each behavior to prevent the situation from escalating
- How to use verbal and nonverbal techniques to defuse hostile behavior and resolve a crisis before it can become violent (CPI, n.d.)

While educators critically need these skills for students with behavior disorders, the program gives educators great strategies they can utilize with all students who are resistant to learning.

Great teachers also possess the skills to track data and responses for behavior and then immediately share that information with both parents and students. When students misbehave, teachers can have them sign a behavior log, and teachers can use the data to conference with students and their parents to help the students overcome their challenges.

Technology can accelerate data collection and make it even more transparent. Web tools such as ClassDojo (www.classdojo.com) or Seesaw (https://web.seesaw.me) provide teachers the opportunity to track both positive and inappropriate behaviors. Best of all, however, these web tools allow parents to see the information in real time, as opposed to waiting for paper communication or a phone call from the teacher.

Classwide supports aim to personalize teacher team–developed routines and procedures in a way that meets the needs of the teacher and the students he or she serves. Personalizing those supports involves determining how to deliver the team's expectations in the classroom. Teachers determine their delivery by how they communicate to students, anticipate and respond to routine problematic behaviors, and clearly and concisely track behavior data so they can share the data with students, parents, colleagues, and administrators. Excellence in routines and procedures depends on how educators and parents support one another in building student independence.

Step 3: Individualized Student Supports

Some students will have difficulty with behavior no matter how effective you are at developing routines and procedures. When misbehaviors persist, we, as teachers, find it easy to become frustrated with the students. But we must remember that when students struggle with learning, we need to personalize instruction based on their greatest area for growth, and the same rule applies to behavior. We need to personalize routines and procedures to better fit student needs but do it in a way that doesn't take away from the consistency we strive for within our teacher team.

When a student is struggling with behavior, we should first check with the student's other teachers. Sometimes, the student has a behavior problem with you but not with other teachers. In this situation, gather ideas and strategies for addressing the misbehavior from teachers who are successfully working with the student. Conversely, sometimes, a student has problems in most if not all of his or her classes. In that situation, the team should approach the problem as a unified front to address the behavior consistently.

In order to solve the problem either as a team or as an individual educator, I developed a four-step problem-solving model as the first phase to responding to student misbehavior (Wink, 2017).

1. Simplify the problem or identify its root cause.
2. Develop a plan to address the behavior that most impedes learning.
3. Work the plan for two weeks to see whether the plan changes the behavior.
4. After approximately two weeks, you have given the intervention enough time to elicit data to determine its effectiveness on the student behavior. By using anecdotal records, you can determine whether the behavior has decreased in frequency. If the behavior has improved, continue providing the behavior supports until the student minimizes or corrects the

behavior. If the behavior has not changed or has worsened, then start the process over by simplifying the problem again.

Figure 3.5 offers a flowchart to help educators simplify behavior problems, develop potential solutions, and then gauge improvement.

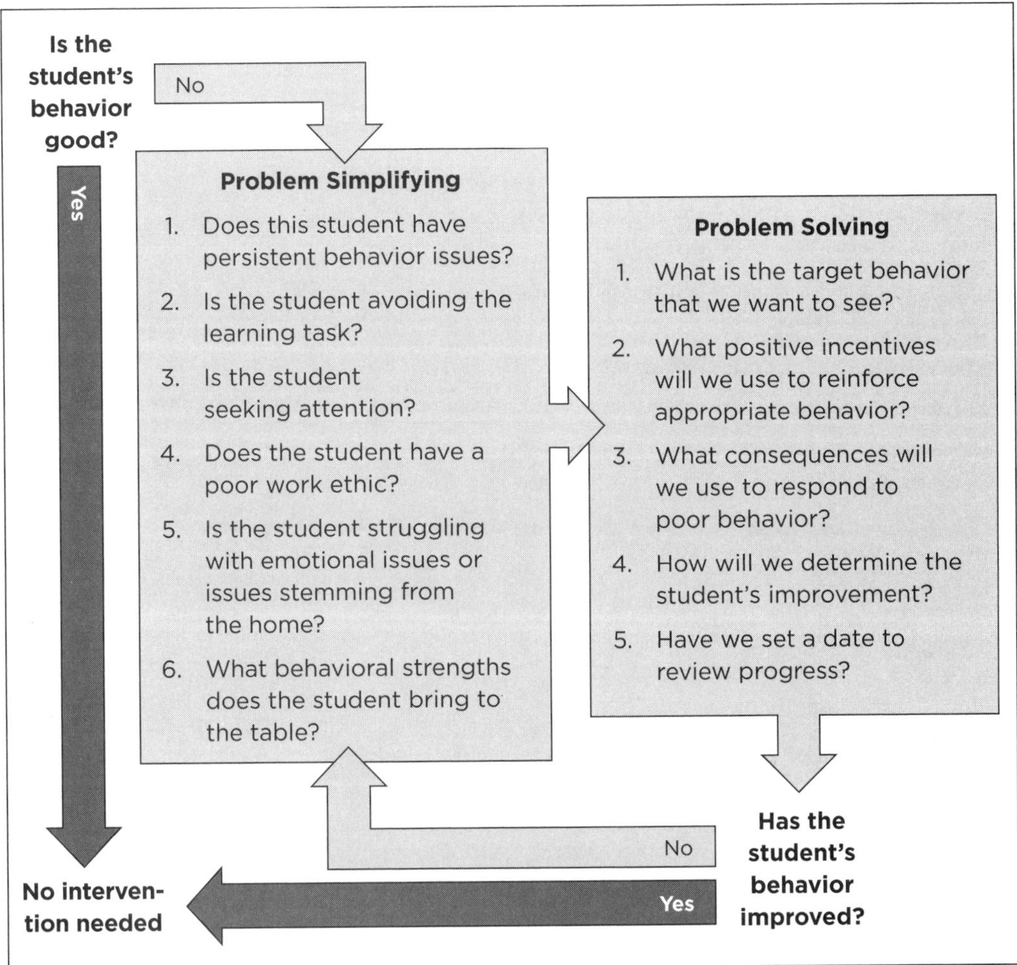

Source: Wink, 2017, p. 155.

Figure 3.5: Response to behavior flowchart.

The problem-solving tool in figure 3.6 (pages 68–69) helps teachers further support students who struggle with classroom routines and procedures. It can help teachers isolate the problem behavior, prescribe a support, and determine the effectiveness of the support.

Individualized Student Support Problem-Solving Tool: Classroom Routines and Procedures	
Question 1: Has the teacher team created common expectations and supports for all students at this level? (Circle yes or no.) (If your answer is yes, continue. If your answer is no, stop and correct this area.)	Yes No
Question 2: Based on the team's work, has the teacher created classwide routines and procedures? (Circle yes or no.) (If your answer is yes, continue. If your answer is no, stop and correct this area.)	Yes No
Question 3: Are the majority of students successfully using the classwide routines and procedures? (Circle yes or no.) (If your answer is yes, continue. If your answer is no, stop and correct this area.)	Yes No

Question 4: Which student is struggling with routines and procedures?

Student: ____________________

Check the boxes next to the routines and procedures that the student struggles with the most.

Classroom Routines

- ☐ Entering the room
- ☐ Leaving the room
- ☐ Transitioning in the room
- ☐ Going to the restroom, office, counselor, or nurse
- ☐ Accessing classroom resources independently
- ☐ Responding to visitors

When Student Struggles With the Routine

- ☐ Beginning of period
- ☐ Middle of period
- ☐ End of period
- ☐ When routine changes
- ☐ When school schedule changes

Learning Procedures

- ☐ Whole-group instruction
- ☐ Small-group instruction
- ☐ Partner work
- ☐ Independent work
- ☐ Technology use
- ☐ Testing

List the student's strengths and difficulties with each component at this level.

<table>
<tr><td colspan="2">Question 5: What is the root cause of the behavior? (Consider the following questions to determine the root cause. Check all that apply.)
☐ Does the student have a history of behavior problems?
☐ Is the student avoiding learning tasks?
☐ Is the student seeking attention?
☐ Does the student have a poor work ethic?
☐ Is the student struggling with emotional issues or issues stemming from the home?
☐ What strengths does this student possess, and am I leveraging those strengths to address behavior?</td></tr>
<tr><td colspan="2">Question 6: What potential supports will help this student be successful with the behavior? (Consider the following questions to determine potential supports.)
☐ What is the target behavior I want to address first?
☐ What positive reinforcement will I provide the student when I see it?
☐ How will I intercept the student when I see signs that the target behavior is not meeting expectations?</td></tr>
<tr><td colspan="2">Question 7: What are the goal and the deadline for the student to be successful with the behavior?
Goal:

Deadline:</td></tr>
<tr><td>Question 8: Did the student meet the goal by the deadline? (Circle yes or no.)
(If your answer is yes, continue the support. If your answer is no, return to question 4.)</td><td>Yes No</td></tr>
<tr><td colspan="2">Notes:</td></tr>
</table>

Figure 3.6: Individualized student support problem-solving tool—classroom routines and procedures.

Visit ***go.SolutionTree.com/instruction*** *for a free reproducible version of this figure.*

Conclusion

In this chapter, we learned that teachers can meet students' safety and security needs by creating routines and procedures that teach students the appropriate behaviors to chase excellence in learning. The second level in the Hierarchy of Student Excellence should challenge all students to learn, grow, and excel as independent learners.

It's important that schools create schoolwide expectations for behavior and learning, but more importantly, teacher teams who share students must create common routines and procedures so students will have common expectations from classroom to classroom. This alignment between teachers provides students with the safety and security that many of them lack.

At this level, the best teachers don't focus on the traditional concept of classroom management with rules and consequences; they build routines and procedures that prepare every student to become a college- and career-ready graduate. They understand that without student independence in learning, behavioral issues might lead to rejection of rules and, ultimately, learning. Student excellence becomes a reality when students believe in classroom routines and procedures and know the teacher supports them in their academic journey.

This chapter concludes with a reflection tool (pages 71–72) that teachers can use to evaluate their understanding of the challenges they face when identifying and making the most effective use of classroom routines and procedures. As you consider the questions and your responses to them, explore possibilities for improving those systems, including teacher team collaboration, classwide supports, and individualized student supports, based on the information and ideas in this chapter.

Reflection Tool: Classroom Routines and Procedures

Answer the following questions to help you create a more engaging classroom where students feel safe and secure through consistent routines and procedures.

Teacher Team Collaboration

- Has our team identified the common routines and procedures that all students will experience?
- How well do team members lead one another in aligning common routines and procedures?
- How well do team members focus on building student independence with each routine or procedure?
- When a teacher experiences difficulty with a student or a routine, what steps does he or she take to seek help from the team?

Classwide Supports

- How well have I aligned my routines and procedures with the routines and procedures developed by the team?
- What evidence do I collect to gauge student success with routines and procedures?
- How well do I communicate expectations for behavior to maintain student independence with those routines?
- How effectively do my positive behavior supports reinforce the behaviors I wish to see in these routines?
- How effectively do I intercept student misbehaviors so I don't have to stop instruction to redirect students?
- What level of independence do my students exhibit with each routine and procedure?
- How can I create student leaders to help me lead each routine and procedure?

Individualized Student Supports

- When a student repeatedly has difficulty with a behavior, how well do I consistently determine the root cause of this behavior?

- Once I determine the potential root cause of student behavior, how well do I verify that the failure is not due to my classroom supports or inconsistency from the team?
- How effective am I at identifying the student's strengths so that I can leverage the strength to address the area for growth?
- When I prescribe an intervention, how committed am I to providing the intervention with frequency and consistency?
- How consistently do I gauge student growth in behavior to determine if my intervention was effective?
- When the student is still unsuccessful, how well do I reflect and refine the intervention to better help the student?
- When my efforts to help the student continue to fail, how well do I reach out to my team members to help me better respond to the student?

CHAPTER 4

Teaching for Excellence: Relationships for Learning

The less stability that students have at home, the more they need a caring, trusting adult at school.

—Eric Jensen

The need for interpersonal relationships motivates behavior. According to psychology researcher Saul McLeod (2018), examples of love and belongingness include "friendship, intimacy, trust, and acceptance, receiving and giving affection and love, affiliating, being part of a group (family, friends, work)." Essentially, the need to belong precedes the desire to learn.

I believe that the love of learning often begins with a relationship with a positive adult role model and ends with an endless thirst for knowledge. Student learning has the potential to accelerate with the help of significant, supportive relationships inside and outside the classroom. In his book *Poor Students, Rich Teaching*, Eric Jensen (2016) reminds us of John Hattie's (2009) research that clearly supports the need for strong relationships for learning. Jensen (2016) writes, "Student-teacher relationships have a strong effect on student achievement, which are easily in the top 10 percent of all factors. . . . For comparison, teacher subject-matter knowledge is in the bottom 10 percent of all factors" (p. 11).

Students of poverty can lack the relationship supports that influence learning because some live in fractured homes or single-parent homes where the sole parent is taking on extra work to make ends meet. Thirty-seven percent of families led by single mothers nationwide live in poverty. Comparatively, only 6.8 perecent of families with married parents live in poverty, according to 2009 data compiled by the Heritage Foundation (My Safe Harbor, 2019). As stated in chapter 1 (page 7), more than half of U.S. students (51.8 percent) live in poverty and receive free and reduced lunch assistance.

This means that not only do most students lack physiological and safety and security needs, but some also lack significant time and support from parents and guardians due to parents working long or irregular hours or multiple jobs trying to support their family. This doesn't mean that all students of poverty lack the relationships needed to foster learning. However, the lack of physiological resources due to poverty can create a roadblock for some students to pursuing meaningful relationships that help to satisfy their growth needs. Those deficits are coming to your classroom.

Through his research and his personal experiences as a disconnected learner, Eric Jensen (2016) provides compelling evidence for why the third level in the Hierarchy of Student Excellence is essential to helping every student find his or her excellence. Jensen (2016) states that relationships between students and teachers are essential to learning, but "are more important to students who don't have a loving parent at home" (p. 29). As the old educational adage goes, students don't care how much we know until they know how much we care. For students who have major gaps in learning coupled with major gaps in their love and belongingness needs, the relationships that we forge with them are the bridges that can close these gaps.

We must better equip ourselves to identify students who are lacking in this need. Teachers can help close the love-belongingness gap; they can leverage this relationship to motivate and inspire students to believe that learning is their golden ticket out of the cycle of poverty, apathy, or any other barrier currently present in their life.

In the next section, you will read about Kelsey, a student of poverty, who has attended multiple schools as a result of lack of stable housing. You will learn how her teacher's frustration with Kelsey's lack of desire to learn turns into resolve, resulting in Kelsey developing a positive relationship with learning as well as with her teacher.

Reaching Students Through Relationships

At the start of a new school year, Kelsey found herself in her third new school in three years, and she felt numb to the point of school. She and her mother were about to be evicted from their apartment due to their rent being several months past due. Kelsey was a sweet but reserved girl in a new home and with no friends, and now, she was assigned another stranger, Mr. Davis, as her fifth-grade teacher. The purpose of school to her now was just to serve as a resting place for the day until her mother got off work.

Mr. Davis was finding his stride, entering his fifth year of teaching. His students' test scores from last year showed his instruction had markedly improved from the previous year, but a new change loomed. The state standards were changing, and the state test was too. Mr. Davis analyzed his new standards and developed a strong plan for not only engaging all students, but also responding to their gaps in learning through intervention. Taking pride in his effectiveness as an instructor, he would not let his students' scores drop. As students started out the year, most were able to transition to the more challenging content, but many, including Kelsey, showed lots of gaps in their learning.

As any great teacher would do, Mr. Davis immediately began making plans to pull students for interventions, identify gaps in their prerequisite skills, and add specific activities to help those students. In spite of all his work, Kelsey made no gains. Her attitude was passively compliant but basically uninterested in what she called "stupid work" to her classmates.

Over the weeks, Mr. Davis grew frustrated in her lack of interest in what he considered very engaging instruction. After all, he was making the learning fun and interesting to students, but she would have none of it. He started to feel that she was just a disrespectful student who needed disciplinary action, so he began doling out consequences for insubordination in the form of referrals to the office.

Not only did the consequences not work, they drove Kelsey to resist Mr. Davis's efforts even more. Losing faith in his ability to meet her needs, he finally reached out to his teammates, the counselor, and the principal. Through research and collaboration, Mr. Davis discovered that this was Kelsey's third school in three years, and she had only had two years' growth in her reading level in the last four years. He learned that her dad was in and out of the picture, so that relationship was weak and inconsistent at best. She was a child of economic poverty and also a child of emotional poverty. This information brought Mr. Davis to tears, because he knew that he was just another unreliable male in her life, and his actions were only making matters worse.

That day, Mr. Davis made a commitment to build a relationship with Kelsey and with every other student he had overlooked. He announced his *star students of the month*, who would have a surprise lunch with him. Mr. Davis selected three students based on one or two of the following criteria: proficiency in learning, growth in acquiring skills, or the need for time to feel special. Mr. Davis committed to this initiative because he knew that every student needed a well-deserved turn at this special and unique time with him and their peers. Surprised that her name was on the list, Kelsey concealed her excitement under her small but skeptical smile.

When the star students went to lunch later that day, to Kelsey's relief, there was no talk about school, learning, or even grades. The students discussed their favorite parts of school, their favorite recess games, and what they wanted to be when they grew up. Mr. Davis thanked his students for their hard work, engaged them in a friendly discussion, and ended the lunch with a quick game of trashcan basketball. The lunch was a hit, and Mr. Davis saw a crack form in Kelsey's wall of resistance, which was the starting point for her growth as a learner and a person.

Over the next few weeks of consistent relationship building, Mr. Davis saw his continued efforts at getting to know Kelsey begin to tear down her walls of resistance while her grades came up. His constant encouragement increased her interest in books, and his interventions caused her mastery of the content to soar. Mr. Davis stopped Kelsey one day after class and said, "Kelsey, I am so proud of how much you are growing in your learning. I have to know how you did it."

Her reply was simple and short: "You make learning fun."

Kelsey went on her way, and Mr. Davis smiled because he had just learned the most important lesson of his career. His mission was to teach students, not content.

Kelsey represents many students in our schools. They come to school with so much emotional baggage and stress that they can't possibly think about learning. Mr. Davis could have blamed Kelsey's apathy or perceived laziness as the reason for her inability to learn; instead, he focused on making Kelsey feel loved and appreciated. It often amazes me how much those little efforts can make an epic impact on students and the trajectory of their education. Relationships precede learning, and they always will. Love and belongingness is the third level in Maslow's Hierarchy of Needs and aligns with the third level in the Hierarchy of Student Excellent—relationships for learning (see figure 4.1). As evidenced in the story, relationships are key to providing the support students need for success in the classroom.

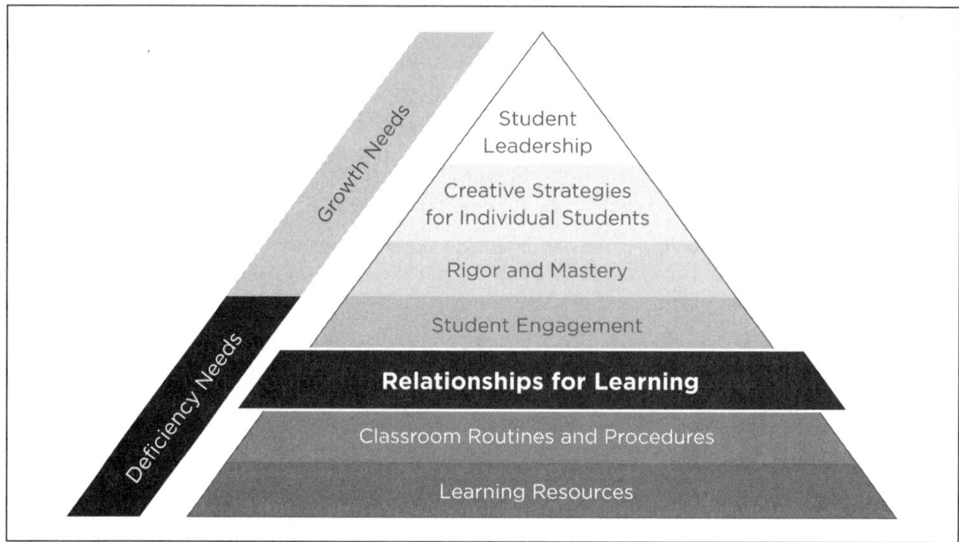

Figure 4.1: Hierarchy of Student Excellence—relationships for learning.

Think back to your days in school. Were you ever left out of a group, or did students ever harass or ostracize you? Did a teacher ever make you feel inferior in front of other students because you weren't as smart, as fast, or as good as them? If we're honest with ourselves, we have all felt that way at one point in our lives. Love, belongingness, and relationships matter in a student's quest for excellence in learning, as Kelsey's story clearly demonstrates.

Building Relationships for Learning

The third level in the Hierarchy of Student Excellence, relationships for learning, corresponds with the third level in Maslow's Hierarchy of Needs, love and belongingness needs, but with one distinct difference. Both focus on fulfilling the need for trusting and loving relationships, but the Hierarchy of Student Excellence leverages the relationships between teacher and student, and among students, to encourage students to fall in love with learning. We can care for students all day long, but if we don't get students to also love or at least solidly appreciate the content we teach, then we will have succeeded as kindhearted individuals but failed as educators.

Relationships for learning are composed of three components: (1) teacher-student relationships, (2) student-content relationships, and (3) student-student relationships. Students can like the teacher, but if they don't like the content or students in the room, they may not be interested in learning. When students like their classmates but don't like the teacher, they may find it hard to develop love for the content simply because they resent the teacher or connect their dislike of the teacher to a dislike for the content. In many cases, students can truly enjoy the content but in time grow weary of learning if they don't trust the teacher or other students in the room. Teachers must aim to facilitate students' development of these three components of relationships for learning to build trust between teacher and student, student and content, and among students themselves, which can provide the support students need to learn at high levels.

Preparation

Making plans to build relationships with students is something that educators often do haphazardly or with little thought. Hattie (2009) claims that building relationships is in the top 10 percent of factors that guarantee growth in learning. Knowing that strong relationships foster learning, we should make the best plan possible to for all students to have a meaningful relationship with the teacher, their peers, and the classroom content. The following sections detail how educators can prepare to build these relationships.

Teacher-Student Relationships

Great teachers make plans to build relationships with students before students even show up. They consider that all students need to feel love and belongingness in the classroom, or to feel like their classroom is their home away from home. Teacher considerations include how they welcome students, how they build relationships with families, and how they help students feel like the learning is personalized just for them.

To get started, take some time to deeply research the two or three most at-risk students in your classroom or the fifteen most at-risk students in your secondary-class rosters. Interview the students' former teachers and administrators, and dig into the cumulative folders in the office or on the student information system to find the following information.

- **Strengths:** What skills does this student bring to my classroom that will help him or her learn?
- **Areas for improvement:** What deficits does the student possess that I need to consider in my assignments for him or her?
- **Home background:** What kind of home support or history of mobility does the student have? Have some significant events or traumatic events occurred in his or her life?
- **Academic history:** What is the student's history of learning? Has the student ever had a year in which he or she excelled in my subject?
- **Discipline history:** What behaviors has the student displayed in the past? Does he or she have a pattern of behavior that I need to be prepared for?
- **Strategies that worked:** What strategies have former teachers used to help this student learn that will help me better connect with him or her?
- **Emotional triggers:** What teacher words, actions, or reactions might escalate this student's behavior? What words or actions by the teacher or classmates might trigger a severe emotional response?
- **Significant adult:** Who is an adult, family member, or school employee who has a powerful relationship with this student? What are the best ways to build a strong relationship with the student through this significant adult?

The key to successful teacher-student relationships is the time teachers put into researching students who need to grow the most in their learning. Without this information, teachers waste precious time experimenting with strategies that may or may not help students connect with learning.

Student-Content Relationships

Teacher-student relationships are critical to connecting students with the teacher, the content, and the other students. However, without student-content relationships, we miss the component that connects students with the content we want them to love. The teacher's skills must include selling the content and coaching students to push themselves to excel far beyond the learning target.

The salesmanship of teaching struggling students requires teachers to sell something bigger than learning. They have to sell what Simon Sinek (2009) calls the *why*. The *why* is something that students lack when they reject the learning. They don't know *why* they have to learn the content or *why* it's important Or they don't understand *why* learning will make a difference in their lives. Salesmanship is about motivating students to believe that not only is the content accessible, but mastery of it is attainable. When students are fired up about learning and believe in what they are doing, they can expect to see an effect size of 0.48 on their learning (Hattie, 2009). In other words, motivation by itself can generate more than a year's growth if nothing changes in your instruction.

Great teachers excel at selling their content and are even better at coaching students to chase growth. After selling the content with motivation, we have to help students set what Eric Jensen (2016) calls *gutsy goals*, personalized goals that students set for both short-term growth and long-term growth. Hattie's (2009) research points out that when teachers leverage gutsy goals by helping students set micro-goals each week, students can expect to see massive growth; this has an effect size of 1.21 or a whopping three years' growth in one year. A *micro-goal* is a short-term weekly or daily goal established for improving in a particular classroom or learning behavior or instructional strategy. At the end of the day or week, the student tracks his or her progress in meeting the goal. If the student meets the goal he or she establishes a new micro-goal or sets a higher goal to continue improving on the behavior. If the student does not meet the goal, he or she reflects on the performance, with guidance from the teacher, and makes a plan to reach the goal next time.

Since 2017, students at Blue Ridge Independent School District in Texas have been setting gutsy goals called *+10 goals*. Students establish their +10 goals by finding their previous year's State of Texas Assessments of Academic Readiness (STAAR) results and then setting a goal to earn ten more points on the test by the end of the year. Every time students take a six-week formal assessment, which are aligned to the standards assessed on the STAAR test, they compare their results to their baseline (the previous year's STAAR result), and then set micro-goals for growth in the next six weeks. Some students establish goals for improving specific skills unmastered, while others establish goals for showing their work, proving their work, or increasing their persistence or stamina on the test. When students own the goal, growth is within their reach.

Teachers also set their own +10 goals to add ten points to their students' STAAR performance that approached the standard, met the standard, and mastered the standard the previous year. Figure 4.2 (page 80) illustrates what +10 goal setting could look like for teachers and how they can use six-week assessments to monitor their effectiveness in reaching goals for improving student learning.

Mrs. Smith's Six-Grade Students	Approaches Standard	Meets Standard	Masters Standard
STAAR Reading Scores for Fifth Graders	70 percent	52 percent	24 percent
+10 Goal for Sixth Graders	80 percent	62 percent	34 percent
First Six-Week Assessment			
Second Six-Week Assessment			
Third Six-Week Assessment			
Fourth Six-Week Assessment			
STAAR or End-of-Year Assessment			

Figure 4.2: +10 goal-setting chart for teachers.

This gutsy goal setting has had tremendous results for students and teachers alike. In 2017, the Blue Ridge Independent School District received an academic rating of C by the Texas Education Agency, and in 2019, it earned the highest rating possible, an A. Goal setting proved to be one of the key strategies used to ensure all students learned at high levels.

Planning strong relationships for learning depends on teachers' researching the best ways to build personal relationships with students, and then leveraging those relationships to sell the content to students and then coach them to believe in their own efficacy and abilities to reach their gutsy goals. Once teachers firmly establish those relationships, the final relationships left to plan for are student-student relationships.

Student-Student Relationships

A culture of learning cannot exist unless students are an interactive part of that culture. The greatest learning occurs when students feel like they matter to their peers; therefore, the best teachers make plans to build a sense of family within the classroom. "Research suggests an especially positive and significant relationship between academic achievement and school belonging, and for minority students, a feeling of acceptance" (Adelabu, 2007; Jensen, 2016, p. 37).

Since a sense of belonging is critical to learning, teachers must consider the climate they want to create for their students. One of the biggest differences between low-performing and high-performing teachers is that high-performing teachers build a positive school and classroom climate (Jensen, 2014). A positive school climate includes the actions and interactions that teachers design for students to work together, learn together, and teach one another. In short, student collaboration greatly impacts a positive climate.

Collaboration, as defined by DuFour et al. (2016), occurs when a group of individuals work interdependently to achieve a common goal for which all members are mutually accountable. You'll find more information about collaboration in chapter 5 (page 101), but note that collaboration begins with a sense of belonging. When students feel like they are contributing members of the classroom, engagement and learning soar. According to Jensen (2016), belongingness and cooperative learning greatly affect academic success. Cooperative learning versus independent learning has an effect size of 0.59 (Hattie, 2009), which is much more than a year's growth. This means students grow more from cooperative learning than they do from independent learning.

The evidence is clear: positive student-student relationships accelerate learning. To begin facilitating these relationships, teachers should consider the following questions.

- How will I arrange students in the classroom so they can interact positively with one another around the content?
- What strategies will I use to build trusting relationships among students so they will want to collaborate with one another around the content?
- What classroom values must I establish to ensure all students are kind to one another and treat each other with respect and support?
- What celebrations will I employ to incentivize the work of collaborative student teams?

When teachers make plans for the structures needed to support collaboration, students are more likely to interact with their peers as well as the content and teacher. Student-student relationships begin when teachers create the conditions for students to learn with and from each other.

Delivery

Delivery of relationships for learning concerns how educators interact with students in the most common situations throughout the school year. "Many teachers consider building relationships with students as a very important part of learning, but excellent teachers make building student relationships their first priority" (Wink, 2017, p. 71). Great teachers execute effective plans for building strong relationships with students to support learning. The following sections discuss how teachers can execute their plans of building teacher-student relationships, student-content relationships, and student-student relationships.

Teacher-Student Relationships

Table 4.1 (page 82) shows common situations and considerations that teachers can leverage to build strong teacher-student relationships. When approached with consistency and positivity, these situations can greatly affect how teachers build relationships with students.

Table 4.1: Considerations for Delivering Teacher-Student Relationships

Common Situation	Consideration
When students enter the room	How will I greet students as they enter the room each day so they will be inspired to learn?
When students leave the room	How will I affirm students as they leave my class so they know they have made a significant contribution to the lesson and their learning?
When students behave inappropriately	How will I correct students in a way that doesn't fracture their relationships for learning?
When students behave appropriately	How will I quickly celebrate students for behaviors that support learning?
When students have a bad day	How will I interact with students when they have bad days, and how will I ensure that bad days don't negatively impact students?
When students learn successfully	How will I celebrate students and the class as a whole when learning is highly successful?
When the teacher communicates with students' parents	In what ways can I engage parents through face-to-face, phone, and digital communication so they will trust me and be partners in their child's learning?

Visit ***go.SolutionTree.com/instruction*** *for a free reproducible version of this table.*

When teachers develop strong, positive relationships with students, students can expect to see one and a half years' growth (0.72 effect size). As stated previously, teacher-student relationships are in the top 10 percent of factors that impact student learning, while a teacher's content knowledge ranks in the bottom 10 percent (Hattie, 2009). Relationships with students must be a non-negotiable if we want students to grow by leaps and bounds.

Student-Content Relationships

Essentially, the goal of student-content relationships is to convince students to believe in their ability to master the content and then coach them to master it. To make this happen, teachers should first make sure they can answer a common question that students introspectively ask before choosing to learn something: "Why do I have to learn this?" If students cannot connect what they need to learn with an understanding of *why* it is important, they are reticent to pursue learning.

Teachers accomplish this goal with their enthusiasm for learning and the content. They leverage their knowledge of the students and their backgrounds to find unique ways to make the content connect to students' personal lives. Teachers build student-content through their passion for learning and inspiring all students to give their best. In addition to motivating students to learn, teachers foster student-content relationships by making the content relevant. Jensen (2016) speaks about the importance of using relevance to build solid student-content relationships. He notes, "Your students want to know 'What's in it for me?' Relevance is everything to your students" (Jensen, 2016, p. 115). Great teachers build relevance into content by showing students how what they are doing now contributes to a positive future outcome. This strategy, according to Carol Dweck (2000), has a tremendous effect size of 1.42, which is more than three years' growth. Great teachers sell their content by telling students the benefits of learning the subject with a great amount of enthusiasm. The teacher's infatuation with the content is not just obvious; it's contagious and rubs off on students, inspiring them to want to learn more.

Content doesn't come to life until passion, purpose, and a plan come to life in students as they set their sights on mastering the content. The best teachers understand this and inspire students to fall in love with the content by convincing them that content mastery is within their reach. After that, they fuel each student's fire for mastery through the use of positive communication and continuous goal setting.

Student-Student Relationships

As discussed previously, student-student relationships can accelerate learning when students work and learn together. It builds a community where every student belongs.

To make collaboration work, students must first know the goal of collaboration; they must know the purpose for learning and the products they create. Communicate norms for behavior so students know how their behavior supports the purpose and product of collaboration. (See figures 3.2 and 3.3 [pages 54–55].)

For collaboration to work well, it has to occur every day. We cannot expect students to collaborate at high levels if they only do so sparingly. Collaboration is a skill that needs frequency and regularity to develop over time. Students grow in their learning when they teach one another through reciprocal teaching. Hattie's (2009) research shows that reciprocal teaching (students teaching peers) has a strong effect size of 0.74 (more than a year's growth).

To promote student-student relationships, Jensen (2016) suggests students work with study buddies or partners. To make this collaborative structure work, group students by their passions or interests, and allocate time for students to get to know each other using questions such as the following:

- What are your academic strengths?
- Where can you use the most help?
- What is the best type of feedback to give you when you are struggling?
- How are you best at helping others? (Jensen, 2016, p. 41)

Collaboration is a relational learning structure based on mutual respect. According to Hattie (2009), student collaboration accelerates learning and generates more than a year's growth, with a 0.50 effect size. Furthermore, the influence that peers have on one another generates even higher gains in learning, with a 0.53 effect size, more than a year's growth.

Celebration also promotes student-student relationships. Think of celebration as the fuel students need on their individual journeys to excellence. Celebration is a ritual that teachers design to "engage more of the class socially and build community" (Jensen, 2016, p. 167).

Different things to celebrate include when students make huge improvements during class, when students achieve short-term and long-term goals, and when the class shows grit in the day's lesson. Great teachers create a positive classroom culture when they empower students to celebrate one another using the same criteria that the teacher uses. Celebration is a class responsibility that affirms each learner for his or her efforts while also raising the bar for other learners. When you praise it, you also raise it, and what gets celebrated gets accelerated.

Reflection

Reflection allows teachers to not only find their strengths and weaknesses but also identify and remove ineffective actions that don't foster positive relationships with students. It also allows teachers to ascertain which students need more support in building stronger relationships with the teacher, the content, or with their peers.

Great teachers reflect on how their relationships with students inspire students to grow in their learning. They analyze their interactions and outcomes with students and the class as a whole to determine how relationship building impacts learning. This reflection enables teachers to gauge the quality of their relationships with students, the students' relationships with the content, and the relationships between and among students.

Beyond assessing their effectiveness, excellent teachers can use reflection to determine how they will respond to students who fail to meet the teacher's expectations for learning. By pinpointing causal factors for student resistance, apathy, or disdain for the content, teachers can determine which relationship component they need to focus on for future growth.

Teachers can use figure 4.3 as a reflection tool to assess their effectiveness with teacher-student relationships, student-content relationships, and student-student relationships.

Relationship for Learning	Reflection
Teacher-Student Relationship	How well do I know my students' strengths and areas for growth? Which groups of students do I have the best relationships with, and which groups of students do I have the worst relationships with? How thoroughly have I researched my students' academic needs or the instructional strategies that have helped students excel? Did my research of students with a disciplinary history reveal the causes of their behavior or simply the fact that they have had challenges with behavior? How effective are my relationship-building strategies for when students enter or exit the classroom? Does my verbal communication enhance or detract from my relationships with students? Do I make effective adjustments when I or my students have bad days? How effective is my plan for parent or family communication in inviting all families to be part of their children's learning in my class?
Student-Content Relationship	How well do students respond to my passion for the content to drive their learning? How well do I sell the importance of learning the content and show students why it's important? How well do I coach students, especially reluctant students, to believe in their own ability to learn the content? How effective are my efforts to help students establish a vision for where they aspire to be in the future and how the content will help them realize their vision? Do students have a gutsy goal (or a +10 goal) that they believe in, and how well do they establish micro-goals to help them achieve their gutsy goal?
Student-Student Relationship	How well do students see each other as learning partners in my class? Is my classroom climate positive for all students, and does the climate inspire even the most reluctant learners to chase excellence in learning? How effectively does student collaboration facilitate every student's learning, empower students to take ownership of their learning, and inspire students to learn with and from one another? How effective are my celebration strategies and rituals at affirming students and reinforcing their efforts to believe in their own efficacy as learners?

Figure 4.3: Relationships for learning reflection tool.

Visit ***go.SolutionTree.com/instruction*** *for a free reproducible version of this figure.*

Building a Student Excellence Support System: Relationships for Learning

Once teachers have established the components of relationships for learning, they need to anticipate student difficulties and build a plan to respond to the most common factors that prevent students from developing relationships for learning. With that in mind, teachers should provide all students with a system of schoolwide supports that helps build strong relationships for learning.

In the following sections, I outline the three steps teachers can leverage to ensure that every student develops strong relationships for learning. In the first step, teacher team collaboration, teachers work in teams to collaboratively build strong teacher-student, student-content, and student-student relationships. In the second step, classwide supports, teachers create their own personalized plan to build these relationships with and for students. The third step, individualized student supports, embodies the spirit of RTI to help teachers create an individualized plan for the most challenging students who have little to no relationship with the content. With this three-step approach, teachers can mend fractured or even broken relationships, and learning can begin to soar for even the most difficult students in class.

Step 1: Teacher Team Collaboration

Through collaborative team structures, teachers can develop a multitude of ways to build relationships with students. They can seek guidance from their teammates on how to help students apply their strengths, background knowledge, and life experiences in pursuit of learning. They can review routines and procedures and hone in on their collective responses to difficult students, and they can spend time in deep study of students before school starts so they have all the information necessary to build strong relationships with all students as a united front.

To build powerful relationships with students, teachers can collaborate in different types of team structures with a preventive mindset. The following sections discuss how teachers can work in teams who share students or content and how to collaborate to build relationships with students and engage parents through communication. This work should begin before the students return to school and be revisited often throughout the year.

Collaboration Among Teachers Who Share Students, Not Content

Through vertical team collaboration, teachers in two consecutive grade levels might sit down and analyze a transition sheet of data about specific students from the previous grade level. They would then discuss specific tactics for students with difficulties from the previous year, which actions were most effective in improving their behavior, and whether those actions should continue in the following year. Finally, the grade-level team could come together to further discuss the information and how the team members plan to implement successful interventions and strategies from previous years or create new ones to strengthen relationships with students and their families.

When teachers who share students collaborate in teacher teams, they can answer the following questions.

- What strengths does the student have?
- What difficulties did he or she have last year?
- What kind of teacher communication can help this student move forward, and what kind of communication shuts him or her down?
- What are the most critical areas in which the team must provide consistency to help the student engage in learning?
- What does the student need from the team to help him or her build positive relationships with other students in the classroom?
- Which of the student's personal, non-school-related characteristics can the team use to build a positive relationship?

In essence, teacher team collaboration ensures that all teachers who share students are collectively one step ahead of students who had difficulty during the previous year and helps them leverage effective strategies from that year to help students improve in the coming year.

Collaboration Among Teachers Who Share Content, Not Students

From an instructional standpoint, teacher teams who do not share students but share content can come together and decide how to approach instruction by building relationships with students, especially those who are reluctant learners. For students who avoid learning tasks, teachers can collaborate on the best ways to incorporate alternative or more accessible tasks requiring varying degrees of ability. They also can collaborate on how they can help withdrawn students connect with classmates, and they can share valuable ideas for how teachers project a passion for the content to their students to inspire learning.

Questions that help teachers who share content collaborate include the following.

- In what ways can we generate excitement about the learning we present to students?
- In what ways can we engage reluctant students when they appear apprehensive about learning?
- How can we challenge students to work hard in learning our content?
- What does consistency look like? What actions should we take to set consistent expectations as well as hold students accountable for meeting them?
- When students are struggling behaviorally, socially, emotionally, or academically, how can we respond with compassion and empathy?

The mindset of *students first, content second* helps teachers, especially those with poor relationship-building skills, develop a useful plan to intercept potential problems in advance.

In order to facilitate the student-student component of relationships for learning, teachers should consider how they will arrange students and give them tasks that build trusting relationships among students. For example, teachers could initially help students build these relationships by having student groups collaboratively do personality or interest inventories. Inventory questions could include the following.

- What is your favorite subject and why? Least favorite subject and why?
- What do you like to do in your free time?
- What is your favorite thing to do after school?
- If you could go anywhere for vacation, where would you go and why?

Having students collaborate around safe topics like these breaks the ice for future academic collaboration. To enhance student-student relationships, teachers can determine ways that students can celebrate one another, help one another, and ask their peers for help. For example, teachers can enhance student-student relationships by using the following questions to engage students as a class.

- Who is one person that made a lot of growth today?
- Who would you like to celebrate for helping you learn today?
- Who would you like to learn more from about the content we are learning?
- Who do you believe has made the most growth in their learning this week?
- Who do you believe has demonstrated the hardest work this week?

Teachers often overlook the student-student element in relationships for learning because they think of this as just students' getting along in the classroom. If they can instead view student-student relationships as a learning accelerant, they will find ways to incorporate this important element into their lessons.

Parent Communication

Teacher teams should collaborate about the various ways to communicate with students' families and the community. A National Education Association (2011) policy brief supports this idea in its statement, "Parent, family and community involvement in education correlates with higher academic performance and school improvement." For example, some interdisciplinary teams that share students might commit to attending students' sporting events to strengthen relationships with students and their parents. Many teacher teams promote positive student relationships by arranging home visits with the divide-and-conquer approach. Through this approach, teachers conduct home visits with students assigned to their homeroom class and then communicate information to all other teachers who have these students in their classes. Teacher teams may also commit to tried-and-true methods of communication, such as phone calls, emails, and take-home papers.

Teacher teams can unleash the power of social media and technology to build strong relationships with students and their families. By using blogs, Facebook (www.facebook.com), Twitter, Remind (www.remind.com), Google Classroom (classroom.google.com), Seesaw, ClassDojo, and other technology tools, teachers make their classrooms more transparent to families by communicating upcoming events, important test dates, accomplishments by the class, or personal messages to individual parents about their children's progress. Teachers can share their lesson plans on a webpage, blog via social media, Remind, Google Classroom or Seesaw for virtually anyone to see at any time, or they may choose to limit access by using a password or controlling the sharing features so only families and students can see the lessons. They can also post pictures and videos that show families the products of student learning. Seesaw is a powerful tool for digital communication. When using any of these types of digital tools, teachers ensure that privacy measures are in place and parents give written permission. The key to parent communication is always showing parents the learning that their children are experiencing.

Some teachers might even flip their instruction for students and their families. In *flipped instruction*, teachers post video lesson lectures online for students to watch before they come to class; then in class, students can practice the work associated with the lesson with the support of the teacher and student groups. While flipped instruction videos are powerful tools for helping students learn, they can also facilitate strong relationships with families. By sharing in their children's learning experiences, families not only know what is going on in the classroom, but also have a resource to help their children successfully learn the content.

Questions to guide teachers in connecting with families include the following.

- How do we initially communicate as a team with every student's family, and what communication tools can we use to engage in this communication on a regular basis?
- What kind of information will the team communicate to every family at the beginning of the year, as well as throughout the year?
- How frequently and in what ways do we communicate the following information to families about their child?
    - The student's overall academic performance or behavior
    - When the student fails a given task
    - When the student commits a minor infraction
    - Upcoming events
- How do we communicate to families the instructions for accessing our lesson plans and other academic information?

- How can we use flipped instruction to help enlist family members to help their children learn at home?
- Which social media or web-based communication tools can we use to convey what students are learning?

These family-centric strategies are in keeping with the overall goal of teacher team collaboration. When teachers develop a common plan for how they will build relationships with students and families, they actually strengthen their instruction. The reason for this correlation is simple. Just as students learn best in an environment in which they feel valued, families will be more willing to assist in the education process when they know that teachers value their children and their support in helping them learn.

Step 2: Classwide Supports

Classwide supports are structures and strategies teachers can employ that are both aligned with the team and personalized to match the teacher's instructional style. The following sections share how teachers can use classwide supports to build teacher-student, student-content, and student-student relationships to address students' diverse needs in the classroom.

Teacher-Student Relationships

The preparation plan for teacher-student relationships includes not only the work teachers do to research students, but also the questions teachers pose to students to get to know them. The following strategies can provide classwide supports for students.

- **All about me:** On the first day of school, teachers can use this worksheet activity to find out more about the students in their class. Students answer questions about themselves, providing a sort of personal inventory for the teacher. This lets students know that the teacher is interested in getting to know them both personally and academically, and it gives teachers the information they need to help students feel more welcome in the class.
- **Personal letters to families:** These letters can express the teacher's excitement to have students in his or her class and ask families for input to better instruct their children.
- **Instructional menu board:** On this board, the teacher lists all the possible activities he or she could use for instruction, such as read independently, write a story or article, work with a partner, work alone, play instructional games on the computer, learn in stations or centers, make videos of their learning, draw pictures of their learning, or any other instructional activity. The teacher can then ask students about their favorite and least favorite activities for future reference.

Building relationships for learning is a daily commitment, and it starts when students enter the room and sticks with them throughout every day's lesson. Table 4.1 (page 82) shows some common situations and considerations for delivering teacher-student relationships for learning. Table 4.2 features common situations teachers encounter every day with students and offers reflective questions to help teachers be more responsive to students who fail to connect with them.

Table 4.2: Considerations for Delivering Teacher-Student Relationships When Students Fail to Connect With Teachers

Common Situation	Considerations
When students enter the room	As students enter the room, what system do I have to strategically build relationships with students who are most disconnected from me on a daily basis?
When students leave the room	What systematic responses can I use as students leave the room to affirm students who had a difficult time learning from me?
When students behave inappropriately	How can I ensure that my responses to disciplinary infractions correct the behavior in a manner that also preserves the relationship for learning?
When students behave appropriately	What specific phrases can I use to praise the class and specific students who display appropriate behavior?
When students have a bad day	How can I gauge the frequency of specific students' bad days so I can anticipate when they will have them and implement a plan of action?
When students learn successfully	What are my celebration rituals for the class and for individual students to build stronger teacher-student relationships? How can I regularly celebrate all students, especially those who may not be the most successful or noticeable but are making progress?
When the teacher communicates with students' parents	What system can I use to reach out often to families of students who have the most difficulty connecting in my classroom? How can I include students as part of my parent communication system?

Visit ***go.SolutionTree.com/instruction*** *for a free reproducible version of this table.*

When teachers have a systematic approach to building teacher-student relationships that incorporates identifying and responding to students who struggle, the majority of students will find success in learning, and it will reduce the need for individual student supports.

Student-Content Relationships

Classwide supports for teacher-student relationships get students excited about the teacher, but student-content supports get students excited about the content. While teachers have a plan to sell the content to students and coach them to grow in their learning, classwide supports evaluate the teacher's effectiveness in responding to students or groups of students who are not connecting with the content. Table 4.3 can help teachers develop classwide supports for student-content relationships.

Table 4.3: Classwide Supports for Student-Content Relationships

Component of Student-Content Relationships	Considerations for Classwide Support
Passion	Which students are not responding to my passion for the content? Which students or groups of students are connected to me but disconnected from the content? What do I do that gets students the most excited about the content?
Purpose	What percentage of my lessons have a purpose that convinces students to learn? How well do I recognize when the class loses interest in the learning or becomes apathetic to the content? How effective is my plan to respond to students when they don't see the importance of what we are doing?
Goals	How compelling is my class goal at convincing students to chase learning? Which students or groups of students believe in their gutsy goals, and which students don't care about their goals? In what ways do I respond immediately to persuade students to work toward their goals?
Coaching	What is my plan to coach the class and individual students? Do I predominantly coach the students to learn specific skills that help them reach their goals, or do I mostly tell them what to do to pass the class? Do I push students to believe in themselves, or do I give up when they don't respond? Do I set micro-goals in activities for students who struggle with content? Which students resent their learning due to my coaching, and which students get more excited about their progress due to my coaching? How flexible are my adjustments in how I coach students?

Mistakes	How do students view mistakes in my classroom? Are they afraid to try? When students become disheartened when they fail, how do I automatically respond to give them the courage and confidence to try again? What is my system to celebrate students who overcome mistakes in their learning? How frequently do I remind students that making mistakes and overcoming them is the only way to grow in their learning?

Visit ***go.SolutionTree.com/instruction*** *for a free reproducible version of this table.*

Excellence in classwide supports for student-content relationships requires having a plan for when students aren't responding. Sometimes, failure or a history of failure is the main barrier that prevents students from connecting to the content, and the teacher's response can remove that barrier.

Student-Student Relationships

As noted previously, student-student relationships involve students' working together, learning together, and teaching one another. A positive, collaborative classroom climate that celebrates student success can help students continue to grow in their learning. Table 4.4 offers questions to help teachers create classwide supports that foster a collaborative climate and strong student-student relationships.

Table 4.4: Classwide Supports for Student-Student Relationships

Component of Student-Student Relationships	Considerations for Classwide Support
Collaboration	What structures do I use to build student collaboration into instruction? What strategies do I use to incorporate socialization strategies into collaboration so students build strong personal relationships? What norms and roles for collaboration have I created so students know how to collaborate effectively? How effectively do I respond to students who engage in off-task behaviors or exhibit disrespectful behavior to other students? How effectively do I affirm students who do well in groups?

continued →

Component of Student-Student Relationships	Considerations for Classwide Support
Climate	What actions do I take to build a positive learning culture where students play an active role in maintaining that culture? How often do I assess the climate of the classroom through both observations and conversations with students? When students conflict with one another, how quick and targeted is my response to guide students to resolve the conflict?
Celebration	What role do students play in leading celebrations in the classroom? What are all the ways students can celebrate one another in my class? Does our celebration primarily focus on high scores, mastery of skills, hard work, or growth in learning, or do we have a healthy balance of celebrations so all students can be exalted for many things? What strategies do I employ to encourage students to cheer each other on in the learning process?

Visit ***go.SolutionTree.com/instruction*** *for a free reproducible version of this table.*

If we want students to learn, grow, and excel, we must create an environment where students drive their learning and the support system for their peers. When these structures are in place, teachers can focus on students who do not respond well to classwide supports through individualized student supports.

Step 3: Individualized Student Supports

When students are unsuccessful and team-level and classwide supports prove ineffective, teachers must develop an individualized plan of action to support those who struggle with relationships. Sometimes, students fail because the teacher has not developed the optimal relationship with them or inspired them to believe in themselves, trust the teacher, or have the confidence they need to pursue learning.

As part of creating individualized student supports, teachers should isolate the root cause of the deficit in relationships for learning. They should evaluate the effectiveness of steps 1 and 2 before building a plan of action for individual students. Sometimes, a lack of team-level collaboration or consistency (step 1) or failure to build effective classwide supports (step 2) is the reason that individual students fail to grow.

Teachers can use the problem-solving tool in figure 4.4 to build a strong plan for providing individualized student supports for relationships for learning.

Individualized Student Support Problem-Solving Tool: Relationships for Learning	
Question 1: Has the teacher team created common expectations and supports for all students at this level? (Circle yes or no.) (If your answer is yes, continue. If your answer is no, stop and correct this area.)	Yes No
Question 2: Based on the team's work, has the teacher created his or her classwide relationships for learning? (Circle yes or no.) (If your answer is yes, continue. If your answer is no, stop and correct this area.)	Yes No
Question 3: Do the majority of students have a positive relationship for learning? (Circle yes or no.) (If your answer is yes, continue. If your answer is no, stop and correct this area.)	Yes No

Question 4: Which student is struggling to develop a relationship for learning?

Student: ______________________

Check the boxes next to the components of relationships for learning that the student most frequently struggles with.

Teacher-Student Relationship	Student-Content Relationship	Student-Student Relationship
☐ Displays a negative attitude	☐ Disengages from activities	☐ Doesn't work well with peers
☐ Is reluctant to respond to me	☐ Lacks pride in his or her work	☐ Will not contribute in a group setting
☐ Appears sad or unhappy	☐ Questions the purpose of activities	☐ Makes fun of others
☐ Argues when redirected or asked to do a task	☐ Won't buy into goals	☐ Interferes with the group
☐ Does not like affirmation	☐ Lacks vision for him- or herself	☐ Will not celebrate others
☐ Has parents who will not support the teacher in difficult times	☐ Stalls to avoid work	☐ Gets others off task
☐ Other: ________	☐ Other: ________	☐ Other: ________

Figure 4.4: Individualized student support problem-solving tool—relationships for learning.

continued →

Individualized Student Support Problem-Solving Tool: Relationships for Learning
List the student's strengths and difficulties with each component at this level. Strengths: Difficulties:
Question 5: What is the root cause of the student's lack of relationships for learning? (Check all that apply.) ☐ Poor home support ☐ History of academic failure ☐ History of disciplinary problems ☐ Struggles with reading ☐ Learning disability ☐ Fear of failure or mistakes ☐ Poor relationships with peers ☐ Struggles with collaboration ☐ A lack of love or belongingness ☐ Other: ____________________
Question 6: What potential supports will help this student develop a relationship for learning? (Consider the following questions to determine the best starting point for potential supports.) • What is the target component in relationships for learning that I want to address first? ☐ Teacher-student relationships ☐ Student-content relationships ☐ Student-student relationships • What one or two specific areas within this component do I need to target first? • Who knows this student best, and what do I need to collaborate about with this person to help me develop a plan of action?

<table>
<tr><td colspan="2">Question 7: What are the goal and the deadline for the student to be successful with relationships for learning?
Goal:

Deadline:</td></tr>
<tr><td>Question 8: Did the student meet the goal by the deadline? (Circle yes or no.)
(If your answer is yes, continue the support. If your answer is no, return to question 4.)</td><td>Yes No</td></tr>
<tr><td colspan="2">Notes:</td></tr>
</table>

Visit ***go.SolutionTree.com/instruction*** *for a free reproducible version of this figure.*

Conclusion

Relationships for learning must be present if we want students to succeed. These relationships include teacher-student relationships, student-content relationships, and student-student relationships. Teachers should research their students as learners and use their research to develop personal relationships with students each and every day. Next, they should leverage their personal relationships with students to inspire all students to connect with the content and set gutsy goals. Finally, teachers can leverage the power of collaboration to create a culture of learning where students work together, learn together, and celebrate each other as learners and colleagues. Remember, when teachers develop strong, positive relationships with students, students can expect to see one and a half years' growth (Hattie, 2009). When relationships for learning are in place, students have the opportunity to grow by leaps and bounds both in their competence as learners and in their confidence as people. Teachers must embrace their powerful role in creating relationships for learning that help students believe in their abilities to master content and support each other's learning through collaboration and peer support. When these relationships are solidly in place, excellence is undeniably attainable.

This chapter concludes with a reflection tool (pages 98–99) that teachers can use to evaluate their understanding of the challenges they face when identifying and making the most effective use of relationships for learning. Consider the questions and your responses to them as you explore possibilities for improving those systems, including teacher team collaboration, classwide supports, and individualized student supports, based on the information and ideas in this chapter.

Reflection Tool: Relationships for Learning

Answer the following questions to help you create a more engaging classroom where students can form strong relationships with the teacher, content, and classmates as a way to support their learning.

Teacher Team Collaboration

- Has our team established plans to build strong relationships for learning with all students that encompass teacher-student, student-content, and student-student relationships?
- How well do team members lead one another in aligning our common language so it facilitates relationship building with students?
- How well do team members inspire students to fall in love with the content and learning?
- How well do team members align their structures to build student-student relationships?
- When a teacher experiences difficulty with a student or a routine, what steps does he or she take to seek help from the team?

Classwide Supports

- How well have I aligned my relationship-building plans with those developed by the team?
- What evidence do I collect to gauge student motivation in learning?
- How well do I build a personal relationship with each student every day?
- How effective am I at displaying my passion for learning so students become passionate as well?
- How effective am I at establishing gutsy goals for the class and empowering individual students to set their own gutsy goals?
- How effectively do my collaborative structures inspire students to learn with and from one another?
- How frequent and personalized is celebration for my students?

Individualized Student Supports

- When a student disconnects from learning, how well do I consistently determine the root cause of his or her frustration?
- Once I determine the potential root cause of the issue, how well do I verify that failure is not due to my classroom supports or inconsistency from the team?
- How effective am I at identifying students' strengths so I can leverage them to address areas for growth?
- When I prescribe an intervention, how well do I provide the intervention with frequency and consistency?

CHAPTER 5

Teaching for Excellence: Student Engagement

Students who are engaged are involved, but not all students who are involved are engaged.

—Phillip C. Schlechty

Every educator desires full student engagement in his or her classroom, but what exactly is engagement? In interactions with your colleagues about the topic, you have probably heard a wide range of attributes used to describe what engagement could or should look like, and you and your colleagues base many of those attributes on your experiences as both learners and practitioners in the classroom. This chapter will clearly define engagement in an effort to clarify your role as educator and your responses to students who fail to engage in learning.

Before we define *engagement*, we must acknowledge that true engagement cannot occur without the first three levels of the Hierarchy of Student Excellence in place. Students must have the ability to skillfully use resources to drive learning, assume their role as independent learners through classroom routines and procedures, and develop meaningful relationships for learning with the teacher, the content, and other students. These three prerequisites all provide a solid foundation on which students can grow. Without any one of these levels in place, teachers might fail to engage students and fail to maximize student learning. Student engagement represents the final deficiency level in the Hierarchy of Student Excellence.

Assuming the bottom three levels of the Hierarchy of Student Excellence are in place, let's explore the topic of engagement. The National Research Council and Institute of Medicine (2004) writes, "Engagement in schoolwork involves both behaviors (e.g., persistence, effort, attention) and emotions (e.g., enthusiasm, interest, pride in success)" (p. 31). In a survey of two hundred eighth graders, students define *student engagement* with the following descriptors: classroom interaction, movement, and variety; the use of technology; the relevance of course material; strong relationships between the teacher and students and among students; and the level of respect and responsibility the teacher extends to the class (Wolpert-Gawron, 2015). This information leads us to view student engagement as students' not following the teacher but leading their own learning.

Education researchers Adena M. Klem and James P. Connell (2005) write:

> An abundance of research indicates that higher levels of engagement in school are linked with positive outcomes such as improved academic performance. In fact, student engagement has been found to be one of the most robust predictors of student achievement and behavior in school. (pp. 1–2)

Skills for building engagement powerfully benefit teachers in the work of promoting learning excellence. For example, these skills lead to more actively engaged, interactive learners; increased student ownership over learning processes; more productive use of class time; and higher levels of academic achievement and student self-esteem. Great teachers build on their strong command of learning resources, well-established routines and procedures, and meaningful learning relationships to structure lessons and classroom activities that promote high levels of student engagement.

Expanding and delving deeper into the definition of engagement, the Schlechty Center (n.d.) add that engaged students "learn at high levels and have a profound grasp of what they learn," "retain what they learn, "can transfer what they learn to new contexts," view classroom activity as "personally meaningful," and have a focus on "getting it right." In the next section, we expose the conflict that all of us have in our definition of engagement. Mrs. Chang has a deep desire to have engaging instruction, but she faces problems with her students' failing to connect with the learning. Eventually, she overcomes those obstacles and delivers on her guarantee of high levels of learning through engagement.

Focusing on Learning Instead of Teaching

Mrs. Chang was a new first year chemistry teacher. Graduating summa cum laude from her university with a bachelor's degree in chemistry, she dedicated her life to following her mother's life path in becoming a great high school teacher. She felt it was her destiny.

As the school year began, Mrs. Chang established her routines and procedures and took time to get to know her students, especially those she heard would cause her the most difficulty. She presented her passion for chemistry, and things seemed to start well. But as the days went on, and the content became more technical and abstract in nature, students began to show frustration, which transformed into quiet disengagement. Her student Jimmy perfectly exemplified what some students were feeling. He was lost but too shy to say a word.

Noticing the disconnect, Mrs. Chang reflected on how she presented her lessons. Her lectures, no matter how entertaining, left students, including Jimmy, bewildered. His eyes slowly glazed over with every passing word. When she asked if anyone had questions, few students, if any, responded with even a remote desire to learn more. Mrs. Chang was losing Jimmy and the other students, and as talented as she was, she had no idea how she would hook them into learning the content. Then she thought of her high school chemistry teacher who inspired her love of chemistry. She reflected on how vastly different his approach to instruction was compared to her lecture approach. The next day, Mrs. Chang met with her science department team. The team members discussed content, assessments, interventions, and extensions. As the focus turned to how the team would respond when students fail to learn, Mrs. Chang chimed in and said, "How do you respond when you know you are the reason students are disengaging from the content?"

The question perplexed her teammates, but the team leader, Mr. Sanchez, patiently probed, "Please tell me more about what's going on."

Mrs. Chang sighed and responded, "I'm so frustrated. I have poured my heart and soul into my standards and thinking of everything I need to do to ensure we reach all of them. With every lesson that I present, students listen to me less and seem more dazed and confused after every lesson. I just don't think they are motivated to learn in my class, and they won't even try to participate in my lessons."

Some in the room nodded, while others began lamenting the lack of student motivation. As the discussion turned into a loud gripe session, Mr. Sanchez said, "All right, all right, everyone. Let's get to some solutions now." He turned to Mrs. Chang and said, "I noticed you say words like *my standards*, *my class*, and *my lessons*. While I understand that you are taking full responsibility for students' learning, it sounds like you are more focused on teaching than learning."

Those in the room sat quietly, and Mrs. Chang was speechless.

Mr. Sanchez continued, "Do you think you are approaching the lessons and content through your lens as a fantastic chemistry student, or as a student who is not very interested in the content? Sure, it's easy to engage in any lesson when you love the content, but it's not that easy when science isn't your thing. Do you understand what I mean?"

A lightbulb went on in Mrs. Chang's head. She realized that all students don't naturally love chemistry the way she does, and she needed to change her focus from teaching to her students' learning. "But how do I get *all* students, especially quiet ones like Jimmy, hooked into learning chemistry if they don't take pride in wanting to learn it?"

Mr. Sanchez replied, "You have to change your instructional focus from teaching to learning. We're not just disseminators of information. We have to create an environment of engagement where students are learning chemistry the minute they come in the door and don't stop until the minute they leave. That is our job, and if you'd like to learn more about making that happen in your classroom, I'll help you with that."

Mrs. Chang smiled and said, "I would like that very much."

Over the next month or two, Mrs. Chang worked with Mr. Sanchez to learn more about engaging students through shorter lectures that incorporate note taking, meaningful collaboration, and better hands-on learning activities. During that time, not only did Mrs. Chang see improvement in her students' interest in learning chemistry, but she saw a remarkable change in Jimmy's desire to complete assignments and his confidence as a student. She learned a valuable lesson. Her engagement with chemistry was due to the self-worth and self-esteem she felt in learning the subject, and her newfound primary responsibility as a teacher was to develop every student's pride and self-efficacy in learning it as well.

As Mrs. Chang learned, self-esteem comes before deep learning, and when our classrooms build students' pride in their own abilities as learners, excellence is attainable. All humans are motivated to have self-worth and self-esteem. They want it in their work, their social circles, and their personal lives. Maslow placed the need for self-worth and self-esteem as the fourth level in his Hierarchy of Needs, and the last level in the deficiency category. This aligns with the fourth level in the Hierarchy of Student Excellence (see figure 5.1). As evidenced in the story, building self-esteem can lead to more confidence in engagement in learning.

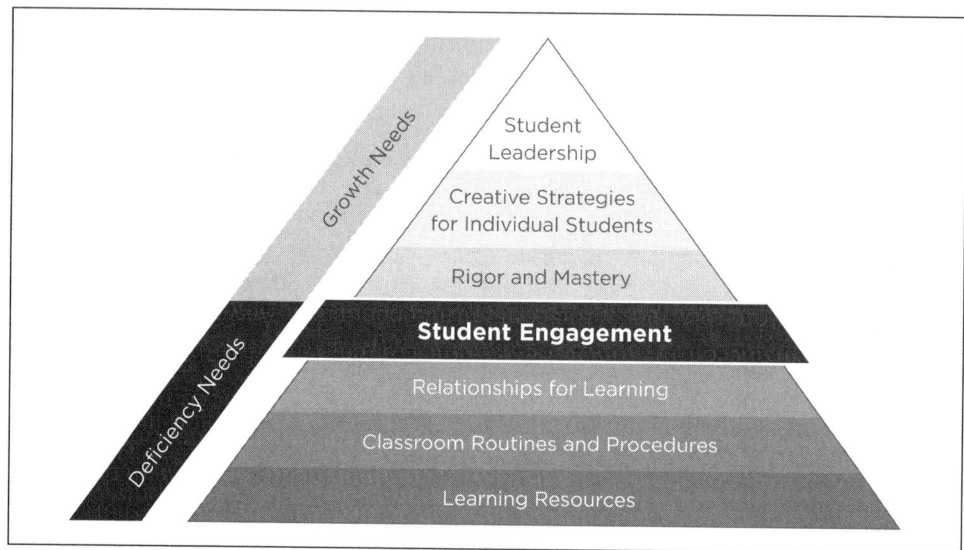

Figure 5.1: Hierarchy of Student Excellence—student engagement.

Mrs. Chang's approach to instruction initially failed to foster pride in student work, and when she made it her priority to build students' self-esteem through more engaging instruction, students beamed with confidence in themselves and generated respect from their peers. Maslow indicated that the need for respect or reputation is most important for children and adolescents and they can gain pride when instruction fosters "esteem for oneself (dignity, achievement, mastery, independence)" and a "desire for reputation or respect from others (e.g., status, prestige)" (McLeod, 2018). If we consider how this pertains to students in the classroom, respect and reputation are at greatest risk when students lose confidence in the work they do or struggle with content or skills while watching classmates succeed. Learning experiences that help students find success grow self-esteem and, while experiences that cause students to dislike learning, fear failure, or resent the content can tear down students' self-esteem.

Self-esteem issues stem from students' unresolved emotions (for example, fear, disgust, sadness, anger) that hinder their cognitive capacity, resulting in lower scores (Jensen, 2016). As educators, we must recognize that barriers to self-worth and self-esteem often enter the room before we start a lesson. Howard S. Adelman and Linda Taylor (2006) write:

> The notion of barriers to learning encompasses both external and internal factors. Some children bring with them a wide range of problems stemming from restricted opportunities associated with poverty, difficult and diverse family conditions, high rates of mobility, lack of English language skills, violent neighborhoods, problems related to substance abuse, inadequate health care, and lack of enrichment opportunities. Some youngsters also bring with them intrinsic conditions that make learning and performing difficult. (page xx)

Developing self-worth and self-esteem begins and ends with the heart, not the head, and great teachers recognize student apathy by looking for their reluctance to learn or hesitance in even making an attempt to learn. Teachers can leverage their relationship with students to discover ways to get them excited or at least confident in their abilities to learn, grow, and excel. The following sections offer suggestions to help reluctant learners engage in the learning process.

Promoting Student Engagement

The connection between Maslow's fourth level (self-worth and self-esteem) and the fourth level in the Hierarchy of Student Excellence (student engagement) is that true engagement builds confidence, self-efficacy, and the belief that deep learning fulfills every person's need for esteem. Phillip Schlechty (2011) confirms this connection in his book *Engaging Students*. He says four components are always present during student engagement:

> 1. The engaged student is attentive, in the sense that he or she pays attention to and focuses on the tasks associated with the work being done.

> 2. The engaged student is committed. He or she voluntarily (that is, without the promise of extrinsic rewards or the threat of negative consequences) deploys scarce resources under his or her control (time, attention, and effort, for example) to support the activity called for by the task.
> 3. The engaged student is persistent. He or she sticks with the task even when it presents difficulties.
> 4. The engaged student finds meaning and value in the tasks that make up the work. (p. 14)

Self-esteem grows when students are authentically engaged, and true engagement fosters a sense of self-worth in students. This leads us to a new question to discover the best definition of engagement: What specific components do we need in order to create an environment of engagement where students are engaged to the degree that Schlechty (2011) defines?

Schlechty (2011) states, "In the highly engaged classroom, most students are engaged most of the time," "all students are engaged some of the time," and there is "little to no rebellion, limited retreatism, and limited ritual compliance" (p. 32). In order to create a highly engaging learning environment, teachers should consider the following three questions.

1. **Relevance:** Is the learning related to students' strengths, affinities, and interests?
2. **Gradual release of responsibility:** Does the learning process gradually transition the responsibility for learning from teacher control to student control?
3. **Time management:** Are students actively, interactively, and productively pursuing learning throughout the majority of class time?

Teachers committed to maximizing student engagement should consider these components when preparing for and delivering instruction with engagement in mind.

As figure 5.2 illustrates, when educators prepare and deliver lessons using a model that incorporates relevance, gradual release of responsibility, and time management, it results in optimized engagement (Wink, 2017).

The following sections explore how teachers can prepare engaging lessons through strong lesson plans that optimize time and the gradual release of responsibility model. Finally, we will discover how teachers can reflect on their effectiveness in the delivering those plans to ensure students are truly engaged in learning.

Preparation

Before teachers can begin the process of preparing a lesson on any concept, they should know two pieces of information: (1) the lesson's goals and student learning

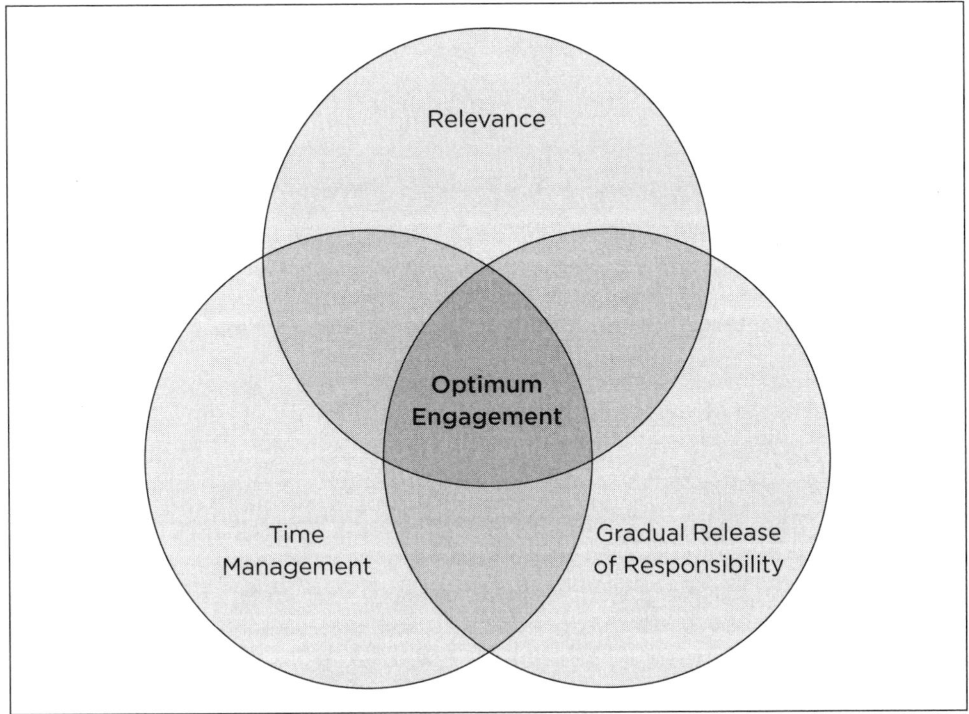

Figure 5.2: The components of optimum engagement.

target and (2) the relevance of those goals to students' existing abilities, interests, and personal goals for learning. Knowing this information helps teachers devise a plan to make the content relevant to students and their background knowledge. It helps them determine how to best engage students by slowly releasing responsibility for learning into their ownership, and finally how to allocate time effectively to ensure each student has access to learning.

Relevance

As discussed in chapter 4 (page 73), relevance is essential to connecting students to the content. It answers, "What's in it for me?" and "Why do I need to learn this?" for students. When students don't know why the content is important or at least interesting, student engagement will not take root. To build a relationship between students and the content that fosters engagement, teachers build lessons that connect to topics that students are currently engaged with.

Great teachers connect learning to current trends on social media. They equate historical events to current events. They find ways to connect what students need to learn to pop culture icons, and even to content from one of students' other subjects. Jensen (2016) states that "students feel respected when teachers understand where they are coming from and apply that understanding by making connections in the classroom" (p. 115).

To plan for incorporating relevance into engagement, teachers can ask questions such as the following.

- How could I connect my lesson to fads that my students are currently interested in?
- What appropriate music do my students like that I can incorporate into my transitions or fun activities?
- What major current events could I connect to my lesson?
- What are some common things my students experience at home that I can connect to my lesson?
- What are students learning in other subjects that I can connect to my lesson?
- How will I sell the point that the learning in this lesson will benefit students in the future?

By asking these questions, teachers gain valuable information they can use to pique student interest in the content. When students understand how the lesson benefits them and their future, they are more likely to see the relevance in academic achievement.

Gradual Release of Responsibility

While addressing students' interests through relevance is important to engagement, teachers can't maximize student learning by simply dumping the responsibility for that learning onto students. Douglas Fisher and Nancy Frey's (2008) gradual release of responsibility model offers educators a framework for delivering lessons in a way that gradually prepares students to assume responsibility for learning tasks and transitions them smoothly through that process. Through eight years of research, Frey, Fisher, and Gonzalez (2010) determined that "this instructional framework leads to significant improvement in student engagement and achievement" (p. 11).

The gradual release of responsibility model establishes that, every time students and teachers meet, class time involves the following four components (Frey, Fisher, & Gonzalez, 2010).

1. **Focus lesson:** This ten- to fifteen-minute lesson establishes (or re-establishes) the purpose of the lesson and models how the teacher thinks about the content, or what questions and issues represent the teacher's or other expert's thinking in regard to that content. This modeling gives students "access to academic language and thinking as well as information about expert problem solving and understanding" (Frey, Fisher, & Gonzalez, 2010, p. 12), access that helps prepare students to engage in complex content.

2. **Guided learning:** Teachers can help prompt students' own thinking about the content using strategic questions or prompts, directed toward either the whole class or small groups. By encouraging students to go beyond the information they learned in the focus lesson to begin to explore their own questions and ideas, teachers are better able to scaffold learning to meet individual learner needs, even as they begin to shift the focus for content exploration to students.
3. **Collaborative learning:** Frey, Fisher, and Gonzalez (2010) note that "to really learn, students must be engaged in productive group tasks that require interaction" (p. 13). Their participation in these groups, the language that they use to describe task elements, and their contributions to those tasks are just some of the ways students indicate their level of comfort with the content and control over the learning experience. Collaborative learning, therefore, is effective when students are interactively engaged in discussing and pursuing the task at hand and when they are accountable for their individual contributions to that task.

   "To effectively impact academic achievement, teachers should split class time equally between social time and individual time" (Jensen, 2016, p. 37). This *fifty-fifty rule*, as coined by Jensen (2016), is a cooperative learning strategy that has a greater impact on learning than independent learning. When researchers compared the impact of cooperative learning to individual learning, they found that cooperative learning had a 0.59 effect size, greater than one year's growth.
4. **Independent learning:** This is the portion of class time in which students apply their learning by creating, for example, quick written summaries of daily lessons or ideas for future goals or plans for tasks associated with the lessons. Frey, Fisher, and Gonzalez (2010) recommend that teachers accommodate this independent practice time before they assign students the related homework.

Adapted from Fisher and Frey's (2008) book, *Better Learning Through Structured Teaching*, figure 5.3 (page 110) illustrates how the responsibility for learning initially begins with the teacher and slowly progresses from guided learning to collaborative learning and, finally, to independent learning.

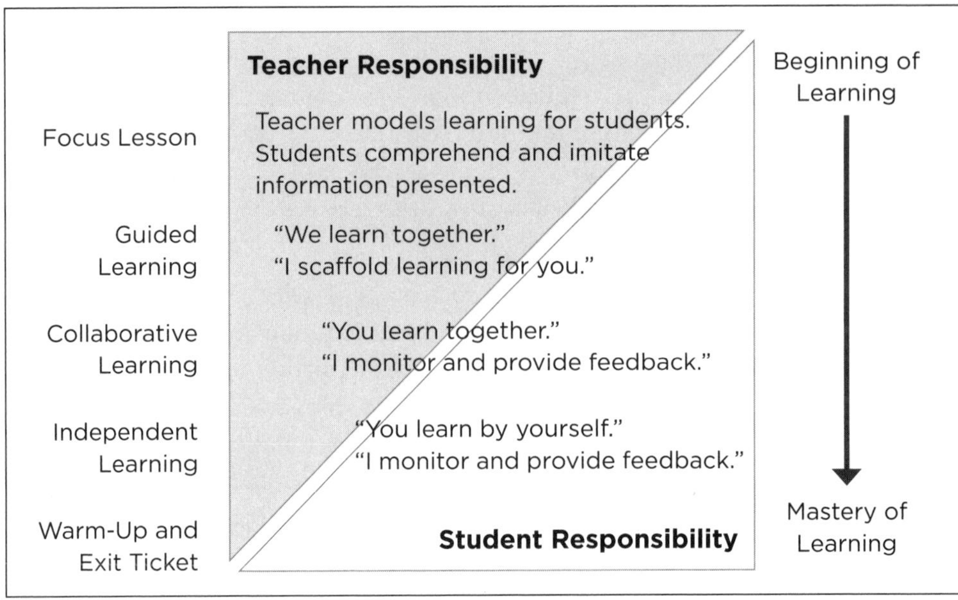

Source: Adapted from Fisher & Frey, 2008.

Figure 5.3: Gradual release of responsibility model.

To optimize class time and provide an engagement structure that yields actionable data, I have added two more components to the gradual release of responsibility model—(1) the warm-up and (2) the exit ticket.

1. **Warm-up:** Teachers provide this student-led activity to students upon entry to the classroom. It is designed to prime student thinking on content that they previously learned anywhere from the previous day to the previous year. The goal of the warm-up is to get students thinking about the learning they will do in the day's lesson. Thus, it warms up the brain.
2. **Exit ticket:** This student-led activity serves as a quick formative assessment that teachers give at the end of the period or lesson, and the purpose is to know which students learned and which ones didn't. Teachers use the data gained from this activity to drive the next day's lesson.

The warm-up and exit ticket serve as the bookends of the instructional period or block. No matter where students are progressing in the lesson, warm-ups prime the brain for the learning students are about to do, and exit tickets wrap up learning to give both the teacher and the students powerful information about how much students have learned. Both these activities, and the cognitive demand that they require, maximize engagement.

By gradually transitioning responsibility for those processes over to students, teachers increase learners' cognitive investment in learning the content. Further, they demonstrate trust in the students' competence and control in the learning process. Structuring class time within a framework of introduction to content and its associated models of thinking, guided interactive activities, collaborative group work, and independent study guarantees that teachers are filling the majority of class time with productive learning activities.

Using Google Sheets (www.google.com/sheets) or another collaborative digital spreadsheet, teachers and leaders can view and edit teachers' plans for student engagement and use the spreadsheet's commenting features to have asynchronous dialogue about the plans.

Figure 5.4 (pages 112–113) features a lesson-planning template that teachers, teacher teams, and leaders can use to collaboratively plan and deliver content by keeping the focus on relevance, gradual release of responsibility, and time management. In Blue Ridge Independent School District in Texas, teachers use the lesson-planning template not only for planning but also as an observation instrument for administrators to give teachers targeted feedback on how well their plans for instruction align with their instructional delivery. They identify where the plans successfully promote engagement, miss opportunities for engagement, or contribute to disengagement in the classroom.

When teachers leverage student interests, cultural affinities, and existing competencies, they can creatively design lessons that intentionally advance learning targets through various components of engagement: student-directed learning, productive group collaboration, active independent study, and other classroom activities. When the preparation for engagement is detailed and aligned to the nature and needs of students, teachers can expect to see an increase in ownership of and pride in the learning process. By planning lessons designed to accomplish learning goals and align with student abilities and interests, teachers well position themselves to both connect students with their learning and inspire them to want to know more about the content.

Time Management

Teachers should plan for time management simply because we don't have enough time in the day to fit everything in. Great teachers seem to make the time by managing and optimizing every minute of instruction, while others run out of time.

In order to ensure students are engaged, we must consider how we optimize time, or in more simplistic terms, we must ensure that students don't waste a single minute in the lesson. Great teachers optimize time by first identifying where they are giving up precious minutes of instruction. Great teachers anticipate how long activities should take, and they make plans to watch the clock to ensure all lesson components optimize time.

English 1 Skills									
Instructional Component	**Number of Minutes**	**What to Document**	**Monday**	**Tuesday**	**Wednesday**	**Thursday**	**Friday**	**Students Will**	**Teachers Will**
Depth of Knowledge Level 3 Question		Questions students must answer by the end of instruction						Be able to answer the questions or tell how they are working toward answering the questions.	Probe student thinking and remind students that what they are doing should help them answer the questions.
Bell Ringer		Question or independent activity						Engage in a task tied to content they will learn in the lesson.	Submit attendance and complete managerial tasks.
Vocabulary		Vocabulary to emphasize in the lesson						Learn the vocabulary and use it in their dialog with the teacher and classmates.	Explicitly teach vocabulary and expect students to use the words in their conversations.
Focus Lesson		Concept to cover						Follow along with the lesson and take notes as directed by the teacher.	Teach the concept at the front of the room and ensure all students are following along.

Guided Reading		Tier 1, 2, and 3 activity tied to the focus skill						Work in groups or pairs with the teacher on focus skills, which should include fluency and comprehension.	Guide students in a small-group activity tied to a deficit in an essential skill.
Collaborative Learning		A coopera-tive group activity for students						Work on a task tied to the focus lesson in groups.	Monitor students to ensure they are working and learning, and pull students for addi-tional support.
Independent Learning		An indepen-dent activity for students						Work independent-ly on a task tied to the focus lesson or their greatest area of need.	Monitor students to ensure they are working and learning, and pull students for addi-tional support.
Wrap-Up or Exit Ticket		Homework expectations or ques-tions to ask to gauge learning						Complete the task prior to leaving class or transitioning to the next subject.	Communicate progress in the day's lesson and set expectations for homework and tomorrow's lesson.

Figure 5.4: English 1 lesson-planning template for student engagement.

Following are a few ways that we are most prone to waste instructional minutes.

- **Long transitions:** In a classroom of excellence, transitions are quick and efficient and maintain the momentum for instruction. Set a goal of having thirty-second transitions.
- **Material mismanagement:** In a classroom of excellence, students do the work. And when it comes to materials, great teachers identify the students whose job is passing out and managing materials.
- **Lengthy lectures:** Great teachers know that the longer they talk, the more students disengage. The general rule of thumb for effective lectures is one minute of lecture per year of the students' age. For example, a ten-year-old's attention span for a lecture is ten minutes, and a fifteen-year-old has a fifteen-minute attention span (Day2Day Parenting, 2013).
- **No work upon entering the classroom:** Great teachers believe that learning begins the minute students enter the classroom; therefore, they prepare work for students to do upon entry so students engage in the first minute of instruction.
- **No extension work:** There are always students who finish early, and great teachers prepare for this by having extension work that enriches students' learning or gives them additional practice. You can find more information on extension work in chapter 7 (page 165).

While addressing these common issues prevents students from disengaging from learning, teachers need to think of minutes as units of time for engagement. For example, assume you have fifty minutes to teach a lesson, and you have twenty students in your classroom. If you think about the fifty minutes in terms of how much time you have to engage every student, each student would have fifty minutes to learn the lesson. Therefore, you would not have fifty minutes of teaching but one thousand minutes for learning (50 instructional minutes × 20 students = 1,000 minutes for learning). Through the lens of student engagement, each student has fifty minutes to be either engaged or disengaged.

If students are engaged, they will learn. So let's assume a student is disengaged for five minutes of instruction in a fifty-minute block of instructional time; that would amount to 10 percent of the lesson. If that student were disengaged for five minutes of that block every day, that student would be disengaged for 10 percent of the block that year. The moral of the story is time is valuable. Five minutes of disengagement is not just five minutes. If five minutes is wasted every day, it can add up to days or perhaps weeks of lost instruction and opportunities for students to learn.

Preparing for engagement requires more than just making good lesson plans. You must consider the students you wish to sell your learning to, how you will put them in the driver's seat of learning by giving them the appropriate levels of responsibility, and how you will not waste time. When teachers make plans to guarantee the highest levels of engagement in every student, those great plans have the potential to transform ordinary lessons into powerful instruction.

Delivery

Great delivery of instruction packs instructional time with work related to students' interests and adapted to students' learning needs. This section provides suggestions for how to enhance engagement, and how to monitor engagement for the purposes of adjusting pacing and using timing structures to ensure students work diligently on relevant work that keeps them engaged from the moment they enter the classroom until they leave.

Beginning of the Lesson

Once students enter the room, the instructional clock starts ticking. The first five minutes of instruction are all about priming the brain for learning. High levels of engagement won't happen instantaneously; therefore, students need to prime their brains with familiar content. Warm-ups work best when students engage in an activity on familiar content that they can do independently.

During these five minutes, great teachers can connect with each student, discuss the homework from the previous night, or help a student arrange a time for additional help during the period. Additionally, this time allows the teacher to make final adjustments for the work that will take place during the lesson, so the warm-up is designed for students as well as teachers.

A warm-up in reading could ask students to reread a familiar passage or review their notes from the previous day's lesson. In writing, teachers might ask students to edit or revise a paragraph or generate ideas for a new essay. In mathematics, teachers might ask students to solve a problem or answer questions on a series of mathematics facts to probe fluency. In science, teachers might ask students to draw what they know about a food chain, list the components in the life cycle of an insect, or draw or write about an example of erosion. In social studies, teachers might ask students to write about the meaning of a political cartoon or generate three causes of World War II.

The key to a successful warm-up is not that students' work is correct but that students are thinking about the right work—work that is familiar and aligned to the day's learning. If students have incorrect thinking or develop misconceptions during a warm-up, the teacher should address those later in the lesson. The warm-up should engage student brains with work that is familiar on an independent level. Students should find the work relevant and easy to complete.

Focus Lesson

After the warm-up, the teacher is ready to give students purpose in learning. During a whole-group focus lesson, the teacher models proficient learning for students, and students imitate what the teacher models by writing it down. Time is of the essence here because when teachers do most of the talking or leading, students are most susceptible to disengagement.

During a focus lesson, great teachers expect students to follow along by taking notes in a manner that works best for them. Some students thrive with a more traditional mode of note taking, such as *Cornell note taking*, a text-based note-taking strategy in which students take notes on the lecture by including key topics, details, and a summary of the learning, while other students use strategies such as visual note taking (note taking that uses a combination of drawings and words). Some students can use a personal device to take pictures and then write notes beside the pictures, or they can use speech to text technology to take notes on a laptop. In kindergarten, teachers can provide students with dry-erase boards and markers to imitate writing letters or words as part of the teacher's direct instruction and erase as they progress through the lesson.

To make a focus lesson relevant, the teacher should display his or her passion for the content to generate excitement in students. If the teacher is apathetic about the lesson, chances are that students will be apathetic as well. A great focus lesson gives students what they need to maintain the momentum of engagement after the focus lesson is over so they can do a collaborative learning or independent learning activity without the teacher's direct help.

Remember, a focus lesson works best when it doesn't exceed the students' attention span (one minute per year of students' age). Teachers should set a timer to complete the lesson and constantly scan the room to see if any student's engagement wanes. When they want to ensure students note critical content, they tell students, "Write this down" or "This part is really important."

A great focus lesson encompasses exactly what its title says: it focuses students on the lesson's purpose. It is concise and precise, and centers students on the day's work. It gets students excited and makes the learning for the day challenging as well as attainable. Finally, a focus lesson sets the tone for the work students will do for the remainder of the period.

Guided Learning, Collaborative Learning, and Independent Learning

Once the focus lesson sets the tone for the lesson, teachers must ask themselves three questions: (1) "Which students need more of my instruction or guidance?" (2) "Which students need to stretch their learning by interacting with their peers?" and (3) "Which students need to show mastery of their learning independently?"

Learning is a not rigid order of activities, and sometimes, teachers develop lessons that require all students to work at the same pace. We must recognize that students learn in different ways and at different speeds, and our plans allow flexibility in order to make the lesson adapt to students' various learning needs through small-group instruction with the teacher, collaboration with peers, or independent work.

However, if teachers focus on learning rather than teaching, they will recognize that some students don't understand information in the focus lesson and need more instruction. In those situations, great teachers build instructional time for students to receive additional time and support through guided learning. In this short five- to ten-minute instructional block, students with common deficits meet with the teacher for a minilesson where the teacher scaffolds the content for students with more concrete supports, such as manipulatives, graphic organizers, or guided practice.

Some students need time to wrestle with the content with their peers in collaborative learning before they tackle the content independently. As we learned in chapter 4 (page 73), collaboration generates high levels of growth when students teach one another more about the content. During collaborative learning, every student needs to know the purpose of his or her work, what kind of product he or she must generate through collaborative work, and the deadline to complete the work. Students also need to know that the teacher has a plan to hold students accountable for using the time wisely to produce evidence of learning. When collaboration is specific, structured, and accountable, students are more prone to engage in the lesson.

A quick and effective collaboration structure that students can use is turn and talk, in which teacher asks students to take one minute to talk to their partners about a question or concept. Another collaboration structure is having two to four students work on a problem together and come up with a couple of different ways to solve it.

To ensure effectiveness, teachers monitor students and gather evidence of their learning by taking notes, having conversations with groups, and giving feedback to groups. The key to effective collaborative learning activities lies in the coaching and facilitation work the teacher does with students to ensure they continue working and learning together.

All students should experience independent learning daily. In order for the delivery of instruction to come to fruition through independent learning tasks, the teacher should consider where students are in their mastery of learning and give them specific tasks to stretch their knowledge. This may mean that some students receive a different independent learning activity than others. It also means that some students will have modified tasks within the activity. The teacher's ability to gauge student learning determines what students do. The teacher adjusts by encouraging students to work on tasks independently without additional support or by keeping struggling students back for guided learning with the teacher, so they have more time to master content that is challenging for them.

End of the Lesson

Great teachers stop instruction five minutes before the period ends and ask students to provide a learning artifact. In fact, some teachers even set an alarm on their phone to remind them to conduct this important engagement activity. The exit ticket is as much an assessment for learning as it is an assessment for instruction. The exit ticket may ask students to answer a question or generate feedback about the student's comfort with the content. But remember that at the end of a lesson, teachers should gather evidence to reflect on the day's lesson and plan for upcoming lessons. (You can find more information on formative assessments in chapter 6 [page 131].)

Great teachers focus on analyzing student learning as an effect of their instruction and teaching. They gauge student interest or students' desire to persist in tasks that they may find a little challenging or uninteresting. If every minute of instruction counts, then every minute of student learning counts more. Great teachers monitor all students' responses to instruction, especially those of students who are most apt to disconnect from learning, in an effort to monitor what Robert Marzano (2003) refers to as *withitness*, which means to stick with a task for a long period of time. Great teachers gather real-time information of those who connect with the content and those who withdraw from the content, and then they quickly re-engage those withdrawn students. Withitness has a massive effect size of 1.42, which means when teachers monitor and respond to students who show lack of interest in learning, students can expect to see almost three years of growth in one year (Jensen, 2016).

Reflection

The best teachers reflect on their effectiveness for meeting students' needs. They evaluate how effectively they promote student engagement by assessing how much class time students spend actively involved in interactive, collaborative, and independent learning. Excellent teachers ensure that every minute of classroom time has students actively pursuing learning. They ensure that their lessons provide relevant activities that engage all students, especially those who are quick to reject learning, and that their lessons focus on learning by providing students with multiple engagement structures found in the gradual release of responsibility model.

Pérsida Himmele and William Himmele (2011) state, "By the time many students hit middle school, disengagement has become a learned behavior" (p. 8). This means that the instruction we provide students has the potential to teach students to *disengage* from the learning, not engage them. In order to avoid passive learning, great teachers constantly monitor interest, persistence with tasks, and withitness from all students, especially those who struggle the most.

Teachers can use figure 5.5 as a reflection tool to help them plan and deliver effective student engagement.

Component	Reflection
Relevance	**Planning** How effectively do my lesson plans connect to the background and life experiences of my students? How well do my lesson plans incorporate other subjects, pop culture, or current events that students are most familiar with? How well do my plans incorporate my students' learning styles? **Delivery** How well do I gauge and respond to my students' responses to lessons? Which lessons generate the most interest? The least interest? Which activities foster greater or lesser student independence? How consistent am I at using exit tickets to get students' feedback regarding their feelings about the lessons or activities?
Gradual Release of Responsibility	**Planning** How well do my lesson plans incorporate all gradual release of responsibility components? How specific are my plans for engaging students with warm-up activities to prime their minds? Are my focus lessons organized enough that they hook students into the learning and get them excited about learning? How well planned out are my guided, collaborative, and independent learning activities? How specific are my plans for exit tickets to gauge learning? **Delivery** How well does my instructional delivery match the plans I create? How effectively does my communication promote engagement and commitment to the lesson? How effective am I at monitoring student behaviors and engagement in each component of my lessons? How well do I adjust my lessons based on student engagement and the beginning signs of disengagement? How consistent am I at ensuring that students complete an exit ticket prior to the end of the period?

Figure 5.5: Student engagement reflection tool.

continued →

Component	Reflection
Time Management	**Planning** How committed am I to predicting the amount of time that activities in my lessons should take? How well do I create focus lessons that don't exceed students' attention span? How well do my plans limit passive engagement (lengthy lectures, material mismanagement, and time-consuming transitions)? **Delivery** How consistently do I monitor my instructional time to ensure that I waste little to no time? How effectively do I notice and respond to students who are wasting time or are disconnected from the lesson or activity? How well do I monitor my instructional time to ensure that I get to my exit ticket prior to the end of my lesson?

Visit ***go.SolutionTree.com/instruction*** *for a free reproducible version of this figure.*

Building a Student Excellence Support System: Student Engagement

The Student Excellence Support System for engagement begins with strategies to strengthen teacher effectiveness and ends with specific structures that teachers give to individual students so the students can more successfully stick with the content they are expected to learn. The Student Excellence Support System begins with teacher improvement because our own instructional gaps create or exacerbate the gaps in student learning. Therefore, in order to help students, we must ensure that we close our gaps first.

The steps in the following sections explain how teachers can work together to create a Student Excellence Support System for engagement. Step 1 asks teachers to collaborate around commonalities they will provide in engagement. Step 2 asks teachers to leverage the collaborative work to each create a personal plan for engagement, and step 3 helps teachers dissect a student's difficulty with engagement when steps 1 and 2 prove ineffective.

Step 1: Teacher Team Collaboration

Collaborative teacher teams need opportunities to have meaningful discussions about how to create an engaging environment for learners. To align student engagement from class to class, teachers should develop activities and lessons as a team. While the way teachers deliver lessons may differ from class to class, effective teams discuss the nuances and steps within specific activities. Team members share strategies for engaging at high levels with the same relevant work. Three strategies that team members can use to help one another with student engagement include (1) instructional planning, (2) instructional rounds, and (3) modeling.

Instructional Planning

During *instructional planning*, teachers work together to develop lessons and plans for instruction that will engage all students through each step of the lessons. Teams can discuss how they engage students through focus lessons, guided instruction, collaborative learning, and independent work, and how effectively the time they spend in each of these components is engaging learners. Teams can also share strategies that ensure their instruction's relevance is high and discuss innovative ways to connect their content to their students' world, background, and interests.

Through honest conversations, teachers can identify and discuss areas where their instructional practice is falling short in promoting student engagement and ask their peers for suggestions. Often, one or more teachers share the same difficulty with student engagement, and collective problem solving for one teacher's challenges can translate into powerful solutions for all teachers. By engaging in conversations about difficulties, teams can move from working together to learning together. Collaborative planning aims to promote active learning at high levels, and the best learning opportunities come from failure, not success.

Collaborative instructional planning is a high-leverage strategy that promotes student learning, but it can't be the only strategy teams use. Instructional planning is a powerful strategy for teacher teams to use, but sometimes they need to collaborate in other ways that will strengthen all teachers' delivery of instruction. The next two strategies we will discuss have the ability to strengthen all teachers' delivery.

Instructional Rounds

Watching other teachers in action with students is a powerful professional development activity. Collaborative teams can use instructional rounds to visit one or more classrooms and observe specific instructional components as a method to learn with and from one another. For example, if teachers want to strengthen the level of engagement during their opening minutes of class, they can schedule their collaborative time to watch anywhere from three to five different teachers as they begin class, so they can see a wide variety of strategies to engage students. Or, to explore ways for improving small-group instruction, collaborative teams can work with the principal to schedule dates to observe teachers when they have small groups in action.

If scheduling time during the school day to do instructional rounds proves difficult, teams can ask their principal to provide videos of different teachers' lessons that the team can review later during collaborative time. With permission from the teachers being recorded, a principal or instructional coach can video a lesson and share the video with the team. By observing strong and struggling delivery models, collaborative teams can glean powerful strategies for improving student engagement from high-performing classes and discover missed opportunities in struggling classes.

When using instructional rounds, teacher teams should agree to focus on one component of instructional delivery and then center their collective learning on that component. They can then use their observation data to help create strategies the entire team can use for optimizing student engagement.

Modeling

As previously noted, modeling is a best practice to help students understand new content through the eyes of the teacher. Sometimes, teams use modeling to help all team members find effective strategies for dealing with difficulties in a particular engagement component.

If a team, for example, has one teacher who is effective in guided instruction, the team should use its collaborative time to have this teacher model how he or she conducts a guided instruction lesson for the team. To ensure success in modeling, the team should include interactive discussions in which the modeling teacher and other team members discuss issues, ideas, questions, challenges, and opportunities associated with the modeled skill. By presenting the structure as well as the mental processes within that structure, an excellent teacher can model for teammates how to make guided instruction and other instructional skills efficient and effective at promoting student engagement.

When modeling, teachers must view one another as learning partners, understanding that all members are there to improve the team's collective approach to instruction. After all, almost all teachers, including the very best, find keeping students engaged in learning difficult.

Step 2: Classwide Supports

Once teacher teams develop consistency in how they engage students, teachers must personalize their own engagement structures based on team norms for engagement. To develop classwide supports, teachers should define the team's common expectations for their own teaching behaviors and their students' learning behaviors for each engagement component. Figure 5.6 can help teams determine their plans for engagement through the gradual release of responsibility model. By using this figure and considering the following questions, teachers can personalize their engagement strategies.

- What range of time do I generally allot to each engagement component on a daily basis?
- What learning behaviors do I expect of my students in each engagement component as it relates to my content?
- What teaching behaviors should I exhibit to ensure I optimize both student engagement and instructional time?

Engagement Component	Time Frame	What Do I Expect of All Students in This Component?	What Do I Expect of Myself in This Component?
Warm-Up			
Focus Lesson			
Guided Learning			
Collaborative Learning			
Independent Learning			
Exit Ticket			

Figure 5.6: Planning form for classwide supports for engagement.

Visit ***go.SolutionTree.com/instruction*** *for a free reproducible version of this figure.*

In addition to mapping out suggested time frames and expected student behaviors for engagement, teachers should prepare for student disengagement behaviors that may cause learning to suffer. Conversely, they should prepare for the times when students complete tasks quicker than expected. In both these situations, teachers must map out their plans to monitor the engagement of the entire class, as well as student groups, and quickly adjust in a wide variety of situations. Figure 5.7 (page 124) helps teachers develop their plan to monitor and adjust to the engagement in the room.

Sometimes, engagement fails not due to lack of planning. It suffers because we fail to monitor student responses to our lesson or we fail to intentionally adjust in order to better engage or re-engage students in the lesson. If we wish to have better engagement, classwide systems necessitate that we articulate the behaviors and time frame in which we wish to engage students for most lessons, and then use those same systems to help us plan for our responses to student engagement. When the classwide system includes planning for engagement and responding to engagement, student learning has a much greater chance of success.

Step 3: Individualized Student Supports

There will be times when students fail to engage, and at this step, we concentrate on students' responses, rather than determining the root cause that created disengagement in the first place. Before we develop individualized student supports for engagement, we need to ensure that disengagement is not caused by deficits in the lower levels in the Hierarchy of Student Excellence. Students might become disengaged due

Situation	Monitoring and Adjustment Response
How will I monitor the relevance of my instruction and gauge student interest? How will I respond when my plans for relevance fail to connect students to the content?	
How will I monitor instructional time and ensure that I don't waste any minutes of instruction?	
How will I notice if the entire class is failing to engage, and how will I respond to the students' lack of engagement?	
How will I respond when students fail to engage in any engagement structure?	
How will I notice when the entire class has completed an activity earlier than planned, and how will I respond quickly so I don't waste instructional time?	
How will I monitor the class for students who master the content early, and how will I further engage them in extension activities or enrichment work?	

Figure 5.7: Monitoring and adjustment plan for engagement.

Visit ***go.SolutionTree.com/instruction*** *for a free reproducible version of this figure.*

to lack of knowledge of the learning resources, failure to be independent in routines and procedures, or lack of relationships for learning.

The following guiding questions help teachers ensure that disengagement is not due to the three lowest levels of the Hierarchy of Student Excellence.

1. Learning resources
    - Does the student know how to independently use learning resources to drive his or her learning?
    - Does the student use the C4B4Me strategy to stay engaged in the lesson, or does he or she quit?

    If the student cannot drive learning with the resources, see the section on individualized student supports in chapter 2 (page 25).

2. Classroom routines and procedures
    - Does the student behave predominantly independently or dependently in the majority of routines and procedures?
    - Do I find myself frequently intercepting and redirecting the student because he or she engages in off-task behaviors?

    If the student's behavior with routines and procedures is detrimental to engagement, see the section on individualized student supports in chapter 3 (page 47).
3. Relationships for learning
    - Is the student apathetic or unmotivated about learning?
    - Does the student reject opportunities to learn with and from peers?

    If the student shows a lack of relationships for learning the content, see the section on individualized student supports in chapter 4 (page 73).

If your reflection on these questions proves that the student is resourceful, independent in his or her behavior, and motivated to learn, then the student might have deficiencies in engagement. In this situation, you can use the problem-solving tool in figure 5.8 to help the student better engage in learning.

Individualized Student Support Problem-Solving Tool: Student Engagement	
Question 1: Has the teacher team created common expectations and supports for all students at this level? (Circle yes or no.) (If your answer is yes, continue. If your answer is no, stop and correct this area.)	Yes No
Question 2: Based on the team's work, has the teacher created his or her classwide structure for engagement? (Circle yes or no.) (If your answer is yes, continue. If your answer is no, stop and correct this area.)	Yes No
Question 3: Do the majority of students regularly engage in my lessons? (Circle yes or no.) (If your answer is yes, continue. If your answer is no, stop and correct this area.)	Yes No

Figure 5.8: Individualized student support problem-solving tool—student engagement.

continued →

Individualized Student Support Problem-Solving Tool: Student Engagement

Question 4: Which student is struggling with engagement in learning?

Student: ______________________________

List the student's strengths and difficulties with each component at this level.

Strengths:

Difficulties:

Question 5: What is the root cause of the student's lack of engagement? Using the following table, evaluate the student's effectiveness with each component as high (H), medium (M), or low (L).

	Warm-Up	Focus Lesson	Guided Learning	Collaborative Learning	Independent Learning	Exit Ticket
Engages in tasks						
Uses time wisely						
Persists when difficulties arise						
Finds relevance in activities						

Question 6: Based on the responses above, what is the student's predominant problem with engagement? What potential supports will help this student better engage in learning? (Consider the following questions to determine potential supports.)

- What target component in student engagement do I want to address first?
  - ☐ Relevance
  - ☐ Gradual release of responsibility
  - ☐ Time management
- What one or two specific areas within the component do I need to target first?
- Which teacher is not having engagement difficulties with the student, and what do I need to collaborate on with this person to help me develop a plan of action?
- What action steps will I take to repair this deficit area?

<table>
<tr><td colspan="2">Question 7: What are the goal and the deadline for the student to be successful with engagement?
Goal:

Deadline:</td></tr>
<tr><td>Question 8: Did the student meet the goal by the deadline? (Circle yes or no.)
(If your answer is yes, continue the support. If your answer is no, return to question 4.)</td><td>Yes No</td></tr>
<tr><td colspan="2">Notes:</td></tr>
</table>

Visit ***go.SolutionTree.com/instruction*** *for a free reproducible version of this figure.*

Conclusion

This chapter emphasized that self-worth and self-esteem appear at the highest deficiency level in Maslow's Hierarchy of Needs, and that students critically need them both in order to pursue growth in learning. It also showed us how teachers can build self-worth and self-esteem through the aligned level in the Hierarchy of Student Excellence, student engagement. Without engagement, no meaningful learning can occur.

The three components of engagement—(1) relevance, (2) responsibility, and (3) time management—are necessary for learning to be engaging. Lessons and activities must be relevant, and they must connect to students' background, life experiences, interests, and learning affinities. And teachers must ensure that students actively pursue learning every minute of the period, from beginning to end.

Engagement requires consistent action from students and continuous supports from the teacher. When the teacher focuses on monitoring student responses to learning, time is rarely wasted, and students find relevance in what they are doing. When the lesson hinges on students doing the work instead of the teacher, the gradual release of responsibility model of learning motivates all students to assume their responsibility in owning their learning. Engagement best happens when teachers focus on learning rather than teaching.

This chapter concludes with a reflection tool (pages 129–130) that teachers can use to evaluate their understanding of the challenges they face when trying to keep students engaged in learning. As you consider the questions and your responses to them, explore possibilities for improving those systems, including teacher team collaboration, classwide supports, and individualized student supports, based on the information and ideas in this chapter.

Reflection Tool: Student Engagement

Answer the following questions to help you create a classroom environment where students are fully engaged with the content from bell to bell.

Teacher Team Collaboration

- Has our team established plans to build high levels of engagement with all students that encompass relevance, gradual release of responsibility, and time management?
- How well do team members lead one another in fostering alignment in our common language and engagement practices?
- How well do we work together to help one another optimize time in our instruction?
- How well do we work together to help one another build high levels of relevance in our instruction?
- How well do we improve our pedagogy in planning, delivering, and reflecting on all components of the gradual release of responsibility model?
- When a teacher experiences difficulty with a student or a routine, what steps does he or she take to seek help from the team?

Classwide Supports

- How well have I aligned my engagement plans with those developed by the team?
- How well have I developed my expectations for my own behavior in each component of the gradual release of responsibility model?
- How well have I developed my expectations for student behaviors in each component of the gradual release of responsibility model?
- How well have I developed structures to monitor and respond to time optimization in my instruction?
- How well do I adjust my lessons during instruction based on the engagement responses I receive from students?

Individualized Student Supports

- When a student is disconnecting from learning, how well do I consistently determine the root cause of the student's lack of engagement?
- Once I determine the potential root cause, how well do I verify that the failure is not due to my classroom supports or inconsistency from the team?
- How well do I ensure that lack of engagement is not due to a deficiency in a lower level in the Hierarchy of Student Excellence?
- How effective am I at identifying the student's strengths so that I can leverage the strengths in engagement to address the area for growth?
- When I prescribe an intervention, how committed am I to providing the intervention with frequency and consistency?
- How consistently do I gauge student growth in the target area to determine if my intervention was effective?
- When the student is still unsuccessful, how well do I reflect and refine the intervention to better help the student?
- When my efforts to help the student continue to fail, how well do I reach out to my team members to help me better respond to the student?

page 2 of 2

CHAPTER 6

Teaching for Excellence: Rigor and Mastery

Our job is not to prepare students for something. Our job is to help students prepare themselves for anything.

—A. J. Juliani

How do you define *rigor*? Better yet, how does your school define *rigor*? Depending on who you ask, you will get a wide variety of responses. All teachers want more rigor in their instruction, but it is hard to put your finger on exactly what that means for students. This chapter offers strategies for inspiring students to chase rigorous learning in their pursuit of excellence.

Before we explore rigor, we need to note that rigor has four prerequisites. First, students must know how to use learning resources to drive their learning and know what to do when they don't know what to do. Second, teachers must have routines and procedures in place to challenge, engage, and inspire students to learn beyond the learning target teachers create for them. Third, students must have strong relationships with the teacher, the content, and their peers that motivate them to develop a strong relationship for learning. Finally, teachers must create a classroom environment where students are optimally engaged from the moment they enter the classroom until they leave.

If the goal of the bottom four levels of the Hierarchy of Student Excellence is to foster student independence in learning, then the definition of *rigor* must encompass the idea of students pursuing rigor rather than the teacher. This means that rigor cannot be one size fits all; rather, it should give students a more personalized pathway, facilitated, rather than dictated, by the teacher. Schlechty (2011) claims that "if schools and teachers are to continue to have a major impact on what students learn, teachers are going to need to learn to direct the learning of their students rather than attempt to control it" (p. 7).

Willard Daggett and Susan Gendron (2015) of the International Center for Leadership in Education describe rigor as involving thoughtful work that prepares students to engage in high-quality learning intentions; high-level questioning, in which students can ask and answer probing questions that can increase understanding and lead to higher levels of thinking; and academic discussion that enables students to engage in "vocabulary-rich, academic conversation with adults and peers" (p. 5). If students have access to high-quality learning intentions, questioning, thinking, and dialogue, profound learning is inevitable. "Profound learning endures and leaves a residue of understanding that provides a cognitive framework to which other learning can be attached" (Schlechty, 2011, p. 22).

Standardized testing has standardized the idea of rigor for many educators, and as a result, it has standardized instruction, formative assessment, and intervention as well. The problem with this idea is that students' abilities and knowledge are not standardized; therefore, they come to us on level, above level, and below level in every subject. With students all over the place in their level of mastery in a variety of subjects, rigor needs a definition that incorporates an attitude of differentiation.

At this level, students are motivated to chase excellence in an effort to satisfy their desire to know and understand the world around them. Rigor and mastery doesn't mean more work for students. It doesn't even mean harder work. To lead all students to the highest levels of rigor, teachers must realize that rigor is always about working toward the next level of proficiency, and every student's next step is slightly different. The rigor we provide must nurture each student's desire to know and understand. If we stretch student learning in the right way, we will greatly enhance every student's desire to know and understand.

If we want to inspire all students to believe in their ability to reach excellence, then rigor must encourage students to take the next and at times more challenging step that helps them move forward. For example, a person, who rarely runs, can't wake up and decide to run a marathon without first training for it. He or she must first run one mile. Then he or she must run two miles, and then maybe increase his or her rigor by competing in a five-kilometer race. The rigor continues to increase with practice, study, reflection, and training until the runner decides he or she is ready for a marathon. An accomplished runner doesn't automatically become the best at running. The runner pushes him or herself with rigorous training and practice, working through each meticulous step to become the better. Learning is no different than running. Training and study are essential to improvement.

In the following story, Grace, an experienced teacher, finds herself on her own rigorous journey toward excellence. Given the last-minute opportunity to teach the most challenging reading students in the school, she realizes that in order to lead her struggling students to success, she first has to discover the real meaning of rigorous learning.

Meeting Students Where They Are

Grace was excited to go back to her school after a restful summer break. In addition to spending time vacationing, she had spent time learning how to be a better reading teacher. Attending conferences, she found all kinds of new and engaging reading activities that inspired students to fall in love with reading. Knowing that her students' scores had gone up every year for the past three years, Grace was more than confident that her students' scores would go up again this year.

A few weeks before school started, Grace's principal, Mr. Hunt called her, saying he needed to change her teaching assignments. One of the school's most exemplary reading teachers, Mrs. Jackson, moved unexpectedly, and he needed a strong replacement to teach the most challenging reading classes in the school. He tapped Grace for the spot. Mr. Hunt felt Grace's hesitance about the reassignment, so he assured her that she was ready to take on the task and that he was fully prepared to help her make the transition. Excited and skeptical at the same time, Grace accepted the position.

The first weeks of school began with great success, and even Grace's most difficult students begrudgingly started to accept some of the newly learned fluency and comprehension strategies that focused on shared reading and independent work. Haley, one of her most challenging and lowest-performing students, started the year hating Grace's reading class, but after three weeks, Haley came in ready to learn. Because Haley was positive and upbeat about reading, Grace felt confident that her academic performance would show growth. Unfortunately, Haley's scores showed only modest improvement, and even worse, the rest of the struggling students were showing similar results.

Frustrated, Grace continued to give her students the same rigorous work, which often was far beyond the level of her least proficient learners. As inspired as the students were to reach their gutsy goals, their hard work never translated into the growth needed to meet their goals. Grace didn't know what to do, so she went to Mr. Hunt for help.

As she entered the principal's office, Mr. Hunt said, "Grace, you came in just in time. Mrs. Jackson has called in to say hello."

Grace responded, "Great! Put her on speakerphone. I need to talk to both of you!"

Surprised by her blunt response, Mr. Hunt put the phone on speakerphone and asked, "What's going on, Grace?"

Grace explained how the students were very engaged but not growing as much as she anticipated. She shared her lessons and activities that just weren't helping the students close their reading gap.

After Grace finished, Mr. Hunt said, "Mrs. Jackson, what do you think she needs to do?"

Mrs. Jackson responded, "Boy, do I know all too well how you feel, Grace. I was in your shoes when I took your position as well. None of my activities that worked for my traditional learners worked for my struggling students. After months of trial and error, I realized that rigor just isn't the same for every student. They're all over the place in their strengths and weaknesses, and they're at different reading levels. It was no wonder that my activities didn't work. They didn't meet every student at his or her level."

Grace responded, "Exactly. My activities don't meet their needs."

Mrs. Jackson said, "But I did start meeting their needs when I created activities that were on their level. I no longer took a one-size-fits-all approach."

"So are you saying that you had multiple leveled tasks for students?" Grace asked.

"Yes," replied Mrs. Jackson. "Every activity assigned was dependent on the essential skills that they needed to master. Once I had this in place, student growth went through the roof."

The conversation affirmed Grace's effort and gave her a new mindset for her own personal growth. She left the meeting determined to inspire every student, especially Haley, to chase growth in his or her learning; now, she would reach out to each student on an individualized level.

Grace learned a valuable lesson from her work with struggling students, especially Haley. Deep down, every student desires to learn, grow, and excel. It's just that some students begin their learning journey at a much lower level than we are prepared to meet. Whether it's improving in reading, mathematics, or music, or getting better at a video game, in my experience, all students have a desire to become excellent at something. But in order to chase growth, they must first satisfy their motivation to fulfill the deficiency needs. If any deficiency need is not satisfactorily met, they will not realize the fifth level in Maslow's hierarchy, the desire to know and understand.

Maslow's fifth level, cognitive needs, encompasses "knowledge and understanding, curiosity, exploration, need for meaning and predictability" (McLeod, 2018). This also represents the first level of a person's growth needs, including the desire to learn, and aligns with the fifth level in the Hierarchy of Student Excellence—rigor and mastery (see figure 6.1).

Think about some of the most successful students you have ever known or taught. They were often more passionate than you about the content they were learning. They posed questions to deepen their understanding, and they were always tinkering with the nuances of the subject.

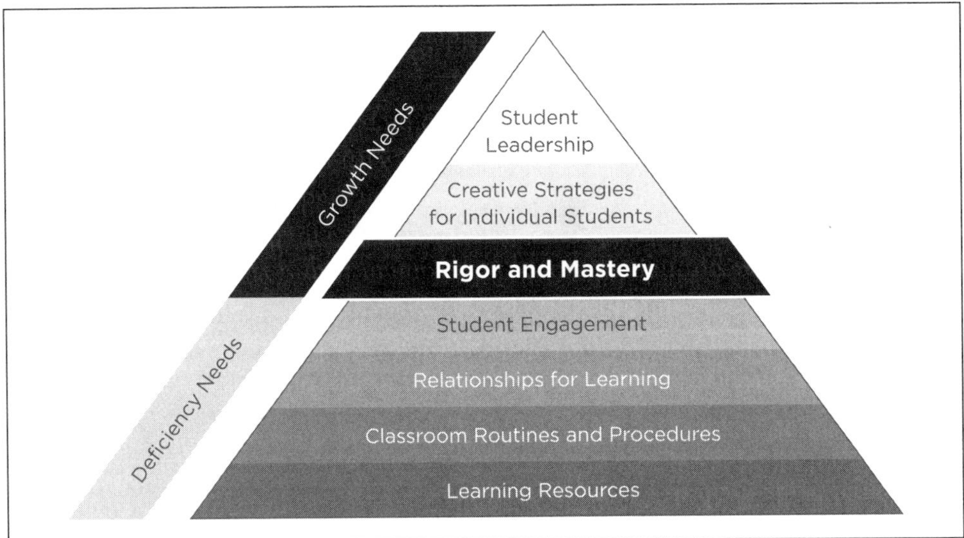

Figure 6.1: Hierarchy of Student Excellence—rigor and mastery.

The following sections explore how Maslow's fifth level in the Hierarchy of Needs—the desire to know and understand—applies to the fifth level in the Hierarchy of Student Excellence—rigor and mastery. You will discover how great teachers design instruction to meet every student's proficiency and inspire them to aspire for mastery in learning.

Implementing Rigor and Mastery

While the need to know and understand in Maslow's (1943) Hierarchy of Needs represents the first level of a person's growth needs, the parallel level in the Hierarchy of Student Excellence, rigor and mastery, asks teachers to develop the skills that will fuel their students' desire to go beyond surface knowledge and deeply understand the content. In order to ensure that rigor leads to mastery, teachers must embrace the following five components of the rigor and mastery cycle.

1. Teachers must possess deep knowledge of the content and the expertise to transfer that knowledge to the students through instruction.
2. Teachers must establish systems of formative and summative assessments that generate actionable data not only for the teacher but for the student.
3. Teachers must provide students appropriately rigorous instructional activities that stretch their thinking.
4. Teachers must establish a learning culture where both the teacher and the students have responsibility for high levels of questioning.
5. Teachers must monitor the success of all students and adjust the cognitive demand of the learning to improve learning outcomes for all students, which then strengthens the first step in the rigor to mastery instructional cycle—content knowledge and expertise.

In the following sections, we will explore these five components of the rigor and mastery cycle, as shown in figure 6.2.

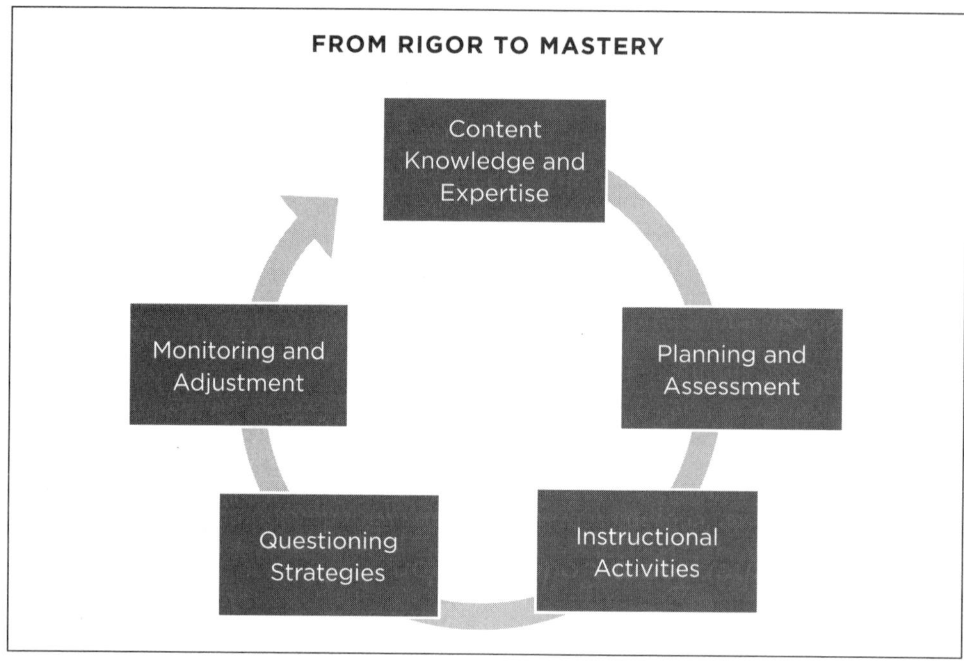

Source: Adapted from Texas Education Agency, 2016.

Figure 6.2: Rigor to mastery instructional cycle.

The following sections explore how great teachers prepare for, deliver, and reflect on instruction that provides students the appropriate rigor that leads to mastery. You will discover how teachers leverage the language within the curriculum to create powerful and differentiated instruction and targeted assessments. Finally, you will learn how the best teachers use feedback to improve their instruction.

Preparation

Two components of the rigor to mastery cycle are essential to the teacher's preparation for excellence. First, the teacher must possess content knowledge and expertise; and second, he or she must determine the assessment criteria that will generate actionable data to drive instruction. In the following sections, we will explore both of these components.

Possess Content Knowledge and Expertise

To prepare students for rigor in a manner that leads to mastery, teachers must first develop their knowledge of the content in order to inspire students to master it. Grant Wiggins (2014) notes that content mastery marks a difference between knowing and understanding learning content. Students who know content can "recall, repeat, perform as practiced" (Wiggins, 2014), and so on. Students who understand content can "*justify* a claim; *connect* discrete facts on their own; *apply* their learning in new contexts; *adapt* to new circumstances, purposes, or audiences; *criticize* arguments made by others; *explain* how and why something is the case; etc." (Wiggins, 2014).

As noted earlier in the book, *if you focus on everything you focus on nothing*. This idea especially applies to rigor and mastery. While most every subject includes a multitude of skills and standards, it is important that educators identify approximately eight to twelve essential skills that they will guarantee that all students master in order to have a strong chance of succeeding in the subject. Austin Buffum, Mike Mattos, and Chris Weber (2012) wrote that these essential skills are the basic skills, content standards, and critical thinking skills students need to use with automaticity and fluency. They provide the endurance, leverage, and readiness for learning other skills and standards. If the teacher doesn't possess a thorough knowledge of both the content and the best ways to help students learn that content, rigorous learning has little to no chance of becoming a reality.

To develop a deep and flexible understanding of the content, teachers must spend time analyzing the standards that compose the content and identify which standards are essential and which are not as essential. Austin Buffum and colleagues (2012) define this as *concentrated instruction*:

> A systematic process of identifying essential knowledge and skills that all students must master to learn at high levels, and determining the specific learning needs for each child to get there. Thinking is guided by the question, Where do we need to go? (p. 10)

To avoid the trap of covering content that is a mile wide and an inch deep, teachers should identify the eight to twelve skills or content standards that all students must master in order to learn the current content and be prepared for next year's content. Douglas Reeves (2002) writes that the essential standards should meet three criteria:

> 1. **Endurance:** Will this standard provide students with knowledge and skills that are valuable beyond a single test date?
> 2. **Leverage:** Will it provide knowledge and skills that are valuable in multiple disciplines?
> 3. **Readiness:** Will it provide students with knowledge and skills essential for success in the next grade or level of instruction? (p. 51)

Teachers must vertically align the essential standards all students must master by first aligning the current year's essential standards with prerequisite and future standards from grade levels above and below the current grade. In this vertical alignment process, teachers determine if their students have successfully met prerequisite standards to ensure they are prepared to undertake the rigorous study of essential standards for the current year as well as the following year.

Figure 6.3 illustrates how vertical alignment of essential content standards translates into developing expertise. This begins with prerequisite skills and eventually leads to students building products that demonstrate mastery of the essential skills to prepare them for mastering future essential skills.

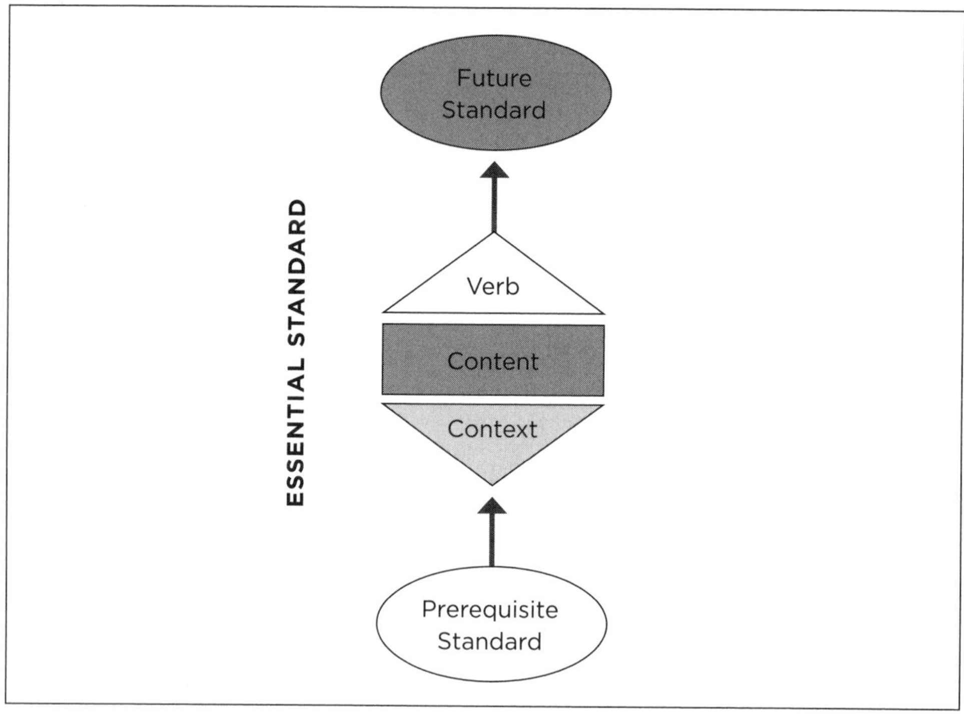

Figure 6.3: Vertical alignment of an essential standard.

Once teachers identify the essential skills, they deepen their knowledge and build expertise of those skills by deconstructing the standards into three parts.

1. **Verb:** The level of thinking that students must use to master the essential skill
2. **Content:** The skills that students must possess to master the essential skill
3. **Context:** The variety of situations in which students must use both the skills and the thinking to demonstrate mastery of the essential skill

Figure 6.4 shows an example of how a teacher might deconstruct an essential skill. First, the teacher writes the skill in its complete language. Then, he or she breaks apart language within the skill by identifying the verbs, the content, and subsequent contextual phrases within the standard. After dissecting the standard, the teacher asks him- or herself, "What does this part of the skill mean for students?" The answer to this question more specifically tells the teacher the assessment criteria, instructional activities, and questioning strategies needed to lead students to mastery. At

Skill	4.5.A: Represent multistep problems involving the four operations with whole numbers using strip diagrams and equations with a letter standing for the unknown quantity.	
Component	**Corresponding Words in the Skill**	**What Does This Mean for Students?**
Verb	represent	Students do not solve but build the equation.
Content	multistep problems	Students do problems with three steps or more.
Contextual Phrase	involving the four operations	Students use addition, subtraction, multiplication, and division (PEMDAS).
Contextual Phrase	whole numbers	Students do not use decimals, fractions, or percentages.
Contextual Phrase	using strip diagrams	Students show problems in strip diagrams.
Contextual Phrase	equations	Students show problems in an equation.
Contextual Phrase	with a letter (variable)	Students' equations and strip diagrams include solving for *x*.
Prerequisite Skill	3.5.A: Represent one- and two-step problems involving addition and subtraction of whole numbers to 1,000 using pictorial models, number lines, and equations.	
Future Skill	5.4.B: Represent and solve multistep problems involving the four operations with whole numbers using equations with a letter standing for the unknown quantity.	

Source for standards: Texas Education Agency, n.d.

Figure 6.4: Example essential skills analysis chart.

the bottom of the figure, teachers can list both the prerequisite skills and the future skills aligned with the essential skill. By listing the aligned standards, teachers can ascertain the skills students already possess that are aligned to the current essential skill, and what parts of their essential skill students will master when they move on to the next year's subject. (You can find a blank reproducible version of this figure, "Essential Skills Analysis Chart," on page 161.)

Essentially, this activity helps teachers align the curriculum while also deepening their knowledge of the content and helping them understand how to deepen students' knowledge of the content as well. This activity sets the stage for the second half of preparing for rigor and mastery—providing assessments to generate data.

Provide Assessments to Generate Data

The purpose of formative assessment is critical to the rigor to mastery cycle. Assessments help teachers determine whether their lessons are effective and which students are doing well and which students need improvement. Effective teachers know "the learning intentions and success criteria of their lessons" (Hattie, 2009, p. 239), and they know how to use formative assessments to drive rigorous learning and produce content mastery. "Formative assessments should shape instruction [just as] our formative experiences are those that have shaped our current selves" (Wiliam, 2018, p. 42).

Figure 6.5 demonstrates how assessment and instruction are interwoven. Once teachers articulate what student mastery looks like and the prerequisite skills that serve as the starting point for instruction, teacher teams, teachers, and leaders determine the summative assessments that will be necessary to gauge mastery of the standard, and the formative assessments that will serve as formal checkpoints along the way to gauge both student learning and instructional efficacy.

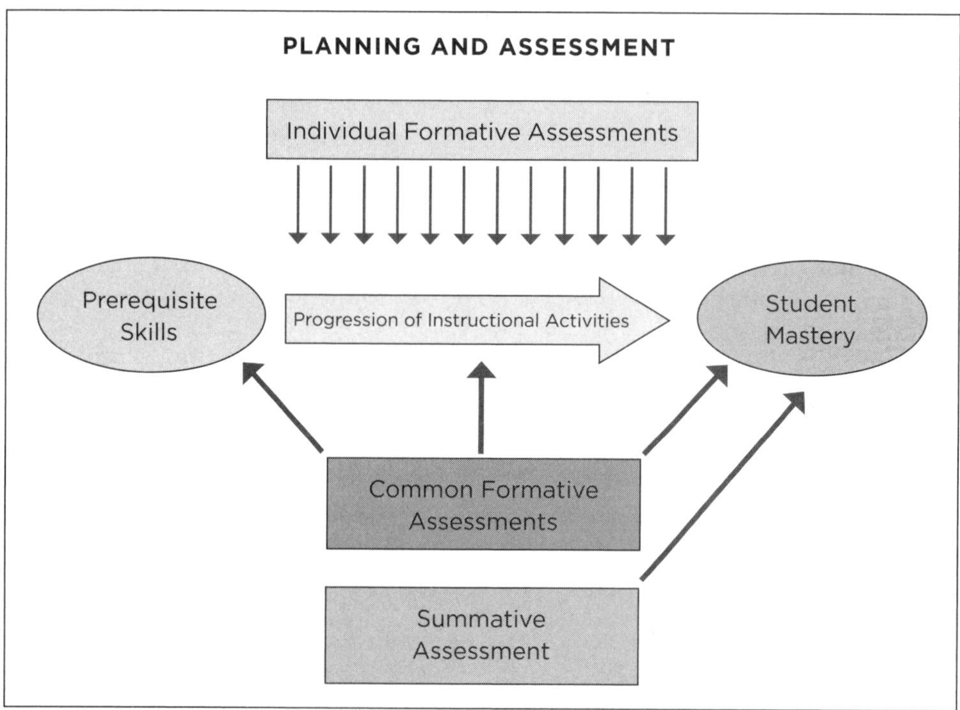

Source: Wink, 2017, p. 125.

Figure 6.5: The relationship between instruction and assessment.

Teachers often fail to consider individual formative assessments. They can use these informal checks for understanding to assess and teach students to self-assess their progress toward mastering the concept. Examples of individual formative assessments include conversations, student collaboration, student work samples, quizzes, quick writes, exit tickets, student feedback, student questions, and any other informal tasks that teachers wouldn't necessarily grade. Think of individual formative assessments as a blood pressure check. Teachers take a minute or two to determine how the student is doing.

To make this idea of rigor and mastery more relevant to students, teachers can create levels of proficiency in their assessments. Instead of giving a quiz with random questions at random levels of proficiency, teachers can create assessment items that assess four levels of knowledge.

1. Level 1 assesses basic knowledge, only the content part of the essential standard.
2. Level 2 assesses the verb and content together at a higher level of complexity.
3. Level 3 assesses the verb, content, and context together, but the rigor of the assessment is based on predictable situations that the teacher has provided to students during instruction.
4. Level 4 assesses the verb, content, and context together; however, the rigor of the assessment is completely unpredictable. Students will have to transfer their knowledge to an unpredictable situation to which they have not been exposed.

Figure 6.6 (page 142) illustrates how teachers might first assess the prerequisite skills at levels 1–4 at the beginning of instruction. Next, they would assess the standards that support the essential skill along the way at levels 1–4. Finally, they would assess the essential skill at levels 1–4. This assessment method generates data by student and by level that drive not only instruction but also intervention.

Planning for rigor and mastery is essential if we hope to deliver them in instruction. By spending time identifying and analyzing the essential skills all students need to learn, we give students a greater chance of successfully finding rigor and mastery simply because we thoughtfully established the road map well before students enter the room. Furthermore, the road map clearly articulates the checkpoints or informal assessments along the way that tell both teachers and students the level of student proficiency on their journey to excellence. Now that they have clearly articulated the direction to mastery, teachers must deliver rigor and mastery through instruction and questioning.

Delivery

As discussed previously, the path to rigor and mastery is concentrated instruction, "a systematic process of identifying essential knowledge and skills that all students must master to learn at high levels, and determining the specific learning needs for each child to get there" (Buffum et al., 2012, p. 10). In preparation for concentrated

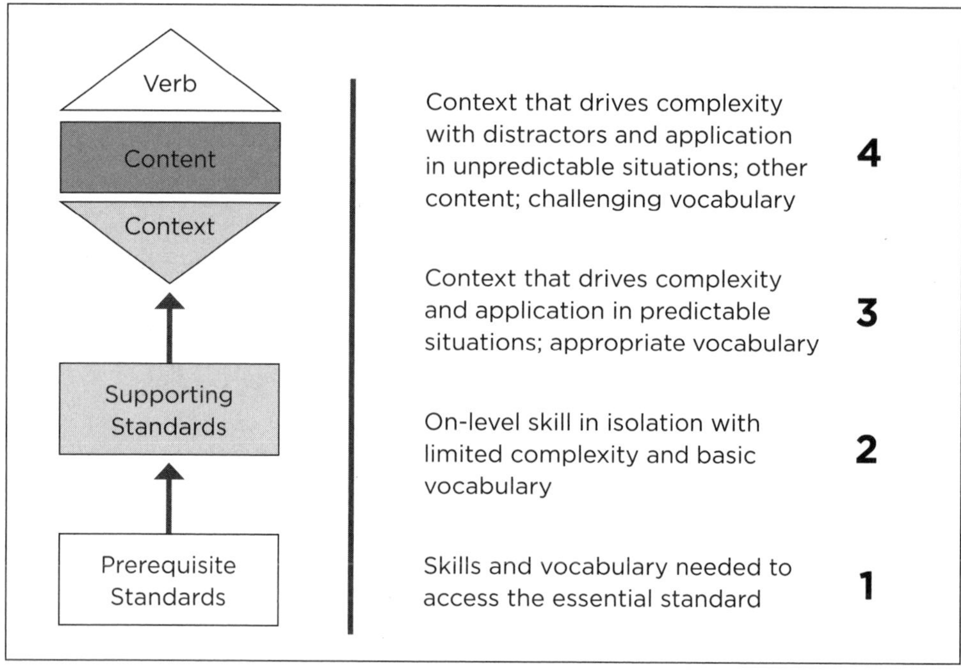

Figure 6.6: Levels of assessment.

instruction, great teachers develop their own content knowledge and expertise and use that knowledge to develop a system of formative assessments that determines each student's level of proficiency in mastering the content.

Teachers now need to deliver rigor and mastery, which includes the remaining three components of the rigor to mastery cycle: (1) provide rigorous instructional activities, (2) establish a learning culture that promotes questioning, and (3) monitor and adjust instruction for student success.

Provide Rigorous Instructional Activities

Instruction for rigorous learning stretches students' understanding from their current level of proficiency so students can create meaningful products that serve as evidence of their growth. It inspires students to evaluate the quality of their own work as well as that of their peers, and it challenges them to ask introspective questions that lead to a deeper understanding of themselves and their learning.

Danielson (2013) writes, "Different disciplines have 'signature pedagogies' that have evolved over time and been found to be most effective in teaching" (p. 6). When selecting instructional activities, many teachers choose those that are aesthetically pleasing first and connected to the standard second. Great teachers, however, consider many factors before choosing instructional activities, and they opt for those that best match and develop students' academic rigor and content mastery. Because they know that they can't leave rigor to chance, great teachers consider the following questions before deeming an activity rigorous enough for instruction.

- Does the activity match the levels of proficiency within the standard?
    - If not, is it aligned to the rigor of the prerequisite standard?
    - If not, can we use it as an intervention for struggling students through guided learning?
- Does the activity challenge students with high-level questions and create opportunities for students to generate their own high-level questions?
- Does the activity inspire students to learn from one another, and does it motivate them to take ownership of their learning?
- Does the activity structure learning so students can set academic growth goals and monitor their growth toward mastery of those goals?

Rigorous learning activities work best when teachers determine where the activity best matches students' confidence and competence levels. As discussed in the Provide Assessments to Generate Data section (page 140), the levels of proficiency range from developing basic skills (level 1) to leveraging complete knowledge of the skills in unpredictable situations (level 4). In order to incorporate rigor into instructional activities, this philosophy of proficiency levels does not change. Figure 6.7 (page 144) shows how the four levels of proficiency apply to instruction.

1. **Level 1:** Basic tasks that build automaticity around the skill or fluency
2. **Level 2:** Skill application in concrete or basic critical-thinking situations
3. **Level 3:** Complex problems that apply the learning in the manner that the teacher taught it
4. **Level 4:** Project-based learning and other situations in which students apply their learning in unique ways for which the teacher did not deliver explicit instruction

Once the teacher determines how the activity aligns with student competencies and meets the criteria for rigor in the preceding questions, teachers can determine where the activity best fits in the gradual release of responsibility model (see chapter 5, page 101). Teachers can use the following questions to gauge how to appropriately place activities in the gradual release of responsibility model.

- Does this activity work best for students working independently or students working with others?
- If collaborative learning is better for this activity, does this activity work best in pairs, groups of three, or groups of four?
- What product must each student generate to demonstrate mastery?

In order to lead all students to the rigor of the essential skill, instruction must meet students' immediate needs along their journey to rigor. Some activities may be remedial in nature, some may be collaborative in order to stretch students through cooperative learning, and some may inspire students to create major products of

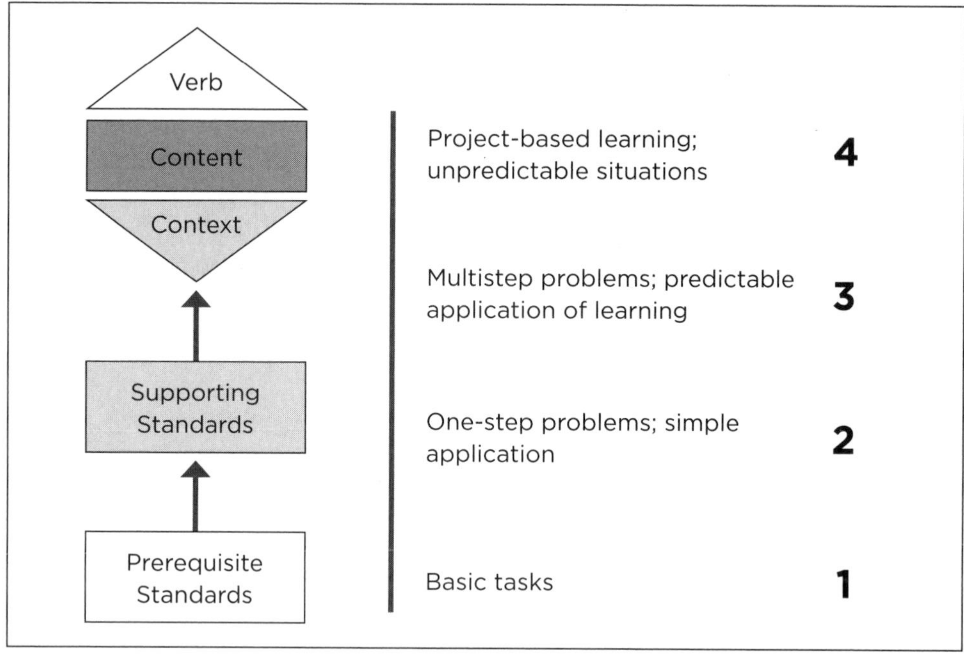

Figure 6.7: Proficiency levels of instruction.

their learning that they can also use as a resource to teach other students about the standard. Instruction is not a one-size-fits-all mentality. It meets students where they are and inspires them to reach for where they want to be.

Establish a Learning Culture That Promotes Questioning

Most teachers periodically ask questions throughout instruction, but excellent teachers intentionally prompt learning and thinking through strategic questioning. Understanding that all students are at different places in their level of mastery, teachers should be prepared to ask three levels of questions throughout their lesson.

1. **Scaffolding questions:** These lower-level questions guide below-level or struggling students to think through the process or concept in smaller, attainable chunks.
2. **On-level questions:** These questions at the appropriate level of rigor and cognitive complexity in the standard lead students to generate answers or products that serve as evidence of their content mastery.
3. **Extension questions:** These high-level questions prompt students to apply or transfer their learning in unpredictable situations, synthesize their thinking about the concept in new or different ways, or create products that expand on their mastery of the standard.

Figure 6.8 illustrates how a teacher can use four levels of questioning aligned to the four levels in assessment and instruction.

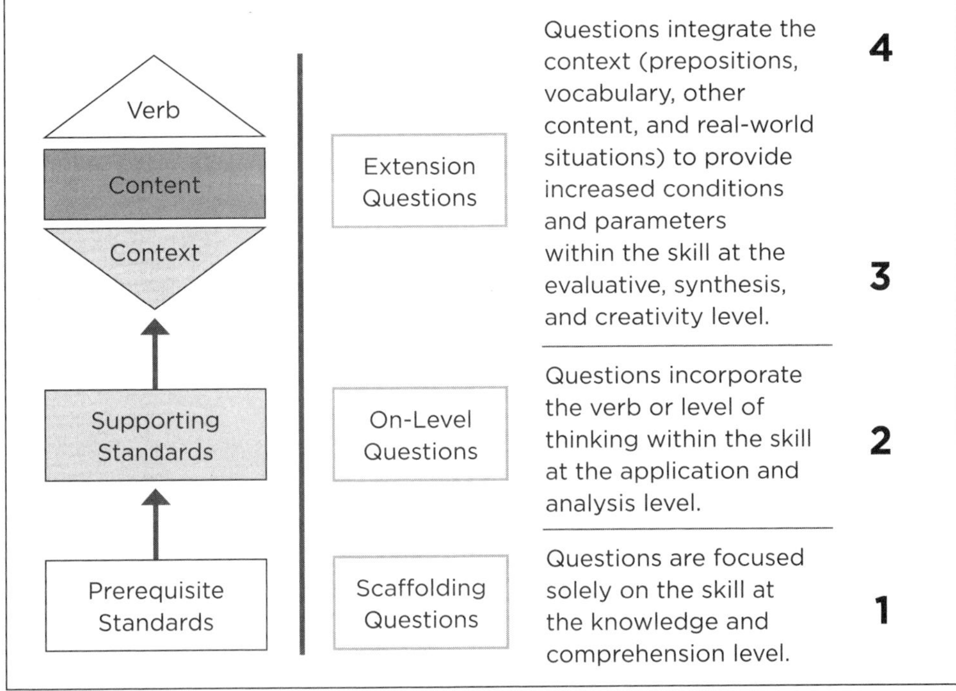

Figure 6.8: Levels of questioning.

Questioning strategies are not just limited to the questions that teachers pose to students. In fact, teachers should encourage students to generate their own questions for each other and the teacher so they can deepen their learning. Students must apply or transfer their learning in unpredictable situations, synthesize their thinking about the concept in new or different ways, or create products that expand on their mastery of the standard; therefore, students must drive the questioning. When students are asking more questions than the teacher, they are using higher-order thinking skills.

Great teachers understand that questioning is a challenging skill in and of itself; therefore, they put as much effort into developing challenging questions as they do in creating rigorous instructional activities. Some teachers post question stem walls in their classrooms that serve as a resource for students to question one another. They also use students' mistakes as teachable moments in the lesson, and they use questioning strategies to challenge students to reflect on their mistakes and determine how they can learn from them. In order to leverage strategic questioning and mistakes to generate questions, teachers can script out the questions they want to ask students and create a list of question stems that cause students to reflect on their mistakes.

Monitor and Adjust Instruction for Student Success

PLC critical question 1, "What do students need to know and be able to do?" (DuFour et al., 2016, p. 251), drives everything in the content knowledge and expertise parts of rigor and mastery. Critical question 2, "How will we know when they have learned it?" (DuFour et al., 2016, p. 251) drives the assessment and questioning parts of rigor and mastery. The answer to question 2 should drive the response to student learning with questions 3 and 4—"What will we do when they haven't learned it?" and "What will we do when they already know it?" (DuFour et al., 2016, p. 251).

Teachers should also pay close attention to question 2 because it drives how they should monitor student learning and adjust instruction to ensure that they maximize the rigor for every student. Throughout the period, most if not all teachers monitor students for behavior and participation, but the best teachers monitor learning to ensure students are getting the most out of the lesson.

Teachers must create systems in which they monitor student progress through assessments and encourage students to provide their own evidence of learning or data. Teachers gauge collaboration to determine if learning is accelerating or sputtering. Their informal conversations with students can provide powerful evidence of the effects of their instruction, and they can analyze student work to determine what students need next.

Essentially, monitoring and adjusting serves as a feedback protocol for teachers, which guides their instruction and helps them make minor tweaks to improve lessons. The more frequently teachers monitor their own instruction, the more efficient their instruction becomes, and the more aligned it will be to student proficiency.

Reflection

Throughout and at the end of every lesson, great teachers reflect on the effectiveness of their instruction and their approach to teaching at each student's highest level. During reflection, "the teacher makes an accurate assessment of a lesson's effectiveness and the extent to which it achieved its instructional outcomes" (Danielson, 2013, p. 62). Great teachers evaluate all aspects of their lessons, including rigor and mastery components, to determine where students struggled, where activities were unable to connect students to the learning target, and where questioning strategies failed to transform rigorous learning into content mastery.

Figure 6.9 offers a tool to help teachers reflect on their learning about the five components of rigor and mastery. As you reflect on these components, determine your next steps for providing more targeted and specific rigor to students. Determine where you need to develop specific protocols for giving all students descriptive feedback to help deepen their knowledge.

Component	Reflection
Possess Content Knowledge and Expertise	Have I identified the eight to twelve essential skills that all students must master in my content? Have I determined the prerequisite skills or supporting skills that serve as foundational skills for the essential skills? Have I determined how my essential skills build a solid foundation for students to be prepared for the aligned future skills? How well have I deconstructed those essential skills to determine the level of thinking in the verbs, the specificity of the skills, and the parameters found in the context needed to fully master the essential skills? How well have I narrowed my focus on those essential skills so that I don't overemphasize skills that are less important than the essential skills? What is my plan to communicate those essential skills to my students so that they know exactly what skills are essential to master my content?
Provide Assessments to Generate Data	How well have I determined the four levels of proficiency for each essential skill? For each essential skill, have I determined how students can demonstrate mastery of the content at the most basic level (level 1)? For each essential skill, have I shown how students can demonstrate mastery of the verb and content (level 2)? For each essential skill, have I shown how students can demonstrate mastery of the essential skill in predictable ways (level 3)? For each essential skill, have I shown how students can demonstrate mastery of the essential skill in unpredictable ways (level 4)? Have I determined how I can gauge student mastery at each level with minimal grading on my part?

Figure 6.9: Rigor and mastery reflection tool. continued →

Component	Reflection
Provide Rigorous Instructional Activities	How well have I created instructional activities that are aligned to each essential skill and the four levels of proficiency that I developed through my analysis of the standard? How well do I inspect the validity of instructional activities to ensure that they are aligned to each level of proficiency in the essential skill? Before I discard an activity, do I determine if the activity would be more appropriate as a remediation activity or as an activity to build prerequisite knowledge needed to master the essential skill? How well do my instructional activities inspire students to own their mastery of the essential skill and teach them to monitor their progress and set goals for future growth? When students reject instructional activities or find them uninteresting, do I have a protocol that students can use to give me feedback about the activity?
Establish a Learning Culture That Promotes Questioning	How well have I developed questioning strategies that incorporate scaffolding questions, on-level questions, and extension questions? For each essential skill, have I developed questions that are aligned to each level of proficiency? Where do I post question stems so I, as well as students, can use them as a reference when creating questions? How well have I taught students to create questions and pose them to one another so that they can deepen their learning at the evaluative, analysis, synthesis, and creativity levels? How well do I generate targeted questions based on student misunderstandings or mistakes with essential skills or levels of proficiency with those skills?
Monitor and Adjust Instruction for Student Success	As students are in the process of learning the content, how well do I monitor student learning to determine their current level of proficiency? How well do I determine the effectiveness of instructional activities as students are learning and use that information to adjust instruction? How effectively do I adjust the pacing of my lesson or adjust future lessons based on the objective student data I gather during instruction? How well do I use data gathered from instruction and assessment to determine the engagement structure (collaborative learning, guided learning, or independent learning) that will best help students learn at higher levels?

Visit ***go.SolutionTree.com/instruction*** *for a free reproducible version of this figure.*

Building a Student Excellence Support System: Rigor and Mastery

In order to guarantee that all students reach high levels of rigor and mastery, the teacher must establish a Student Excellence Support System. These supports include teacher team collaboration, classwide supports, and individualized student supports.

In *A Leader's Guide to Excellence in Every Classroom* (Wink, 2017), I outline some schoolwide supports that leaders should provide to ensure all teachers are equipped with the knowledge and skills to guarantee rigor and mastery in their instruction. These include a guaranteed and viable curriculum that helps teachers determine the concentrated instruction; curriculum guides that help teachers determine the suggested time frames for instructional units, assessment guidelines, and instructional supports; and ongoing professional development on essential skills, formative assessments, questioning strategies, and other important skills that all teachers need to ensure that all students learn at high levels.

In this book, I expand on that information so teachers can deliver a guaranteed and viable curriculum that provides rigor and mastery to build student excellence. In order to build a Student Excellence Support System, teachers leverage the necessary curriculum tools, knowledge, and expertise to accelerate their productivity and creativity in developing more powerful instruction to provide rigor and mastery for every student.

Step 1: Teacher Team Collaboration

Guaranteeing excellence in every student starts with developing consistency among teachers who provide rigorous learning to every student through collaboration. Teacher teams can offer members various tools and strategies for promoting rigor and mastery at every stage of the instructional process, from planning for instruction to designing assessments to reflecting on data.

Great teachers understand that collaborative teams don't have members complete some kind of teaching-for-rigor-and-mastery checklist. Instead, they help members clarify rigorous learning goals for developing content mastery and the most effective instructional processes for delivering it. "Teachers are most effective in helping all students learn when they are clear regarding exactly what their students must know and be able to do as a result of the course, grade level, and each unit of instruction" (DuFour et al., 2016, p. 122).

To build the most effective system for teacher collaboration, teachers can create different kinds of teams that address multiple opportunities and challenges for professional growth in teaching for rigor and mastery. The following sections outline five such teams: (1) content teams, (2) vertical teams, (3) interdisciplinary teams, (4) singleton teams, and (5) virtual teams.

Content Teams

Content, or subject-level, teams are organized around content; therefore, members have a great deal in common when it comes to rigor and mastery. Team members work with the same curriculum, the same standards, the same age group of students, and the same instructional outcomes. As a result of these commonalities, perhaps most importantly, these teams produce an aligned understanding regarding their instructional goals, processes, and assessments. Since content knowledge and expertise is the foundation for successfully teaching rigorous content, content teams can begin by focusing their collaborative efforts on clarifying their understanding of the essential skills. Then, for each skill, they should answer this question: "How would student work demonstrate content mastery within this standard?" DuFour et al. (2016) state, "This strategy of clarifying standards through the lens of student work leads teams through a natural progression of questions" (p. 119).

Careful analysis of the essential skills at all levels can help teams collectively develop a deeper knowledge of their shared subject's content and what form rigorous learning of that content might take. The reproducible "Essential Skills Analysis Chart" (page 161) can help content teams improve their knowledge of the learning standards and the associated rigor while simultaneously designing instruction and crafting assessments that will help students master the standards at the highest levels.

Team members can deconstruct an essential skill and answer the question, "What does this mean for students?" This question both deepens understanding and helps teams visualize what instruction and assessment should look like for students. By collaboratively agreeing on the elements for this chart, teachers develop their collective expertise in guiding students through the rigorous learning processes necessary to master content.

Figure 6.10 shows an example of how a third-grade reading team could complete the Essential Skills Analysis Chart.

Vertical Teams

Vertical teams have less in common than content teams, but they offer huge potential for teacher collaboration around rigor and mastery. Examples of vertical teams include a mathematics team with teachers from grades K–5 or a middle school reading team with teachers from grades 6–8. Like content teams, vertical teams can discuss how they align instructional strategies using the Essential Skills Analysis Chart. Discussions about how essential skills are taught from grade to grade can encourage vertical team members to align their instruction with the prerequisite skills their students learned from the previous year and also prepare students to master content included in following year's standards.

Vertical teams should also carefully consider aligning vocabulary, instructional language, instructional strategies, and problem-solving models. When vertical teams collaborate with the mindset of providing students with three to four years

Skill	3.7.D: Retell and paraphrase texts in ways that maintain meaning and logical order.	
Component	**Corresponding Words in the Skill**	**What Does This Mean for Students?**
Verb and Skill	Retell texts	Give a presentation of the important information, key people, or order of events in any genre of text.
Verb and Skill	Paraphrase texts	In one to three sentences, tell what the text was about.
Contextual Phrase	In ways that maintain meaning	Ensure that students tells the important ideas by not including extraneous information in their presentation.
Contextual Phrase	In ways that maintain logical order	Ensure that students can present information or stories in the order in which they appeared in the text.
Prerequisite Skill	2.7.D: Retell and paraphrase texts in ways that maintain meaning and in logical order.	
Future Skill	4.7.D: Retell, paraphrase, or summarize texts in ways that maintain meaning and logical order.	

Source for standards: Texas Education Agency, n.d.

Figure 6.10: Essential skills analysis chart for third-grade reading team.

of continuity in rigorous content instruction, they have the potential to accelerate student content mastery and, at the same time, strengthen each teacher's content knowledge and expertise.

Interdisciplinary Teams

Interdisciplinary teams share students rather than content, and they have the power to positively affect students and their ability to engage in rigorous learning. While these teams don't necessarily share content standards, they share expectations for learning and a collective responsibility to help students learn at high levels. Interdisciplinary teams can collaborate about positive approaches for improving specific students' learning, and they can collaboratively develop shared strategies for promoting rigorous thinking and content mastery in all students. These shared strategies can help teachers:

- Deepen students' critical-thinking and problem-solving skills
- Utilize technology tools to strengthen instruction
- Set instructional expectations for students
- Establish the level of rigor expected within each component of the instructional delivery model

Because of the diversity of their members, who may represent a broad range of content knowledge and expertise, interdisciplinary teams bring a wide array of strategies to the table. As education administrator, author, and educator Ben Johnson (2014) writes, "We can promote deep learning by encouraging multiple teachers working together in helping students to understand math in the context of science, coordinating timelines of scientific discovery and literature, and demonstrating how a painter uses light to express meaning." Johnson (2014) goes on to describe the power of such interdisciplinary collaborations to drive rigorous learning: "When professional educators combine their energies and reinforce the same deep learning, the stream of information is clearer for the student, the learning activities are more fluid, and the student's reservoir of knowledge and skills fills faster."

Singleton Teams

Great teachers who don't share content or even students still share the same goal—all students learning at high levels. Art, music, and technology teachers frequently are *singletons*, or the only educators within their schools who teach their specific subject. Even in small schools, singletons can form teams that take the work of interdisciplinary teams one step further by focusing collaboration on shared instructional components. For example, an arts-focused singleton team could develop strategies to engage and inspire rigorous learning through collaborative experiments with music genres, dance, or graphic arts technologies. A singleton team of advanced placement (AP) teachers could focus its collaboration on questioning strategies or skill-based activities to help students earn a score of three or higher on the AP test. Career and technical education teachers could form a singleton team to align their instruction with a rigorous, nationally recognized industry certification program or to create plans that help students master content so they prepare to transition into a college or career path after graduation.

Virtual Teams

When determining what types of teacher teams can best address the need for promoting rigorous learning and content mastery, remember that these collaborations don't have to revolve around a common meeting time or place. Schools with dwindling resources and limited time overcome these limitations by providing teachers ample opportunities to collaborate through the use of virtual tools.

Virtual teams can use Google Docs and folders to share documents and simultaneously create planning documents and assessments for rigorous learning, such as those described earlier in this chapter in figures 6.3 (page 138) and 6.9 (pages 147–148). Virtual teams can use a website such as Smore (www.smore.com) to create a library of digital creations or discoveries that help virtual team members develop instruction that is more rigorous for their students. Collaboration that guarantees consistency for every student doesn't have to occur at the same time, in the same place, or even face to face. Teachers can collaborate with other teachers and teams at any time and from locations around the world, and they are helping one another make a huge impact on student learning.

Step 2: Classwide Supports

Once teachers create a support system for their team through collaboration, teachers can leverage the collaborative work to create their own personalized plan for instruction to promote rigor and mastery. This section defines how teachers can create specific plans that also serve as student supports to help all students master the essential skills.

Planning and Assessment

At the classwide supports level, teachers can apply the planning and assessment work of teacher team collaboration to develop formative assessments that are both aligned to the work by the team and to the specific needs of their students. Figure 6.11 offers a chart to help teachers determine how they can build informal formative assessment items for their students at the four levels of assessment described previously. Teachers can also share the teacher's personalized questions with students to be used as a rubric that establishes the goal and roadmap to mastering the lesson's content or to set a gutsy goal for the end of a unit in preparation for the assessments developed by the teacher team.

Skill			
Level	**Components**	**Our Team Assessment Questions**	**My Assessment Questions**
4	Verb + skill + context in unpredictable situations		
3	Verb + skill + context in predictable situations		
2	Verb + skill		
1	Skill		

Figure 6.11: Essential skill assessment chart.

Visit ***go.SolutionTree.com/instruction*** *for a free reproducible version of this figure.*

Level 1 assessments would include basic-level tasks to prove that the student can show mastery of the skill in isolation without any distractors, complex vocabulary, or critical thinking. Level 2 assessment items would add the verb to allow students to demonstrate how they use the skill to solve a simple problem or answer a basic question. Level 3 incorporates the language found in the essential skill's context so students can show mastery of the skill in the most complex ways taught by the teacher, and level 4 assesses students in completely unpredictable situations by incorporating the full language of the essential skill. Level 4 asks students to prove they have fully mastered the essential skill by transferring their knowledge to a situation for which they could never have prepared.

The purpose of assessment is to generate actionable data from the students' work that can inform the student, teachers, leaders, and parents as to which mastery level the student is performing. In the Texas Teacher Evaluation and Support System instrument (Texas Education Agency, 2016) high levels of planning and assessment create environments that have the following results for both students and teachers.

- Students engage in self-assessment and build awareness of their own strengths and weaknesses.
- Students track their own progress.
- Teachers provide consistent feedback to students and their families regarding the students' growth and what steps they need to take next to ensure mastery of the essential skill.
- Teachers gather information about what instructional activities are necessary to help students close the gaps that the assessments revealed.

Assessment without actionable data wastes both the student's and the teacher's time. When done well, assessments should tell teachers how students are doing, and also what instruction is the next best step. Data inform progress and proficiency, and when leveraged through the lens of growth, they also inspire students to believe in their own efficacy.

Instructional Activities

Once teachers have developed assessment items for each level, they must next design instructional activities that prepare students for the assessment items at each level within the essential skill. Instructional activities should serve as precursors to the assessment; therefore, the levels of proficiency within instructional activities should incorporate knowledge and comprehension tasks at levels 1 and 2. Levels 3 and 4 activities should require more cognitive demand with critical thinking that leads students to conceptual understanding behind the essential skill. Figure 6.12 offers a chart to help teachers structure instructional activities so they can determine which activities are aligned to the essential skill and to each proficiency level within the standard.

Sometimes teachers are prone to select activities that loosely align to the standard but don't address all the levels of proficiency within the skill. Some activities may best fit levels 1 and 2, but not levels 3 and 4, while some only address one specific level, such as level 4. This does not mean that teachers shouldn't select the activities. It just means that they will have to assign additional activities that meet

Skill		
Level	**Components**	**What Activities Can We Use to Prepare Students for Mastery at This Level?**
4	Verb + skill + context in unpredictable context	
3	Verb + skill + context in predictable context	
2	Verb + skill	
1	Skill	

Figure 6.12: Essential skill instructional activities chart.

Visit ***go.SolutionTree.com/instruction*** *for a free reproducible version of this figure.*

the unaddressed levels. Simply grading an activity doesn't help students know how well they have mastered the essential skill, and it doesn't prepare students to show mastery through formal assessments. In these situations, teachers should determine which levels the activity addresses so students know ahead of time what level of assessment the instructional activity is preparing them to master. For example, a mathematics activity that works on basic computation would be considered a level 1 activity because it only addresses the skill in isolation, whereas creating a PowerPoint presentation teaching students how to solve a complex problem that has not been introduced or taught would be considered a level 4 activity.

Furthermore, instructional activities lose their impact when teachers present them to students as a checklist of things to do for a grade or as something to keep them busy. The more information students have about the levels of proficiency and where they stand in those levels, the more motivated they will likely become to achieve. Rigorous instruction inspires students to ask, "What's next in my learning?"

Questioning Strategies

If teachers identify assessment levels as checkpoints along the way to mastery, and instructional activities serve as the road map to mastery, then questioning strategies serve as a metaphorical GPS to help students ensure that they stay on the path to mastery. Questions merely serve as the quickest and most informal form of assessment. They gauge student thinking, and they also reveal gaps in student thinking about the essential skill. In order to ensure that students are on the right path in instruction, teachers can script the questions they will pose to students at each level of proficiency.

Figure 6.13 (page 156) offers a chart to help teachers map out the questions they will pose to students at each level of proficiency within the essential skill.

Skill		
Level	**Components**	**What Questions Can We Ask to Probe Student Thinking at This Level?**
4	Verb + skill + context in unpredictable situations	
3	Verb + skill + context in predictable situations	
2	Verb + skill	
1	Skill	

Figure 6.13: Essential skill questioning strategies chart.

Visit ***go.SolutionTree.com/instruction*** *for a free reproducible version of this figure.*

Teachers should determine the appropriate level of questions from their instructional resources and curriculum. Additionally, teachers can use depth of knowledge (DOK) question stems, which you can find on the internet by googling *DOK question stems*. By having question stems handy, teachers can increase the rigor of the question by simply changing the question stem used to probe thinking from students. This search generates a plethora of resources for questioning and instructional activities at DOK levels 1–4. The DOK levels, developed by Norman Webb (2002), align nicely with the levels of proficiency from this chapter.

Monitoring and Adjustment

Once teachers develop assessments, instruction, and questioning for the essential skills with the four levels of proficiency in mind, teachers should monitor student progress and adjust instruction based on their findings. To monitor progress, teachers could develop methods to collect data on student progress. This data could be in the form of anecdotal or qualitative data, written notes about each student's learning, or quantitative data that measures the number of items students correctly answered on a given activity or assessment. No matter how they collect data, great teachers ask, "Based on the data I collected, how do I need to adjust instruction to meet student needs?"

The following questions can help teachers drive next steps for adjusting instruction.

- What method do I use for determining each student's current proficiency level?
- How do I gauge if students are making progress in the current activity?
- Once I know students are struggling, how can I adjust the activity or the engagement structure students are using in the activity (collaborative learning, independent learning, or guided learning)?

- What data do I collect to determine if the class or student groups are unsuccessful, and how prepared am I to reteach the concept using a more structured or scaffolded approach?
- What feedback do students give me to help me improve my instruction?
- How well do I differentiate my feedback to students' needs based on their level of proficiency and their specific learning style?
- As a result of the data that I collect, do I adjust the structure of my lessons to the needs of the class, or am I more committed to sticking to my lesson plans for all classes?

The answers to these questions can provide clues as to the teacher's strengths in the monitoring and adjusting skill set. They reveal instructional tendencies and areas where teachers can make more of an effort in student-centered instructional delivery. Monitoring and adjusting can be a challenging skill for teachers because it requires them to be less in charge of students and more attentive to and reflective of student learning. It impacts the pacing and sequencing of current instruction and tells teachers the best engagement structures to accelerate student learning.

Step 3: Individualized Student Supports

When students struggle with rigor and mastery in spite of teacher team collaboration and classwide supports, they may require individualized instructional supports. For individualized student supports at the rigor and mastery level, teachers must gauge each component of the gradual release of responsibility model (see figure 5.3, page 110) and determine if they have instructional supports in place for assessment, instructional activities, and questioning strategies.

Since assessments are essentially independent tasks, teachers should determine if the rigor provided in assessments works for a struggling student by evaluating the student through an independent learning setting only. Instructional activities and questioning strategies can appear in all structures in the gradual release of responsibility model; therefore, the teacher should determine if the rigor provided in instructional activities and questioning strategies fails to work for the student in guided learning, collaborative learning structures, independent learning structures, or all learning structures.

Monitoring and adjusting through classwide supports may not generate targeted and specific data to fully meet the struggling student's needs; therefore, teachers should determine if they are gathering data that are appropriately actionable for that student and if they are delivering feedback that causes the student to give more effort or less effort in pursuit of learning. This reflection on the rigor and mastery cycle is essential if we want to close the struggling student's gaps in learning the essential skills.

Before teachers develop a specific plan of action for a student, they must guarantee that the student's deficit is not due to a deficiency in the Hierarchy of Student Excellence's first four levels. Then teachers must ensure that they have provided consistency through the teacher team's collaborative work, and they should make sure the student's difficulties do not stem from their failure to provide a classwide system of supports for rigor and mastery. Once teachers have verified those areas for planning and delivery, they can narrow the root cause of the student's failure in rigor and mastery and develop an individualized plan of action to guarantee student growth.

Teachers can use the problem-solving tool in figure 6.14 to isolate the problem in rigor and mastery, prescribe a support, and determine the support's effectiveness. With this tool, teachers can more efficiently develop potential solutions and develop an action plan for implementing rigor and mastery.

Individualized Student Support Problem-Solving Tool: Rigor and Mastery	
Question 1: Has the teacher team created common expectations and supports for all students at this level? (Circle yes or no.) (If your answer is yes, continue. If your answer is no, stop and correct this area.)	Yes No
Question 2: Based on the team's work, has the teacher created his or her classwide structure for rigor and mastery? (Circle yes or no.) (If your answer is yes, continue. If your answer is no, stop and correct this area.)	Yes No
Question 3: Do the majority of students regularly pursue learning at their level of proficiency in your lessons?(Circle yes or no.) (If your answer is yes, continue. If your answer is no, stop and correct this area.)	Yes No
Question 4: Which student is struggling with rigor and mastery? Student: ______ List the student's strengths and difficulties with each component at this level. Strengths: Difficulties:	

Question 5: Where are students proficient or not proficient in the rigor and mastery cycle? The following table is an assessment of the student's response to the rigor and mastery cycle through each component of the gradual release of responsibility model. Place a checkmark to indicate where the student is proficient and an X where the student is not proficient.

	Guided Learning	**Collaborative Learning**	**Independent Learning**	**Exit Ticket**
Planning and Assessment	Not applicable	Not applicable		
Instructional Activities				
Questioning Strategies				
Monitoring and Adjusting				

Question 6: Based on the identified proficiency levels, what is the predominant problem preventing the student from finding rigor and mastery? What potential supports will help this student develop better rigor and mastery in learning? (Consider the following questions to determine potential supports.)

- What is the target component in rigor and mastery that I want to address first?
  - ☐ Planning and assessment
  - ☐ Instructional activities
  - ☐ Questioning strategies
  - ☐ Monitoring and adjusting
- Which essential skills does the student fail to master?
- With which prerequisite skills does the student need remediation to further support him or her in the targeted area?
- What supports do I need to provide in each component to help the student succeed in rigor and mastery?
- What supports, modifications, linguistic accommodations, and instructional accommodations should I make so the work is more accessible to the student?
- What data points must I collect from the student to determine if he or she is growing in this deficit area?
- What is my action plan to support this student in this specific area for growth?

Figure 6.14: Individualized student support problem-solving tool—rigor and mastery.

continued →

Individualized Student Support Problem-Solving Tool: Rigor and Mastery	
Question 7: What are the goal and the deadline for the student to be successful with the behavior? Goal: Deadline:	
Question 8: Did the student meet the goal by the deadline? (Circle yes or no.) (If your answer is yes, continue the support. If your answer is no, return to question 4.)	Yes No
Notes:	

Visit ***go.SolutionTree.com/instruction*** *for a free reproducible version of this figure.*

Conclusion

Rigor and mastery, the first level of growth needs in the Hierarchy of Student Excellence, aligns with the fifth level in Maslow's Hierarchy of Needs—the desire to know and understand. Rigor and mastery has five components: (1) possess content knowledge and expertise, (2) provide assessments to generate data, (3) provide rigorous instructional activities, (4) establish a learning culture that promotes questioning, and (5) monitor and adjust instruction for student success.

This chapter concludes with a reflection tool (pages 162–163) that teachers can use to evaluate their understanding of the challenges they face when implementing rigor and mastery in their instruction. As you consider the questions and your responses to them, explore possibilities for improving those systems, including teacher team collaboration, classwide supports, and individualized student supports, based on the information and ideas in this chapter.

Essential Skills Analysis Chart

Use this chart to deconstruct the language within a specific standard so you can identify what the language within the verbs, content, and contextual phrases specifically means. Once you define the language, determine what the language means for students so you can create actions and tasks for students to complete to demonstrate mastery of all parts of the essential skill.

Skill		
Component	**Corresponding Words in the Skill**	**What Does This Mean for Students?**
Verb		
Content		
Contextual Phrase		
Contextual Phrase		
Contextual Phrase		
Contextual Phrase		
Contextual Phrase		
Prerequisite Skill		
Future Skill		

Reflection Tool: Rigor and Mastery

Answer the following questions to help you create a Student Excellence Support System that provides students with the appropriate rigor to challenge them at their level of proficiency and pursue success in content mastery.

Teacher Team Collaboration

- Has our team established plans to incorporate all five components of rigor and mastery (possess content knowledge and expertise, provide assessments to generate data, provide rigorous instructional activities, establish a learning culture that promotes questioning, and monitor and adjust instruction for student success) into our classes?
- How well do team members lead one another in deepening our knowledge of the essential skills?
- How well do we work together to deepen our understanding of the prerequisite skills?
- How well do we work together to ensure that our knowledge of the essential skills serves as a solid foundation for future skills?
- When a teacher experiences difficulty with rigor and mastery, what steps does he or she take to seek help from the team?

Classwide Supports

- How well have I aligned my plans for rigor and mastery with those developed by the team?
- How well have I developed my informal formative assessments with both those developed by the team and the four levels of proficiency in mind?
- How well have I developed instructional activities that are aligned to my assessments and that are at the four levels of proficiency?
- How well have I crafted my questioning strategies to scaffold learning for struggling students and extend learning for proficient learners?
- How well do I monitor student learning and use those data to adjust my lessons during and after instruction?

Individualized Student Supports

- When a student is disconnecting from the learning, how well do I consistently determine the root cause of the student's frustration with rigor and mastery?
- Once I determine the potential root cause, how well do I verify that the failure is not due to my classroom supports or inconsistency from the team?
- How well do I ensure that the lack of rigor and mastery is not due to a deficiency in a lower level in the Hierarchy of Student Excellence?
- How effective am I at identifying the student's strengths so I can leverage these strengths to address the areas for growth?
- When I prescribe an intervention, how committed am I to providing the intervention with frequency and consistency?
- How consistently do I gauge student growth in the target area to determine if my intervention was effective?
- When the student is still unsuccessful, how well do I reflect and refine the intervention to better help the student?
- When my efforts to help the student continue to fail, how well do I reach out to my team members to help me better respond to the student?

CHAPTER 7

Teaching for Excellence: Creative Strategies for Individual Students

Those who make the most progress are those who take the most action.

—Richard DuFour, Rebecca DuFour, Robert Eaker, and Gayle Karhanek

Chapter 5 (page 101) explores the importance of student engagement, and chapter 6 (page 131) defines how the appropriate instructional rigor can lead students down the road to true mastery of the content. This chapter discusses how teachers can reach individual students through creative strategies, also known as *differentiation*. Once teachers have provided students with the proficiency levels found in the rigor and mastery cycle, the next step for teachers is to create learning environments that differentiate the learning modalities and opportunities within the proficiency levels.

Ultimately, every teacher aims to inspire students to become lifelong learners or leaders of their learning. Campus leaders typically use the term *lead learner* to describe themselves, and that makes sense. Instructional leaders need to lead learning for the campus, but now, I invite you to think about how we, as teachers, could create classrooms where students lead learning. That means we would transform learners from consumers of content to leaders of learning. To that end, the work in this chapter expands on our work in rigor and mastery from chapter 6 by personalizing the proficiency levels developed for the essential skills by establishing targeted and prescriptive intervention and extension for each student.

Personalized learning is a strategy that teachers employ to create an environment where students have access to individualized instruction that meets them where they are in proficiency and leads them to mastery of essential content. *Personalized learning* and *creative strategies for individual students* are synonymous terms, meaning teachers can allow students to self-select instructional activities or intervention activities with the teacher that are strategically aligned to how the student learns best.

Educational consultant Glen Heathers (1977) describes personalized learning this way: "Individualized instruction consists of any steps taken in planning and conducting programs of study and lessons that suit them to the individual student's learning needs, learning readiness, and learning characteristics or 'learning style'" (p. 342). Another description of personalized learning or individualized instruction shows that "learning strategies are based on student readiness, interests and best practices . . . to help each student master the skills they will need as defined by established academic standards" (Basye, 2018).

Personalized learning requires teachers to master their knowledge of content, students, and pedagogy. Hattie's (2009) research has yielded a wealth of data that support the need for differentiation in the classroom. Teachers might consider using the Goldilocks principles with students. This strategy asks students to sift through activities or problems and determine which are too low, too high, or just right for their current proficiency level. Next students select the best activity to stretch them appropriately. According to Hattie (2009), when students adopt the Goldilocks process, they can expect to see a 0.74 effect size (one and one-half years' growth). When students become leaders of their own learning through personalized learning activities, their learning is accelerated.

Personalized learning requires us to see students with different capabilities and aptitudes for learning. As previously noted, great teachers are able to categorize students into three broad groups: (1) high-performing learners, (2) average performing learners, and (3) low-performing learners. While we need to do this analysis of student ability to give students the best level of supports and equity so they can reach mastery, sometimes, the labels we place on students limit our expectations for students and the instruction we give them. Jensen (2016) states the following:

> In education, we often get desensitized to the process of labeling students. However, labeling students as a *minority* or being a *low* (bottom 25 percent in classroom scores) student is pejorative and detrimental to student achievement. In fact, not labeling students ranks an impressive 0.61 effect size (top 20 out of 138 factors) in contributing to student achievement (Hattie, 2009). High-performing teachers would never label students as low. (p. 134)

In order for personalized learning to work, we must stop making academic decisions about students based on their labels of ethnicity, poverty, disability, language, gift, or performance and start accepting the fact that educators are the great equalizers for students and their learning trajectory. According to Jensen (2016), the classroom teacher has the most significant influence on student achievement. Furthermore, "research shows that above-average teachers (those who get one and a half years or more of student gains per school versus one year) based on year-after-year progress can completely erase the academic effects of poverty in five years" (Jensen, 2016, p. 16; Hanushek, 2005).

The following story illustrates the importance of differentiating instruction to meet students where they are in their learning. Mr. Harris's classroom contains students with all levels of proficiency, and Mr. Harris realizes that he must modify his instruction to be sure all students have opportunities for success.

Differentiating Instruction for Individual Student Success

Marcus and Roberto felt excited and anxious about the upcoming school year, when they would enter middle school as sixth-grade students. Their excitement and their assignment to Mr. Harris's sixth-grade mathematics class were about all that they had in common. Marcus, a bright African American student, won every award you could possibly win as an elementary student. Gifted in academics and in virtually everything he pursued, he had high aspirations for the upcoming year. Roberto didn't have quite the same history of academic success. He was new to both middle school and America. As a beginning English learner, he was below grade level in almost every skill, and his scores proved it. He was served by every special program his elementary school offered, and besides the labels of *economically disadvantaged*, *English learner*, and *potential special education student*, all the teachers knew he was at a low level of learning.

Mr. Harris was a fantastic and perennial favorite teacher. Every year, his students had among the best scores in the school. As the new school year approached, he talked with his principal about making a bigger impact on the school. Knowing that his school was starting to see greater diversity as well as poverty, he wanted to be on the front lines by helping the school's students who struggled the most. His principal gladly accepted his wish; as a result, his classes would have a mixture of students with varying abilities and successes.

As the school year started, Mr. Harris quickly realized that he would soon have to modify his previously successful teaching strategies in order to meet his students' needs. He instantly noticed that Marcus was brilliant and motivated, while Roberto struggled in virtually every task, and the class contained a wide variety of mathematics students. Some were doing well, but others were struggling or completely falling apart. To meet every student's needs, he would have to differentiate in ways that he had never done before.

First, Mr. Harris researched his students—those at the highest levels and those who appeared several grade levels below sixth grade. He pored over cumulative folders, and he pulled up data in the student information system. Knowing that he had only quantitative data, he called Marcus's teachers from last year and reached out to the counselor for more information on Roberto. He also spoke to the special programs coordinator and other support personnel to find out as much as he could about his students' learning styles.

Next, he met with his team to conduct an in-depth study of the essential skills students needed to master in sixth-grade mathematics. He identified the prerequisite and future standards that aligned with the skills and ensured that his strategies aligned with those of the fifth- and seventh-grade mathematics teachers. Finally, he analyzed his instructional block to ensure that all students, especially the students who struggled the most, had intervention time with him every day, and that all students had extension and enrichment activities aligned to the skills that they still needed to master. He was committed to creating a personalized instructional plan that offered innovative extension activities for high-performing students, like Marcus, so those students could work on projects that developed each student's creativity. Meanwhile, low-performing students, like Roberto, received targeted interventions focused on basic or prerequisite skills through the support of prescriptive modifications and accommodations to help those students close their learning and language gaps.

As a result of Mr. Harris's resolve to devise creative strategies for learning for each student in his class, not only did all students grow in learning that year, but Roberto saw two years' worth of growth in mathematics, and Marcus became the highest-performing mathematics student in the entire grade level. That year, Mr. Harris modeled for all teachers that excellent teachers can help any student grow regardless of his or her challenges if they put a plan of excellence in place for the student. The secret to excellence in every student lies in an intentional, individualized learning plan.

This story examines how providing individual students with creative instruction geared toward their specific proficiency levels and skills can help students succeed. The purpose of the sixth level in the Hierarchy of Student Excellence (see figure 7.1) is to push students to go beyond content mastery through the use of personalized or individualized intervention and extension activities.

The sixth level creates a learning environment that helps students grow in the sixth level in Maslow's Hierarchy of Needs—aesthetic needs—a person feels motivated to leverage his or her knowledge to create and design. Maslow said that those at this level possess an appreciation of life, and they search for beauty, balance, and form in the world around them (McLeod, 2018).

Take a moment to think about the most creative or the most passionate students you have ever taught. They sought not only to know more about what they were learning, but also to apply that learning in creative ways. They built unique projects. They represented their learning in unique ways, or perhaps they performed at levels that exceeded your instruction. In essence, they were infatuated with their learning, and they sought levels of understanding that far surpassed what the content standards listed.

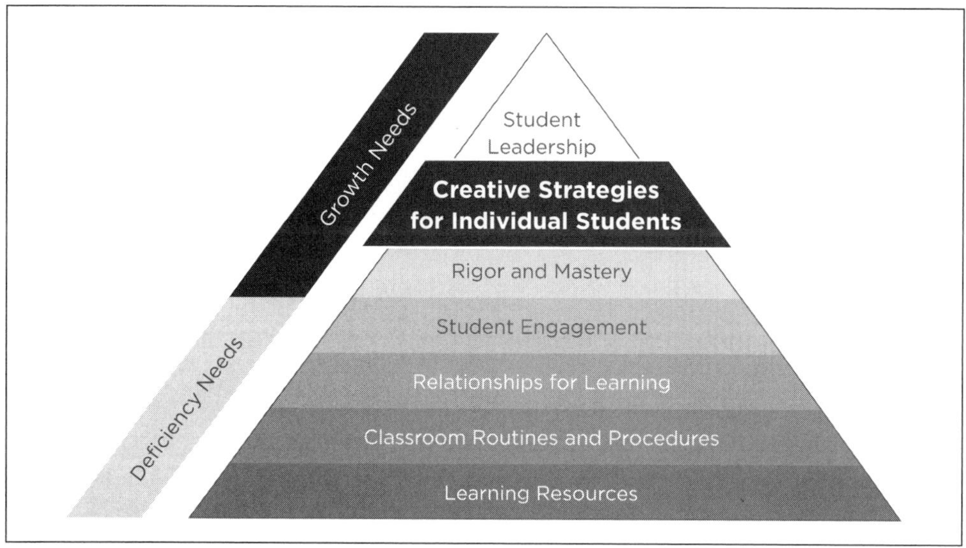

Figure 7.1: Hierarchy of Student Excellence—creative strategies for individual students.

When a student functions at this level, he or she is not necessarily the top-performing student; however, he or she is creative in finding new and innovative ways to get better at mastering learning and comes to school every day with the purpose of taking mastery to a higher level.

The following sections discuss how great teachers plan for, deliver, and reflect on designing learning opportunities that promote creativity. They also explore how teachers can build a Student Excellence Support System that provides creative strategies for individual student success.

Developing Creative Strategies for Individual Students

Because students have varying starting points for learning and different affinities for learning content, students each need a personalized, creative education plan in order to have meaningful learning experiences and reach academic excellence. But what does that mean for teaching?

It means that teachers must be able to leverage their knowledge of students, differentiate learning and create instruction that meets all students where they are, and guides them to where they need to be. Hattie (2009) writes:

> The art of teaching, and its major successes, relate to "what happens next"—the manner in which the teacher reacts to how the student interprets, accommodates, rejects, and/or reinvents the content and skills, how the student relates and applies the content to other tasks, and how the student reacts in light of success and failure apropos the content and methods that the teacher has taught. (p. 2)

According to the Texas Teacher Evaluation and Support System (T-TESS; Texas Education Agency, 2016), differentiation by distinguished teachers includes the following four elements: (1) adapting "lessons with a wide variety of instructional strategies to address the individual needs of all students," (2) consistently monitoring "the quality of student participation and performance," (3) always providing "differentiated instructional methods and content to ensure students have the opportunity to master what is being taught," and (4) using "multiple strategies to teach and assess students" (p. 52).

To synthesize this information for better precision in meeting the needs of students at this level, I have found that three components (see figure 7.2) must be present in order for powerful personalized learning to occur. They include (1) knowledge of students through relationships for learning, (2) content knowledge and expertise, and (3) differentiation. If one or two components exist without the third component, true personalized learning cannot occur.

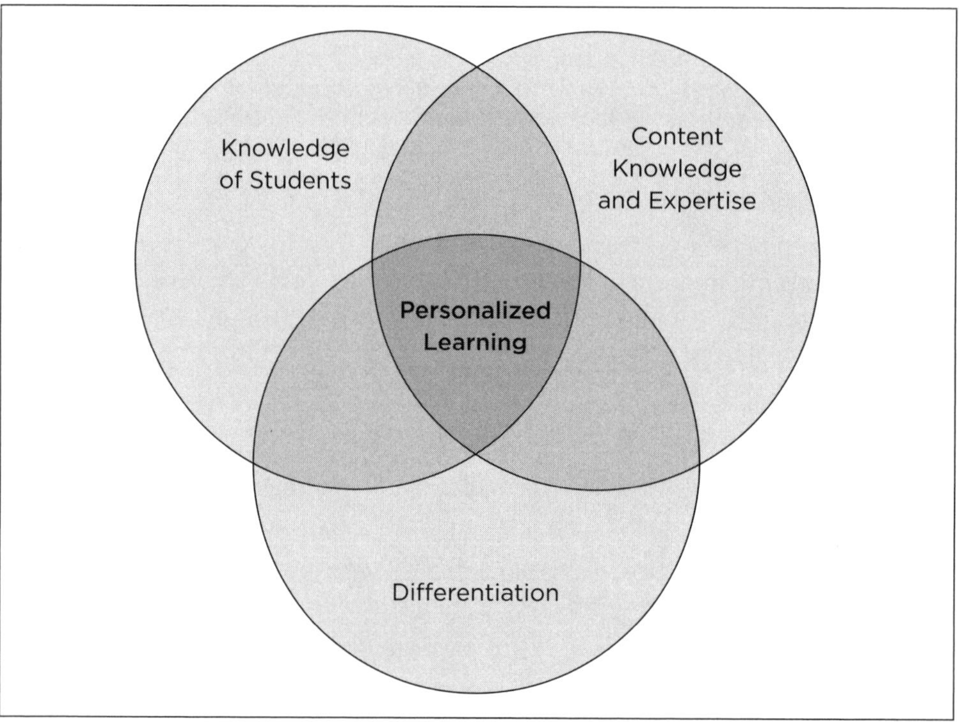

Figure 7.2: Components of creative strategies for individual students.

The following sections, Preparation and Delivery, discuss how PLC critical questions 3 and 4— "What will we do when they haven't learned it?" and "What will we do when they already know it?" (DuFour et al., 2016, p. 251)—drive teachers' work to individualize instruction for each student. Question 3 challenges teachers to respond to students who fail to learn through a simultaneously proactive and reactive approach. Question 4 asks teachers to empower students to take their learning to the next level through extension or enrichment. The Reflection section gives teachers tools to analyze their work in planning and delivery to assess how well interventions and extensions have been developed to optimize learning for individual students. The goal of these sections, and this chapter, is to help prepare teachers to provide every student with a personalized learning plan that possesses both intervention and extension.

Preparation

Designing creative strategies for individual students requires teachers to constantly pose this question: Did the student learn the standard? This question drives all the work that students need to pursue learning. Without an answer to this important question, teachers are left to prescribe work that they think or hope students need, and hope is not an effective strategy for designing meaningful work for students.

If the answer to this question is *yes*, the teacher's responsibility shifts from teaching to extending the student's learning with enrichment opportunities. If the answer is *no*, the teacher's response includes providing targeted and prescriptive interventions to the struggling student. The flowchart in figure 7.3 illustrates the mindset that teachers should have when answering this question so they can determine whether the student's personalized learning should be below level, on level, or above level.

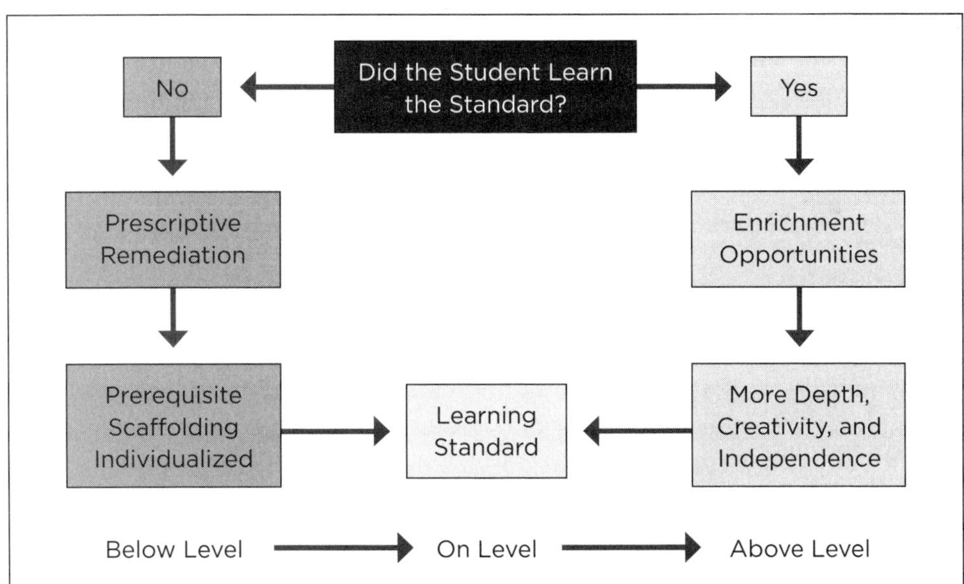

Source: Wink, 2017, p. 154.

Figure 7.3: Learning progress flowchart.

Creative strategies for individual students aim to give students purpose or meaning in their learning. These creative strategies include *purpose-driven learning*, which involves leading students in activities that encourage communication, collaboration, critical thinking, and creativity. As William Ferriter (2015) writes in *Creating Purpose-Driven Learning Experiences*, "Meaning drives motivation for any learner" (p. 3). Ferriter has designed purpose-driven learning strategies for enrichment purposes by offering students project-based exercises, such as studying global poverty and then creating and participating in micro-lending activities (involving making small loans to individuals in developing countries to fund business ventures) and blogging to raise awareness of current issues such as obesity.

Another example of an extension activity for students includes designing choice boards. A *choice board* is a menu of enrichment opportunities that students can use to extend their learning through either consumption activities, such as instructional games or basic skill drills that develop automaticity or fluency with a particular skill, or through creation activities, which allow students to develop skills by helping other students or the community through service projects, tutoring other students, making videos or blogs, or conducting and sharing research. See figure 7.4.

Creativity	A service project	Project-based learning	Flipped videos
Evaluation	Peer tutoring	A review	A blog
Extension	A personalized learning activity	Instructional games	Basic skill practice or drills
Research	Research on college and career	Research on a topic of interest	A compare-and-contrast presentation

Source: Adapted from Wink, 2017, p. 155.

Figure 7.4: Choice board of extension activities.

For consumption purposes, for example, students could engage in peer tutoring with another student, play instructional games, explore academic websites, or complete a personalized learning activity for a particular standard. For creation purposes, students could engage in project-based learning, create flipped videos on their knowledge of standards, write a blog or review of their learning, research colleges and careers around content, or create a compare-and-contrast presentation.

In order to prepare extension for students, teachers must determine which choice-board activities best meet students' learning needs as well as their learning style. Danielson (2013) comments, "The teacher's adjustments to the lesson, when they are needed, are designed to assist individual students" (p. 58). Choice boards and enrichment work best when students find the learning relevant and meaningful. When they have choice in the work, they decide to engage with the explicit purpose of deepening their learning.

In order for teachers to be successful at providing interventions for students, they must first ensure that students can successfully work independently through extension activities without help from the teacher. Once teachers provide enrichment activities for students that require minimal assistance from the teacher, they can prepare interventions. They should design these interventions by student and by skill. Too often, teachers provide interventions just to students who are failing. If we aspire for every student to excel through creative strategies, every student needs feedback and support from the teacher to move to their next level of growth.

Students fail to grow in their learning for a variety of reasons, and they don't all share the same learning challenges. When some students share learning deficiencies, we provide intervention supports with groups, and when they do not, we provide more targeted and individualized interventions. Failure is an effect of learning, and great teachers respond by adjusting the instruction that could have contributed to the student's difficulty.

Great teachers build intervention groups based on common deficits. This means that they pull students for intervention based on deficits in prerequisite skills or supporting skills, or specific skill deficits that prevent them from moving to the next proficiency level. Figure 7.5 (page 174) illustrates how teachers could use their work from content knowledge and expertise to identify students who are lacking skills and then create interventions for them based on common deficits.

Planning for intervention is challenging because it requires teachers to anticipate failure with the understanding that their predictions may not necessarily match the deficits walking in the door. This means that creative strategies for intervention must incorporate adjusting to students' ever-changing needs. Here, Buffum and Mattos (2015) describe the reason for constantly adjusting to individual students:

> Because all students do not learn the same way, develop at the same speed, enter school with the same prior knowledge, or have the same academic supports at home, students will be provided additional time and support to achieve these rigorous expectations. (p. 5)

Preparation for creative strategies results in plans for both interventions and extensions that all students can access. After careful planning, teachers are now ready to deliver those strategies.

Delivery

Preparing for individualized interventions and extensions is very important if we want students to pursue learning at the highest level, but preparation doesn't work without execution. In order to deliver creative strategies for individual students, teachers need to leverage the structures they developed in classroom routines and procedures (see chapter 3, page 47) and the gradual release of responsibility model in engagement (see chapter 5, page 101). This will create a classroom where students are pursuing mastery of content (see chapter 6, page 131) on their specific level in

Prerequisite Skill, Essential Skill, and Future Skills		What are the interventions we will use to remediate students when they don't know it?	What ways will we enrich and extend all students in more challenging ways when they do know it?
Prerequisite Skill	3.5.A: Represent one- and two-step problems involving addition and subtraction of whole numbers to 1,000 using pictorial models, number lines, and equations.		
Essential Skill	4.5.A: Represent multistep problems involving the four operations with whole numbers using strip diagrams and equations with a letter standing for the unknown quantity.		
Future Skill	5.4.B: Represent and solve multistep problems involving the four operations with whole numbers using equations with a letter standing for the unknown quantity.		

Source for standards: Texas Education Agency, n.d.

Figure 7.5: Planning interventions based on content knowledge and expertise.

their own way. Personalized learning means that students drive their own learning and the teacher facilitates that learning.

Teachers can employ a variety of strategies to create personalized learning opportunities for students, including the following.

- Students can do independent learning tasks in which they work on enrichment based on their current level of proficiency.
- Students can do collaborative learning activities in which they work and learn together to either create a product of their learning or research more about the content. Remember that collaborative learning works best when it involves reciprocal teaching (students teaching peers; Hattie, 2009).
- Once students are engaged in meaningful enrichment on their level through independent or collaborative learning, the teacher can be available to provide targeted and prescriptive interventions through guided learning.

The most challenging part of intervention, especially when instructional blocks are short, is structuring the time to provide interventions. Teachers can use figure 7.6 as a tool to organize time so that both teachers and students know the student groupings for intervention and the specific skills to address in intervention.

Date:		
Group	**Students**	**Focus Skill**
Group 1 (fifteen minutes)		
Group 2 (fifteen minutes)		
Group 3 (fifteen minutes)		

Figure 7.6: Intervention grouping.

Visit ***go.SolutionTree.com/instruction*** *for a free reproducible version of this figure.*

Grouping students by deficit is the first step to successful intervention, not the final step. The second step for intervention is providing accommodations and modifications that would help students better access the content. For example, teachers could utilize graphic organizers to help students generate or flesh out their ideas. Interventions could include scaffolding a problem-solving strategy into smaller steps or guiding students through the steps of solving a mathematics problem.

For English learners, specific groups could include explicit instruction of important vocabulary to ensure that language acquisition doesn't become a barrier to learning. For struggling readers, teachers could pull groups to work on specific strategies in developing fluency or phonemic awareness. Guided learning gives students specific strategies they can leverage when teachers send them to independent learning activities later on.

The following sections explore how teachers can use micro-goals, proficiency levels, and student feedback to accelerate learning by guiding individual students to create a laser-like focus on their learning.

Micro-Goals

To keep students engaged and focused on their growth goal, as described in chapter 4 (page 73), teachers can introduce students to micro-goals. Setting micro-goals enhances the work of setting gutsy goals (see chapter 4, page 73). In fact, when students set weekly or even daily micro-goals, they can expect to experience three years' growth in one year, or a 1.21 effect size (Hattie, 2009).

Students articulate a daily or weekly micro-goal that they establish to help them reach their overarching goal. Teachers could use figure 7.7 as a tool to guide students in setting micro-goals for the week. On Monday, the students would set personal micro-goals for behavior, study skills, academic strategies, grade improvement, or any other academic endeavor. Throughout the week, the teacher would review the goals with students and monitor progress. Finally, on Friday, students would assess their progress in reaching the goal, which would, in turn, drive the micro-goals students set for the following week. Micro-goals give students choice and voice in what they want to improve in their learning, and this structure gives students the opportunity to set the course for how they want to improve.

Proficiency Levels

In addition to micro-goals, teachers could create folders for essential skills, prerequisite skills, or future skills that offer differentiated activities, projects, or choices boards that match the proficiency levels of those skills (see chapter 6, page 131, for more information on proficiency levels). The folders could range in work from basic work that reinforces automaticity of information or fluency (level 1) to choice boards that ask students to create products that demonstrate mastery of the essential skill (level 4). This work allows students to select a specific leveled activity for the essential skill that they would like to use to pursue growth in their learning.

Student Feedback

The use of student feedback also helps teachers make creative strategies for individual students. At this level, students generate the feedback, not the teacher. They give and receive feedback from one another and the teacher as part of their quest for higher levels of learning. In their book *Creating a Culture of Feedback*, William Ferriter and Paul Cancellieri (2017) cite three critical questions that support meaningful student feedback: (1) "Where am I going?" (2) "How am I doing?" and (3) "What are my next steps?" (pp. 7–8).

What is my +10 goal or learning goal?		
Week	**What Is My Micro-Goal (Monday)?**	**Did I Reach It (Friday)?**
Week 1 micro-goal		
Week 2 micro-goal		
Week 3 micro-goal		
Week 4 micro-goal		
Week 5 micro-goal		
Week 6 micro-goal		

Figure 7.7: Micro-goals chart.

Visit ***go.SolutionTree.com/instruction*** *for a free reproducible version of this figure.*

Teachers can provide students with structures to seek feedback from their peers. For example, teachers can give students sentence stems to articulate their strengths and areas for growth in a one-minute turn-and-talk. In the first thirty seconds of a turn and talk, student pairs talk to each other and complete the sentence, "I feel like I am strong at . . ."; and in the second thirty seconds, they complete the sentence, "I would like to know how to . . ." This allows students to converse with one another, seek feedback, and give feedback.

Teachers may also use the feedback protocol called a *brain dump*, which is more introspective in nature. In this three-minute activity, students spend the first minute reflecting on their work for the day by considering their learning strengths and the areas where they currently experience difficulties. In the second minute, students write about their strengths and weaknesses. In the final minute, students reflect on their writing, make a plan for growth in their learning, and decide which students they would like to seek feedback from to make their plan work. Reflection teaches students how to give themselves feedback and use that feedback to create their own strategies for individual growth.

In order to deliver creative strategies for individual students, teachers must structure the learning environment so students can take charge of their learning. By creating extension opportunities that meet specific learning needs and supporting students with targeted and prescriptive interventions, teachers give students a greater chance of experiencing growth. At this level in the Hierarchy of Student Excellence, students are not the recipients of instruction but the designers and teachers of their own learning.

Reflection

Teachers can use figure 7.8 as a reflection tool to help them create personalized learning opportunities for students with both extensions and interventions. As you review the questions, generate a list of action steps and then prioritize them in order of importance.

Component	Reflection
Personalized Learning	How frequently do I determine whether each student is learning? How consistently do I prescribe guided learning, collaborative learning, and independent learning activities based on the informal data that I gather on students? How well do my students create and take ownership of gutsy goals and the micro-goals to achieve those goals? How well do students seek feedback from me? How well do students give feedback to and receive feedback from their peers? How effectively do I scaffold feedback protocols so students feel comfortable giving feedback to and receiving feedback from their peers?
Extensions	How well do my enrichment opportunities inspire students to learn at higher levels? How well do my enrichment activities match the learning needs of my high-performing students, average-performing students, and low-performing students? How often do I add extension activities to my choice boards? Do students have the opportunity to choose projects that apply their learning? How effectively do I assess the effectiveness of my extension activities by generating student feedback?

Interventions	When a student is not learning, how well do my interventions match the learning need and learning style of the student? How well do my preventive interventions match the learning needs and actual difficulties that students experience? How consistent am I in planning for interventions? How well do I take into account the learning disabilities or learning barriers of individual students in my interventions? How well planned are my guided learning activities? Are my guided learning groups based on common deficit or overall failure?

Figure 7.8: Creative strategies for individual students reflection tool.

Visit ***go.SolutionTree.com/instruction*** *for a free reproducible version of this figure.*

Building a Student Excellence Support System: Creative Strategies for Individual Students

To keep students at, below, and above level continually striving to grow requires a broad range of creative instructional strategies that apply directly to each student's interests, background, learning style, and capabilities. Even the most experienced teachers find this difficult.

To support teachers in this endeavor, schools should offer professional development that sharpens teachers' skills in providing leveled interventions as well as extension opportunities through the use of choice boards, technology, and other new and innovative ideas to help in building the Student Excellence Support System.

The following sections outline how teachers can create a Student Excellence Support System that offers creative strategies for individual students. Step 1 discusses how teachers can collaborate to develop individual strategies for students. Step 2 outlines how teachers can design classwide supports to address students' diverse needs. Step 3 articulates how teachers can create personalized support plans for students who struggle through intervention or extension.

Step 1: Teacher Team Collaboration

The primary purpose of teacher team collaboration in this area lies in strengthening Tier 1 instruction as a first step in meeting all students' individual needs. An intervention created in isolation has as much chance of remediating student failure as instruction and assessment created in isolation. In fact, RTI processes are collaborative by design.

As Tom Carroll (2009) says:

> The idea that a single teacher, working alone, can know and do everything to meet the diverse learning needs of 30 students

> every day throughout the school year has rarely worked, and it certainly won't meet the needs of learners in years to come. (p. 13)

Teacher teams design effective interventions based on two shared assumptions: (1) teams must anticipate student failure and plan to minimize and prevent it wherever possible; and (2) when students are failing, teachers must respond collectively. This section outlines both preventive and responsive team interventions. First, however, let's address teacher team supports for learning extension.

Choice Boards for Extension

The Preparation section defined the concept of choice boards (see page 172). To guarantee that teacher teams develop the very best choice boards, they can create a wide variety of extension activities that students can access independent of the teacher. When teacher teams collaborate to create one menu that all students can access, teachers also have a broader menu of options to offer students based on individual students' challenges, capabilities, and needs. The broader the variety of these activities, the more support they provide to individual students.

To ensure that collaboration is optimized through both synchronous (same time, same place) collaboration and asynchronous (on your own time, as your own place) collaboration, teacher teams can meet to share Google Docs that serve as the choice board for all students. Through commenting, teachers can collaborate with one another about the choice board ideas as each teacher adds new activities. Once the team adds plenty of activities to the board, members can distribute a choice board of activities to students. As teachers and students generate new ideas, they can update the Google Doc choice board without having to meet.

Teacher teams can use the "Choice Board Template" on page 197 to develop a Google Doc choice board for essential skills, and they can also align student choices to proficiency levels, as described in chapter 6 (page 131). This allows students to choose not only the activity but also the rigor within the activity. Collaboration about extension activities can take many forms as teachers work together to learn new ways to empower students to own their learning. The team can, for example, have a teacher or instructional coach model how to incorporate choice boards into instruction. Alternatively, the team can visit and observe a classroom where a teacher is successfully using extension activities to empower students.

Preventive Interventions

Teacher teams can design preventive interventions before students begin studying a new concept. During this stage of the intervention process, teacher teams, with the support of curriculum coaches and administrators, can discuss the challenges they predict students will have during initial learning. By familiarizing themselves with student histories, transition sheets, and other academic and behavioral background information, team members can take student learning styles and previously learned content into consideration. Additionally, they can prepare for students who do not have prerequisite skills necessary to learn the new content, and they can discuss how they will remediate those skills from the start. Responding to these students with instructional strategies and language from the previous year's instruction is a great starting point for remediating foundational skills. Finally, teacher teams can discuss common misconceptions that students form when learning a new concept and create effective responses for students who demonstrate these misconceptions during initial instruction.

Teacher teams can utilize templates and tools for planning preventive interventions, such as that shown in figure 7.9. Teacher teams can use this template to gather insights and strategies from vertical team members for preventing student failure with a given skill. I have had great success in using this template to encourage deep conversations among teachers about their practices. In the first row, the team identifies the individual skill it will address. In the second row, team members (either independently on separate templates or collaboratively on a single template) list three common mistakes students make when initially learning the skill. The team then seeks collaborative input—from team members teaching at the skill's grade level, above it, and below it—on strategies for preventing or responding to these common mistakes. Teachers can use the Notes section to record supplemental information and suggestions to help team members hone their methods for teaching the skill.

Skill	
Three Common Mistakes Students Make When Initially Learning the Skill	
Interventions	
Grade-Below Suggestions	
Grade-Above Suggestions	
Notes	

Source: Wink, 2017, p. 164.

Figure 7.9: Preparing for student success.

*Visit **go.SolutionTree.com/instruction** for a free reproducible version of this figure.*

Responsive Interventions

If team collaboration focuses on preparing and continually updating and improving effective tools for preventive responses in advance of learning, fewer students will need responsive interventions. Responsive interventions become necessary when students continue to fail to demonstrate progress in learning after teachers have delivered initial instruction and preventive intervention responses. In designing responsive interventions, teacher team, coach, and administrator discussions center on students, not content. In these situations, teams can employ the 1-2-3 process (Buffum & Mattos, 2015), as shown in figure 7.10. This three-step process helps collaborative teams respond to an individual student's repeated failure.

When teachers struggle with an individual student, and their interventions fail to address the student's difficulties, they should seek assistance from their colleagues. The 1-2-3 process allows teachers to seek assistance from colleagues through the following three-step process: (1) identify students' greatest areas of need, (2) define the results of current interventions provided by the teacher, and (3) generate ideas or ask clarifying questions in an effort to help the teacher develop more targeted or prescriptive interventions. The following sections describe these three steps in more detail.

Identify Students' Greatest Areas of Need

The referring teacher's responsibilities in this step are to (1) identify a student struggling in academics or behavior; (2) name the biggest issue that prevents the student from learning; and (3) share samples of student work or data. "Without greater clarity regarding what is causing the failure, [teachers] will be unable to intervene effectively" (DuFour & Marzano, 2011, p. 178). In this step, the teacher provides samples of student work or behavior logs to support his or her prognosis of the student's difficulties, barriers to learning, and potential. The team can then determine if the teacher needs to change core instructional practices or classroom management procedures to further support the student.

Define the Results of Current Interventions

In this step, the referring teacher (1) names two classroom interventions that the teacher has tried; (2) describes the frequency of those interventions; and (3) describes the student's response to the interventions. DuFour et al. (2016) write, "Intervention will offer a setting and strategies that are different from those that have already proven to be ineffective for the student" (p. 180). By listening to the referring teacher's detailed descriptions of interventions that have failed, the team has more information to assess the fidelity of those intervention efforts and to create more targeted and specific interventions.

Generate Ideas for More Prescriptive Interventions

In this step, it is the teacher team's responsibility to (1) ask questions about student behavior or learning; and (2) recommend interventions that may help the student.

<table>
<tr><td colspan="2">Student Name: ______________________ Date: ____________
Teacher: ______________________________</td></tr>
<tr><td rowspan="2">1</td><td>Referring Teacher Responsibilities
a. Name one student who struggles in academics or behavior.
b. Name the biggest issue that prevents the student from learning.
c. Share samples of student work or data.</td></tr>
<tr><td>Notes</td></tr>
<tr><td rowspan="2">2</td><td>Referring Teacher Responsibilities
a. Name two classroom interventions that have been tried.
b. Describe the frequency of the interventions used.
c. Describe the student's response to the interventions.</td></tr>
<tr><td>Notes</td></tr>
<tr><td rowspan="2">3</td><td>Team Member Responsibilities
a. Ask questions about the student behavior or learning.
b. Recommend interventions that could be tried to help the student.</td></tr>
<tr><td>Notes</td></tr>
</table>

Source: Buffum & Mattos, 2015, p. 92.

Figure 7.10: Response to failure with the 1-2-3 process.

Visit ***go.SolutionTree.com/instruction*** *for a free reproducible version of this figure.*

Ferriter et al. (2013) state, "While it is important to create an initial list of approved interventions, it is also important to provide PLTs [primary lead teachers] with some flexibility to innovate" (p. 71). Here, the team can revise current interventions to make them more effective, or it can recommend new interventions to better address the student's needs. For example, if a student with reading difficulties is not responding to small-group instruction due to peer distractions, a logical response would be to pull the student individually at a time without distractions to see if he or she responds positively.

The 1-2-3 process offers teacher teams a viable method for finding creative strategies to help individual students who struggle with academic or behavioral issues. There are times, however, when even the most effective and committed teacher team fails to produce effective solutions. That's why we must ensure that it also includes procedures for encouraging teachers to seek assistance from an instructional coach, a counselor, or an administrator.

If the 1-2-3 process doesn't address the student's issues the first time, the teacher then returns to the team to complete the 1-2-3 process again before referring the student to the campus-based student intervention team. This allows the team to support the teacher twice, and if the teacher continues to have difficulty, then he or she could refer the student to the campus-level student intervention team. The 1-2-3 process leverages the power of collaboration to build all team members' shared knowledge around interventions for problems that most teachers face.

When teachers collaborate about how they can inspire students to take ownership of the learning, they are able to create targeted and powerful interventions for all students, and they can share all kinds of creative ways for students to extend their learning through the higher cognitive levels of creativity, evaluation, synthesis and application. If teacher teams can create norms for how they desire to intervene and extend all learners' learning, the next step for teachers, classwide supports, has a better chance of success.

Step 2: Classwide Supports

Since personalized learning encompasses knowledge of students, content knowledge and expertise, and differentiation, providing class-wide supports for differentiation can prove to be a challenge, especially if the teacher lacks competence in one or more of those areas. It is critical that the teacher make plans for how they will evaluate the effectiveness of interventions or extensions provided to the student and then use that information to quickly prepare responses to students' lack of progress. Based on this knowledge of students and the content knowledge and expertise, teachers can use preassessment data and ongoing assessment data to determine student strengths and weaknesses. The strengths identify which content students have mastered and can be further strengthened through extension activities, while the weaknesses drive both intervention for direct remediation from the teacher and extension for additional practice on the student's proficiency level. Formative assessment data drive the personalized learning that students need.

The following sections provide specific strategies for individual students through intervention, extension, micro-goals, and feedback protocols.

Interventions

For intervention purposes, figure 7.6 (page 175) shows how teachers must build intervention groups around a common deficit. To expand on that concept, figure 7.11 (page 186) offers another tool to help teachers determine which students need remediation on multiple essential skills. In the first row, the teacher lists the essential skill for focus in intervention. Next, the teacher determines how to group students based on their proficiency level with the skill (see chapter 6, page 131, for the four proficiency levels). Finally, the teacher prescribes the specific intervention that he or she would offer students to remediate them based on their current level of proficiency. Then he or she documents individual students' response to the intervention. When teachers base an intervention on a common deficit, plan it with precision, and document the results, students have a greater chance of responding positively to the intervention.

To ensure that an intervention meets diverse student needs, teachers can differentiate the intervention for students in a group setting by providing them with personalized modifications and accommodations that are often reserved for students with identified disabilities.

In a differentiated classroom, teachers provide all students with modifications and accommodations that give them a concrete model of how to mentally process the content successfully. For example, an intervention group focusing on reading fluency could have a student with dyslexia provided the accommodation of colored overlays, while a student with tracking deficits could use an index card to place under the line of words as he or she reads the passage. In a mathematics group focusing on problem-solving with multiplication, one student could use a multiplication chart to quickly find mathematics facts, while another student uses a calculator to quickly multiply numbers. Teachers can later withdraw the modification once the student demonstrates independence without the need for the support.

In order to determine if interventions have met student needs, the teacher should gather anecdotal evidence of student responses to the intervention and document the information in the results section of figure 7.11 (page 186) by proficiency and skill. This is essential to gauge the effectiveness of the teacher's response to student failure. Without a system to gather quantitative or qualitative data, teachers will not have a systematic way to determine if what they are doing is working for students, and teachers will base their work on thoughts and feelings that are often unreliable.

Extensions

PLC critical question 4 asks: What will we do when they already know it? In other words, how will we extend student learning? (DuFour et al., 2016). In order for extensions to work, students must find relevance in the work they have to do independent of the teacher. Without meaning, students merely go through the motions when it comes to extension, and that leads to busyness instead of learning.

Skill 1:	Skill 2:	Skill 3:
Level 1 students: Intervention: Results:	Level 1 students: Intervention: Results:	Level 1 students: Intervention: Results:
Level 2 students: Intervention: Results:	Level 2 students: Intervention: Results:	Level 2 students: Intervention: Results:
Level 3 students: Intervention: Results:	Level 3 students: Intervention: Results:	Level 3 students: Intervention: Results:
Level 4 students: Intervention: Results:	Level 4 students: Intervention: Results:	Level 4 students: Intervention: Results:

Figure 7.11: Intervention groups by proficiency level and by skill.

Visit ***go.SolutionTree.com/instruction*** *for a free reproducible version of this figure.*

A meaningful extension has a purpose for learning and a product to demonstrate mastery independently. The best extensions also serve as artifacts of learning that can later serve as resources for the student or the entire class. One extension idea that works well is having students chose the option of creating flipped videos of what they are learning; for example, they can use their cell phones to record a video of them explaining how to solve a problem. Another extension opportunity involving technology would challenge students to share a picture of their efforts to solve a problem or draw a picture representing their knowledge of a specific concept. Then students can upload their videos or pictures to the teacher's Google Classroom (https://classroom.google.com) or Pinterest (www.pinterest.com) board. When students create resources that successfully demonstrate their knowledge and expertise of a specific essential skill, these resources can become virtual resources that other students can access to deepen their learning when they don't fully understand the content.

Another tool that teachers use in extension is Google Slides (www.google.com/slides). Teachers can ask students to create a three- to five-slide presentation to demonstrate their mastery of a particular topic or skill. Students can embed images and import YouTube videos into the presentation, and like in the previous flipped-video example, they can make their presentation available through the teacher's webpage or Google Classroom or a Pinterest board for all other students to access.

For students who need more structure in extension activities, personalized learning software, such as iStation for reading or Dreambox for mathematics, allows students to answer questions, and the incorrect and correct answers in the software prompts questions of increasing or decreasing complexity in future units of study. Additionally, these systems provide real-time data that teachers can use to create other extensions or interventions that students can complete through performance-based instruction or traditional pencil-and-paper work. This is a viable option that teachers can also assign to students who thrive with technology or need more structure to stay engaged in personalized learning tasks.

For students who are extremely creative and need less structure to deepen their learning, teachers can offer passion projects. A *passion project* is an independent or collaborative learning activity completely created by one student or a group of students. The students identify a problem that they want to address or a cause that they would like to support or bring awareness to, and their project essentially involves making a plan that is central to their passion. For example, a group of science students could learn more about plants by creating and maintaining a garden in the school courtyard. Another group of students might be interested in eliminating hunger in the community and create a plan to hold a food drive. The plan would also include the necessary written and verbal communication to reach out to the community. Another group could research careers associated with a particular subject of interest. Passion projects don't necessarily have a specific essential skill that they address, but they do address the critical-thinking skills needed to master the essential skills in the content area. Finally, they inspire students to learn with little to no support from the teacher, to explore without boundaries, and to dream with no limits.

Micro-Goals and Feedback Protocols

Using micro-goals and feedback protocols, the final part of providing classwide supports, ensures that both interventions and extensions fully optimize learning for all students. Providing classwide supports for individual students can be challenging, but it is important that teachers create structures that all students access and create for themselves individually by addressing goal setting first, micro-goals second, and then feedback protocols last.

Since goal setting occurs periodically, teachers can use the goal-setting sheet in figure 7.11 (page 186) to help students set +10 goals (see chapter 4, page 73) each time they take a common formative assessment, and then they can compare students' performance to the previous year's end-of-year state assessment. Students can also use the sheet to measure their growth in mastering essential skills throughout the year. Figure 7.12 illustrates how students can use their data over time to establish goals for a particular content area.

Once students set their overarching goal for a particular subject, the teacher could help students establish micro-goals as weekly targets to help them reach their gutsy goal. To scaffold student thinking around micro-goals, teachers should have students brainstorm the characteristics scholars exhibit to reach their goals. Next, teachers could ask students to analyze the list of characteristics and categorize that list into strengths and weaknesses. After that, students would select a weakness that they would like to focus on for the next week and track their progress each day. Once they accomplish their micro-goal, students would then select another weakness that they would like to improve on and begin the process again. Teachers could use the worksheet in figure 7.13 (pages 190–191) to have students complete their micro-goals each week and review them as a part of their daily work.

Effective communication is the glue that holds all progress together. The best communication to drive student learning is feedback. To ensure success at this level, students seek feedback as well as offer it to their peers. When students engage one another in feedback, they can expect their learning to grow. To help students get started engaging in feedback with one another, teachers might post or provide students with feedback sentence stems to guide their thinking. Figure 7.14 (page 192) offers a list of feedback sentence stems that students can use either to seek help or to offer help to their peers.

MY EXCELLENCE PLAN (+10 GOAL)

Student: ______________ Grade: ______ Subject: ______________ Teacher: ______________

Instructions

- Grid: Color in your overall performance on each test.
- Table: List essential skills for the subject, and chart your progress on each skill throughout four-week or six-week grading periods.

100 percent							
80 percent							
60 percent							
40 percent							
20 percent							
0 percent	End-of-Year Test From Previous Year or Beginning-of-Year Test From This Year	Formal Assessment 1	Formal Assessment 2	Formal Assessment 3	Formal Assessment 4	Formal Assessment 5	End-of-Year Assessment or State Assessment

Figure 7.12: Student goal-setting sheet.

continued →

Standard Number	**Skill**	**Formal Assessment 1**	**Formal Assessment 2**	**Formal Assessment 3**	**Formal Assessment 4**	**Formal Assessment 5**	**End-of-Year Assessment or State Assessment**
Example Texas Student Expectation 4.2.B	Use context clues to determine meaning.	1/3	Not tested	2/4	1/2	1/1	3/4

Visit ***go.SolutionTree.com/instruction*** *for a free reproducible version of this figure.*

Student Name:	My Gutsy Goal:

1. List the characteristics of an outstanding learner.
2. Mark each characteristic as a strength (S) or weakness (W).

__ ______________ __ ______________ __ ______________

__ ______________ __ ______________ __ ______________

__ ______________ __ ______________ __ ______________

__ ______________ __ ______________ __ ______________

Based on the weaknesses you identified, set your micro-goal for the week, and measure your progress daily and at the end of the week.

Micro-Goal	**Monday**	**Tuesday**	**Wednesday**	**Thursday**	**Friday**	**Goal Met? (Yes or No)**

Figure 7.13: Micro-goals worksheet.

Visit ***go.SolutionTree.com/instruction*** *for a free reproducible version of this figure.*

Building classwide supports at this level is not about building individual supports for specific students. It's about creating a plethora of individualized activities at varying levels in different modalities that all students in the class can access and complete individually or through group learning. These structured supports allow students to gauge their proficiency and determine their next course of action to make progress toward mastery of content and essential skills.

Giving Feedback	Seeking Feedback
I like how you . . . I noticed how you . . . This is great work because . . . What is making this difficult for you is . . . Would it be better if you . . . ? Here is a way that worked better for me . . . You might try . . . I suggest more (or less) . . .	Can you help me with . . . ? Can you tell me more about . . . ? Can you show me how to . . . ? Do you know a better way to . . . ? Can you show me how to get better at . . . ? What does . . . mean? Do you have another suggestion for . . . ? Where can I show more or less . . . ?

Figure 7.14: Feedback sentence stems.

Visit ***go.SolutionTree.com/instruction*** *for a free reproducible version of this figure.*

Step 3: Individualized Student Supports

No matter how experienced we are as classroom teachers, we can be certain that we will eventually struggle with trying to meet the needs of individual students. Since all students are different, any student can present a new challenge that individual teachers may not be prepared to address. That's the primary reason why great teachers continuously develop creative strategies for individual students.

We know, for example, that students who excel need meaningful and relevant extension opportunities, and we also know that students who have a history of academic failure need ongoing specialized supports if they are to close their learning gaps. Individualized supports for students will always present challenges that teachers are unprepared to respond to, no matter how much experience and training they have had.

Many schools have personnel whose sole responsibility is to work with at-risk or struggling students by providing them Tier 2 and Tier 3 interventions through independent intervention labs. There are multiple ways this arrangement can suffer from disconnects. Sometimes, for example, the regular classroom teacher doesn't reinforce the interventions provided by intervention staff. Other times, student struggles that occur in the classroom are never communicated to the interventionist. To avoid these situations, teachers should work with intervention personnel to incorporate specific strategies for aligning the work of intervention staff with the work the teacher provides students in the classroom. The same applies for providing extension opportunities for students who are proficient in their learning but fail to pursue opportunities to extend their learning.

Teachers can use the problem-solving tool in figure 7.15 to determine how to best support individual students with creative strategies. The first step has the teacher ensure that the teacher team has created common expectations and strategies for intervention and extension, and the second step ensures that classwide supports have been developed for all students. Once the teacher has determined that team-level and classwide supports are in place that support the majority of students, he or she must determine if the student's difficulty derives from intervention or extension issues. From there, the teacher can develop the best type of support to help the student grow in his or her learning.

Individualized Student Support Problem-Solving Tool: Creative Strategies for Individual Students	
Question 1: Has the teacher team created common expectations and supports for all students at this level? (Circle yes or no.) (If your answer is yes, continue. If your answer is no, stop and correct this area.)	Yes No
Question 2: Based on the team's work, has the teacher created his or her classwide structure for creative strategies for individual students? (Circle yes or no.) (If your answer is yes, continue. If your answer is no, stop and correct this area.)	Yes No
Question 3: Which student is struggling with extensions or interventions? Is the student's failure due to difficulties with extensions or interventions? (Circle extensions or interventions.) (If extension is the difficulty, please answer question 4, and then proceed to question 6. If intervention is the difficulty, please answer question 5, and then proceed to question 7.)	Yes No
Question 4: What are the student's strengths and difficulties with extensions at this level? Strengths: Difficulties: Move to question 6.	

Figure 7.15: Individualized student support problem-solving tool—creative strategies for individual students.

continued →

Individualized Student Support Problem-Solving Tool: Creative Strategies for Individual Students
Question 5: What are the student's strengths and difficulties with interventions at this level? Strengths: Difficulties: Move to question 6.
Question 6: Based on your responses to question 4, what is the root cause of the difficulties with extensions? Based on the identified difficulties, prescribe potential supports. (Consider the following questions to determine potential supports.) • Does the student genuinely enjoy the content, or does he or she find it boring? • Is the student an introvert or extrovert? Does the student enjoy working alone, or does he or she enjoy working with peers? • Does the student enjoy peer tutoring other students? • Is the student a kinesthetic, visual, or auditory learner? • What interests does the student have outside of school? • Does the student have an interest in creating products with technology? • Does the student enjoy writing or speaking? • Does the student need extensions that are independent or collaborative? • Does the student need to work on projects that require a written, graphic, or spoken medium? • Does the student need extension work that integrates technology? • Does the student need extension work where he or she teaches others? • Does the student need work that is more connected to his or her background or interests? Notes:
Question 7: Based on your responses to question 5 , what is the root cause of the difficulties with intervention? Based on the identified difficulties, prescribe potential supports. (Consider the following questions to determine potential supports.) • Does the student have a history of poor performance with this content? • Does the student have a reading problem?

• Does the student have a vocabulary deficit? • Is the student a kinesthetic, visual, or auditory learner? • Does the student possess the prerequisite skills for this content? • What strengths does this student offer to learn the content? • What is the biggest barrier to the student's learning? • What steps should I take to correct and address the student's barrier to learning? • Do my interventions match the student's learning style and essential skill in need of remediation? • What data will I generate to gauge the effectiveness of the intervention? • How will I determine if progress is being made? Notes:
Question 8: What are the goal and the deadline for the student to be successful with extensions or interventions. Goal: Deadline:

Question 9: Did the student meet the goal by the deadline? (Circle yes or no.) (If your answer is yes, continue the support. If your answer is no, return to question 4.)	Yes No
Notes:	

Visit ***go.SolutionTree.com/instruction*** *for a free reproducible version of this figure.*

Conclusion

At the sixth level in the Hierarchy of Student Excellence—creative strategies for individual students—the teacher's goal is to creatively design instruction so students have a personalized learning plan to meet their specific needs. In order to accomplish this, teachers must understand the three components of personalized learning:

(1) knowledge of students, (2) content knowledge and expertise, and (3) differentiation. Creative strategies for individual students address students' needs for interventions when they are struggling and extensions when they are proficient and need more challenge.

When the support systems for both interventions and extensions are targeted, specific, and aligned to individual student needs, teachers can expect to see learning take root and grow.

This chapter concludes with a reflection tool (pages 198–199) that teachers can use to evaluate their understanding of creating and prescribing interventions and extensions. As you consider the questions and your responses to them, explore possibilities for improving those systems, including teacher team collaboration, classwide supports, and individualized student supports, based on the information and ideas in this chapter.

Choice Board Template

Use this template to create your own choice boards for extension activities in the classroom.

1. List the essential skill to be reinforced through the choice board in the first row.

2. In each cell, add activities that reinforce the essential skill at varying proficiency levels. You can leave some cells empty to allow students to create a task that they would like to complete that addresses the skill on their level.

3. Place the choice board in a folder or station with the activities, and ask students to choose activities to complete to demonstrate mastery independently.

Essential Skill:		

Reflection Tool: Creative Strategies for Individual Students

Answer the following questions to help you create a more engaging classroom where students have access to interventions and extensions to meet their individual learning needs.

Teacher Team Collaboration

- Has our team established plans to provide consistency with creative strategies for individual students?
- How well do team members lead one another in deepening our knowledge of interventions?
- How well do we work together to deepen our understanding of extensions?
- How well do we work together to incorporate micro-goals into our instruction?
- How well do we create feedback protocols so students give and seek feedback among themselves?
- When a teacher experiences difficulty with any component of creative strategies for individual students, what steps does he or she take to seek help from the team?

Classwide Supports

- How well have I aligned my plans for creative strategies for individual students with those developed by the team?
- How well do I leverage the data from my informal formative assessments to identify students in need of intervention and group them by common deficits?
- How well do I offer students choice in my extension activities so they are aligned with their current proficiency level and learning affinities?
- How well have my students taken ownership of their micro-goals to achieve the larger goal?
- How well do my students give feedback to and seek feedback from one another in relation to their learning?

Individualized Student Supports

- When a student is disconnecting from the learning, how well do I consistently determine the root cause of the student's frustration within interventions or extensions?
- Once I determine the potential root cause, how well do I verify that the failure is not due to my classroom supports or inconsistency from the team?
- How well do I ensure that the student's difficulty is not due to a deficit in a lower level of the Hierarchy of Student Excellence?
- How effective am I at identifying the student's strengths so I can leverage those strengths to address areas for growth?
- When I prescribe a support for intervention or extension, how committed am I to providing the support with scaffolding, frequency, and consistency?
- How consistently do I gauge student growth in the target area to determine if my intervention was effective?
- When the student is still unsuccessful, how well do I reflect and refine the intervention to better help the student?
- When my efforts to help the student continue to fail, how well do I reach out to my team members to help me better respond to the student?

CHAPTER 8

Teaching for Excellence: Student Leadership

A leader is one who knows the way, goes the way, and shows the way.

—John C. Maxwell

The final chapter of this book explores the top step in the Hierarchy of Student Excellence—student leadership. At this level, the student is a resourceful learner. He or she exhibits excellent learning behaviors, strong relationships for learning, and work ethic by engaging in learning. This student possesses a zest for learning rigorous content and thrives through personalized learning. When students reach this level of success in learning, we must challenge ourselves by asking what is the next step for these excellent students.

While students can demonstrate excellence at every level in the Hierarchy of Student Excellence, the pinnacle of excellence for a student is helping other students, the school, or the community through student leadership. The reason is simple. Leadership is not about title or position, and it's not about telling people what to do. Effective leadership sees a need in other people and finds a way to fill that need. All students can be leaders; they can lead in very visible ways, or they can lead in quiet and not so obvious ways.

Every school's mission statement aspires for students to be contributing members of society. If we want to accomplish this mission, we must recognize that contributing members of society lead in a myriad of ways. Our job as educators is to create classrooms that develop the leadership skills in every student.

The future of the world hinges on the leaders of the future. To that end, formal education can help ensure the security of humankind by guaranteeing that all students possess the knowledge and skills needed for leadership. Communities rise and fall with leadership. When communities have leaders focused on helping others, those communities thrive. Conversely, when communities or organizations have self-serving leaders, those communities eventually crumble. As educators, we have a moral imperative to make our world better for tomorrow by creating academic environments that build self-actualized leaders today.

Before we get too far into this chapter, we need to define *leadership*. In *School Leadership That Works*, Robert Marzano, Timothy Waters, and Brian McNulty (2003) describe the traits of transformational leadership found in the research of leadership studies scholar Bernard Bass (1985). Bass (1990) characterizes transformational leaders as offering the following four qualities.

1. **Individual consideration** is characterized by giving "personal attention to members who seem neglected" (p. 218).
2. **Intellectual stimulation** is characterized by enabling "followers to think of old problems in new ways" (p. 218).
3. **Inspirational motivation** is characterized by communicating high performance expectations.
4. **Idealized influence** is characterized by modeling behavior through exemplary personal achievements, character, and behavior.

Too often, students think of leaders as being the boss or manager of others. That is not transformational leadership, but *transactional* leadership. While transactional leaders get things done, transformational leaders motivate others to get things done. Leadership is influence. It is guidance and service, and we, as teachers, have an obligation to not only teach the traits of transformational leadership to our students but model them as well.

In this chapter, I discuss the importance of leadership as well as how teachers can inspire all students to assume leadership responsibilities both inside and outside the classroom. This chapter offers high-impact ideas to integrate student leadership into our current work with students.

In my career, I have worked with many students who have become effective leaders. In the next section, I will highlight a student in my school who was one of my best exemplars of excellence in every student; I have changed his name to Jake. Jake saw a need in his school, developed a plan of action, and ensured that his vision of saving every student became a reality.

Supporting a Student's Mission

Early in the summer of 2017, Jake, who was entering his senior year at Blue Ridge High School, called me to schedule a meeting about an idea he had. In virtually all cases when I have had students request to meet with me as superintendent or principal, they have made these requests for personal reasons or to discuss making the school a better place for themselves. Little did I know that I was in for a surprise. This meeting request was going to change the entire culture of the school.

Upon arrival, Jake greeted me and thanked me for the opportunity to meet. His first order of business was to inform me that the Dallas Cowboys organization had awarded him the Jason Garrett leadership scholarship. To apply for the scholarship, applicants had to write an essay about an idea that could make the student's world or community a better place. Out of hundreds of applicants, Jake had earned Coach Garrett's scholarship for his idea.

Then he informed me of his idea. Jake's mission was admirable. He wanted the school to offer students more than mastery in learning or extracurricular opportunities. His vision, called Green Saturday, would provide food, fun, games, fellowship, and—most importantly—a safe alternative to the temptations that many students often succumb to on Saturday nights. Knowing that many students had exposure to underage drinking and drug use, Jake wanted to give students a safe place to go and have fun with their friends, and he wanted the school to be an integral part of making this alternative available to students. But he didn't want adults to be responsible for running the event. He only wanted their support and supervision. He wanted other students to lead the event with him because he knew that if students took part in owning the responsibility for organizing, running, and leading the event, they were going to enjoy it even more.

After hearing this outstanding presentation, I answered his proposal with a resounding *yes*! But I knew that conquering the distance from his vision to reality depended on his ability to organize and communicate his plan so that students, parents, and educators would not only attend but take an active role in this initiative.

After the initial presentation of his vision for Green Saturday, I told Jake to develop an organizational and communication plan, and then I set an appointment where he and I could meet with campus leaders and teachers to roll out the plan. Within his plan, I gave him things to consider in his presentation and readied him for other ideas, potential roadblocks, and questions from those in attendance. Since his mother was a teacher at the school, I encouraged him to seek her support prior to the meeting.

When Jake came back a few weeks later to make his presentation, in addition to blowing everyone away with his PowerPoint, he inspired a room full of adults to envision the school in a manner they had never imagined. He not only described his idea with great enthusiasm but also delivered a plan of action that would rival that of many adults. Those in attendance accepted his plan, and many of them agreed to join him in its implementation.

After one year of many successful Green Saturday events, Jake graduated and left Blue Ridge for college, but Green Saturday did not leave with him. He developed an exit strategy to build student leaders along the way who would continue the Green

Saturday initiative, and in its second year, Green Saturday continued to offer students a safe place to come together in fun and fellowship.

Jake impacted the school around him because he thought more of others than himself. He was self-actualized, and he was a student leader. In Maslow's Hierarchy of Needs, the paramount human need is self-actualization or transcendence. In order to achieve self-actualization needs, a person must realize his or her personal potential, reach self-fulfillment, and seek personal growth and peak experiences. To reach transcendence, "a person is motivated by values which transcend beyond the personal self" (McLeod, 2018). In other words, people can never fulfill self-actualization or transcendence needs, because they are constantly seeking ways to make the world around them better. This highest level of Maslow's hierarchy is aligned with the highest level in the Hierarchy of Student Excellence—student leadership (see figure 8.1).

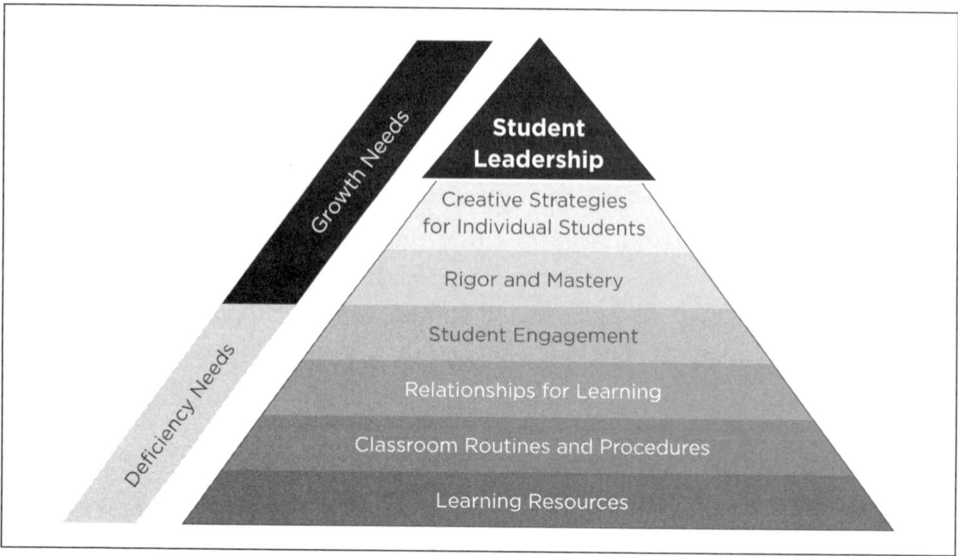

Figure 8.1: Hierarchy of Student Excellence—student leadership.

At his school, Jake saw a need for something besides himself. He wanted his classmates to reach their full potential, and he knew that he had to give them other options for interacting with their peers in socially appropriate settings outside of school. He turned his ambition into a reality.

Leadership is service to others and when people are self-actualized, they think of others before they think of themselves, and they take action to transform the thoughts of others into action. It is important that we acknowledge that some people lead for selfish reasons, such as notoriety, titles, and recognition, but we should reinforce through both our words and actions that the pinnacle of leadership is based on selfless service to others. With that said, while many students have the potential to become great leaders, they will not realize that potential until teachers ensure that building leadership capacity in all students becomes an integral part of their moral imperative. Jake reached the pinnacle of student leadership because he inspired and empowered other student leaders to take complete ownership of his idea even long after he graduated and left high school. Leadership is not defined by what you do; it's defined by what you inspire others to do after you're gone.

Fostering Student Leadership

To expand on our definition of student leadership, we will need to be more concrete in the behaviors we want students to emulate in order to grow as leaders. But before teachers can build leadership in every student, teachers must remember that they must first build the leader within themselves. Without teacher leadership, student leadership will never come to fruition in the classroom.

I believe all great leaders possess four basic characteristics of leadership, as follows.

1. They display great commitment to a cause and to the people who work toward that cause.
2. They are great communicators, and they can articulate their vision to all people, especially those who would otherwise reject such ideas.
3. They motivate others, and they celebrate the achievements and efforts of others because they know that when people are celebrated, it accelerates their efforts.
4. They model trust and respect to everyone, because they understand that no great accomplishments are achieved without a culture built on trust and respect for all people and all ideas.

So what does *student leadership* mean? In one of Joe Sanfelippo's (2019) weekly #LeadershipChallenge posts on Instagram, his daughter delivers a powerful message that asks educators whether they actually let students lead or merely have them do announcements and other superficial tasks in the name of student leadership. The post makes the point that student leadership is more than delegation of simple tasks. Educators must create the conditions in which every student can become a leader and positively impact his or her classroom, school, district, community, and even world.

The following sections offer a variety of ideas for how teachers can prepare for and deliver strategies to build student leadership. These ideas align with instructional outcomes that teachers want all students to achieve in the classroom, but they also push beyond that limited environment to encourage students to become leaders outside the school as well.

Preparation

In *The Student Leadership Challenge*, James Kouzes and Barry Posner (2018) perfectly describe the seventh level in the Hierarchy of Student Excellence:

> Everyone can lead, whether or not they are in a formal position of authority or even part of an organized group.... It's about knowing your values and those of the people around you and taking the steps, however small, to make what you do every day demonstrate that you live by those values.... Leadership is about transforming values and goals into action. (p. 591)

To turn this idea of leadership into action, Kouzes and Posner (2018) frame their belief about student leadership in the Five Practices of Exemplary Leadership, which educators can implement into their instruction: "When students do their best as a leader, they model the way, inspire a shared vision, challenge the process, enable others to act, and encourage the heart" (p. 474). If you reflect on these five practices, you'll find they're not five more things for teachers to do; these practices show teachers how to build leadership capacity in all students in order to inspire them to own their learning by leading themselves and each other. In essence, our job as educators is to inspire students to take full ownership of their learning and the world around them.

Consider challenging students to embrace the following five areas of leadership (Wink, 2017): (1) self-leadership, (2) group leadership, (3) class or club leadership, (4) interschool or civic leadership, (5) global leadership. These areas of leadership are important because when students become leaders, they become more invested in their own learning and the learning of others, and ultimately develop their skills to lead beyond the goals of the classroom.

1. **Self-leadership:** Before people can successfully lead others, they must first know how to successfully lead themselves. As educators, we must inspire students, motivate them, and teach them how to have the discipline to lead themselves in their own growth and development. When we teach students to monitor their own behaviors and actions, they can use that ownership to build self-esteem and leadership skills in themselves and others.

2. **Group leadership:** All students need opportunities to lead one another in small groups. Too often, we delegate leadership to the "best" or most responsible student. While this is a safe way to ensure completion of tasks, it fails to teach all students how to assume the responsibility for leading others, which also reinforces the false idea that leadership is reserved for the select few. Again, we teach students group leadership through structures for working and learning together and monitoring students and giving them timely feedback about their leadership skills.

3. **Class or club leadership:** This more formal type of leadership leads many students to accomplish meaningful goals for an organization. Often, it is easy for educators to take over as the formal leader because students lack the organizational skills to quickly accomplish goals. We must remember that the teacher's taking control usurps the instruction of student leadership. Leadership is messy, and we must allow students to learn the art of leadership through trial, error, and multiple mistakes. Our role is to guide them to learn how to become more efficient and effective leaders every day.
4. **Interschool or civic leadership:** Almost every student fails to experience this rare form of leadership simply because it doesn't take place inside the school and few organizations seek student involvement as part of their work. As educators, we must challenge students and civic leaders to find meaningful ways that students can take an active role in helping the community around them and working with other schools to accomplish goals that matter.
5. **Global leadership:** Many educators positively impact the world of education. They use the power of social media and the internet to inspire millions of educators to become better at what they do. Students also have the ability to positively influence others around the world. Sadly, many students use their social media presence for superficial purposes that can often delve into inappropriate and nefarious topics. As educators, we must teach them about digital citizenship and how to make a powerful and positive impact on the world.

To help students develop leadership skills in these five areas, we should identify students' leadership strengths and abilities (commitment, communication, celebration, and trust and respect), and then adapt and use the four critical questions of a PLC (DuFour et al., 2016) to articulate the expectations and supports for student leadership. Teachers can use figure 8.2 (page 208) as a planning tool to incorporate student leadership into their instruction.

Teachers can also powerfully inspire student leadership by defining the jobs and responsibilities that they want to relinquish to students. In elementary school, teachers use line leaders, lunch-count leaders, and materials leaders. In secondary classes, teachers can assign students jobs such as technology support leaders, materials managers, content support specialists, and other similar responsibilities. Beyond that, teachers can consider how to identify students who have mastered concepts and who can lead tutoring for other students on those particular concepts. Students who master the use of specific tech tools or accommodations can lead other students who reach out for assistance. Teaching should equip students with the knowledge, skills, and confidence to become teachers of themselves and then their peers. If teachers can create a culture of learning and leadership among students, content mastery is almost a certainty.

Question 1: What do we expect students to know and be able to do to be leaders in the classroom?	
Question 2: What will we look for to determine if students are meeting our expectations for student leadership?	
Question 3: How will we respond when students struggle to lead themselves or their peers?	
Question 4: How will we extend students' leadership opportunities when students meet our expectations?	

Source: Adapted from DuFour et al., 2016.

Figure 8.2: Four questions for student leadership.

Visit ***go.SolutionTree.com/instruction*** *for a free reproducible version of this figure.*

Delivery

In order to deliver student leadership, teachers should remember that providing explicit instruction is extremely important. Explicit instruction requires building relationships with and among students in the classroom. As discussed in chapter 4 (page 73), relationships for learning incorporate connecting all students with the teacher, the content, and their peers.

Then, teachers should explicitly define leadership for students. Too often, students believe *leadership* means being the boss of others, but great leaders don't have to be bosses because they exhibit powerful influence to support and serve those whom they lead. In lessons about leadership, teachers should illustrate what leading looks and sounds like. They should teach leadership lessons about serving and influencing others. Teachers should routinely share and review communication strategies and scripts for resolving conflict with students based on the behaviors students display when they are leading. Figure 8.3 can help students identify their leadership roles and their accompanying responsibilities.

Beyond jobs and responsibilities, teachers should create leadership engagement structures such as collaborative learning and guided learning. Teachers can also meet with students to build personal leadership plans for helping them lead by working with and influencing others, especially those who are difficult to work with. While these conversations can be time-consuming, remember that regular investments of time in developing student leadership pay huge dividends in student engagement,

What is my job title?	
What responsibilities must I assume to do the job well?	
What responsibilities must I delegate to other students?	
What phrases can I use to communicate responsibilities to other students?	
What phrases can I use to praise and encourage students when they are doing a great job?	
When I experience difficulty with students who are doing their job, what can I say to them to get them back on task in a positive way?	
What should I not do or say when I am frustrated with other students?	

Figure 8.3: Questions for identifying student jobs and leadership responsibilities.

Visit ***go.SolutionTree.com/instruction*** *for a free reproducible version of this figure.*

relationships for learning, and rigor and mastery. Great teachers are great leader builders, and "to be a great leader, we have a responsibility to develop a leadership pipeline that will continue to grow" (Martin, 2017).

Finally, in order to keep students engaged at high levels, teachers must remember to keep students busy and challenged. When students have mastered the content, they pursue rigor and mastery by learning through powerful extension opportunities beyond the learning target. This kind of learning environment can develop leadership skills.

Chapter 7 (page 165) discusses meaningful extension activities that incorporate passion projects and service projects. These projects can be independent or collaborative in nature. Within these projects, teachers can develop student leadership skills by asking the student or group to create a plan of action to carry out their project. If the project is collaborative, then students must create jobs and responsibilities along with a timeline for completing critical tasks. Groups can create norms for working together and resolving conflicts when they arise. Education should teach students how to think critically, communicate effectively, and collaborate in meaningful ways to create a better world.

The key principle of a PLC (DuFour et al., 2016) teaches us that a professional learning community is a school or district working interdependently to achieve a common goal. This principle provides a powerful framework for building student leadership skills. Sometimes, we think that PLC strategies for collaboration apply solely to adult learning, but we should remember that students are adults in the making. We owe it to students to teach them how to lead like adults and provide structures to lead in a manner that supports instruction.

Reflection

To conclude this section on student leadership, you can use the reflection tool in figure 8.4 to challenge your thinking about leadership. Do you reserve leadership in the classroom for the best and brightest, or do you believe leadership is everyone's responsibility? Use these questions to reflect on your plan for leadership.

Have you created leadership expectations and structures that help all students know how to successfully lead their peers? Where have your leadership plans come to fruition, and where do you need to grow in your skill set for developing leadership in every student?

After you make your list of actions and improvements, prioritize your list. As previously noted, if you focus on everything, you'll focus on nothing. You don't build leadership by doing everything well; you build it by developing one skill at a time.

Building a Student Excellence Support System: Student Leadership

In order to ensure that every student develops leadership skills, we must build a support system so all students have access to supports in the Student Excellence Support System on their way up the ladder to the pinnacle of self-actualization—leading others.

For this Student Excellence Support System, I created a three-step approach to supporting all students in their growth and development as leaders.

1. Teacher teams align their efforts to build leadership capacity in every student.
2. Teachers leverage the work of their team to create classwide supports for student leadership.
3. Teachers respond to individual students who need additional leadership support beyond what the first two steps provide.

Component	Reflection
Planning for Student Leadership	What is my philosophy of student leadership? Do I have a plan to develop student leadership in all students or just a select few? How well have I taught the four characteristics of leadership to my students (commitment, communication, celebration, and trust and respect)? Have I answered the four questions for student leadership (What do I expect? How will I know? How will I respond? and How will I extend leadership opportunities?)? How well have I prepared my students about the five areas of leadership (self, group, class or club, interschool or civic, and global)? What are the jobs that I need to delegate to students so they can learn how to be leaders of their peers? What is my personal learning plan to develop a better understanding of student leadership?
Delivery of Student Leadership	In how many jobs or roles have I empowered students to lead, and what jobs do I need to incorporate into my student leadership plan? For each job, how effectively have I articulated the responsibilities of that job so students know their role? When students struggle with their leadership role, how have I provided them with a written support structure they can independently refer to for support? What passion or service projects can students take on so they can both extend their learning and enhance their leadership skills? What are some team structures that I can employ to help students develop their collaboration and leadership skills? What supports do I need from my campus leader or other teachers to ensure that student leadership is developed in every student?

Figure 8.4: Student leadership reflection tool.

Visit ***go.SolutionTree.com/instruction*** *for a free reproducible version of this figure.*

As with all other levels in the Hierarchy of Student Excellence, to ensure all students have the opportunity to succeed, we must invest in all three levels of the Student Excellence Support System: teacher team collaboration, classwide supports, and individualized student supports.

Step 1: Teacher Team Collaboration

In the Preparation section of this chapter (page 206), I gave an example of how teachers could build leadership into their classrooms using the four critical questions of a PLC (DuFour et al., 2016; see figure 8.2, page 208). Teacher teams can use the four questions to guide their collective thinking in developing a unified vision for student leadership. Before using those questions to define expectations and responses for leadership, teams should articulate their vision for student leadership and then use that vision to define how to distribute leadership among all students through jobs and responsibilities. Teachers can use the tool in figure 8.5 to define student leadership with team members.

What role do students play in leading learning in the classroom?	
Do we believe that leadership is reserved for a select few, or do we believe that all students must lead in some capacity?	
What is our definition of student leadership, and what are our expectations for student leadership?	
How will we, as a team, communicate our expectations for leadership to students?	
How will we teach leadership to all students, and how frequently will we teach leadership to all students?	
How will we provide and reinforce extension opportunities for students who meet our expectations for leadership?	
How will we respond to students who struggle with leadership or leading their peers?	

Figure 8.5: Questions for defining student leadership.

Visit ***go.SolutionTree.com/instruction*** *for a free reproducible version of this figure.*

After the teacher team defines its vision for student leadership, it can address the student leadership topics of classroom jobs and grade-level leadership teams or representatives. The best way to develop student leadership as a team is by creating common jobs and representative leadership in all classrooms.

Classroom Jobs

Beyond asking general questions about student leadership, teacher teams can create job descriptions that are universal in all classrooms. To ensure consistency among teachers and clarity among students, teachers should consistently define the components of the job for students. Teachers should align the job responsibilities as well as the expectations for communication from classroom to classroom so all students know how to answer the questions in figure 8.3 (page 209). Remember, leadership is service, support, and influence, as opposed to mandating and dictating. When teachers create a common expectation for leadership, students have a greater chance of making it happen in all classrooms.

Grade-Level Leadership Teams or Representatives

Some students are natural leaders for the entire class, but we often fail to develop classwide leadership in our students. We, as teacher teams, should remember that the future of our local, regional, state, and national government is sitting in our classrooms. If we begin developing those leadership skills in a purposeful manner, not only will we generate more ownership among students, but we will do our civic duty of preparing future leaders.

In class teams or groups, teachers can select student grade-level leaders or allow students to vote for class representatives to advocate for the class. We shouldn't position these leadership roles as superficial titles. We must create structures so student leaders can advocate for things that matter to students. For example, student leadership teams can take on responsibilities for teachers in the following areas.

- **Lunch dismissal:** Student leadership teams can work together to create lunch dismissal rotations so all classes have the opportunity to be first in line on a regular and fair basis.
- **Recess decisions:** Student leadership teams can meet to develop a needs list for recess or create a presentation to improve recess and share it with the principal.
- **Minor disciplinary infractions:** Student leadership teams can create and manage a student court. In this court, students with disciplinary infractions could elect to have their issue heard before the court, and the court could decide (with principal or teacher approval) how the students could make reparations for their minor disciplinary infraction.
- **Student incentives:** Student leadership teams could work together to generate a list of incentives or positive behavior supports for recommendation to the teacher or principal. Furthermore, the

leadership team could create a plan to raise funds to support the student incentive plan.

- **Service projects:** Student leadership teams have created canned food drives for families in need. Through the Angel Tree Christmas project, they might provide Christmas gifts to needy students. Or students might create improvement projects in the community.
- **Tutorial projects:** Colleges everywhere establish tutoring centers where college students can provide services or take advantage of services to improve their grades. Student leadership teams can create tutorial stations in their school where students tutor peers or study together to help all students grow in their learning.

Teacher team collaboration offers all teachers the opportunity to work together to achieve the common goal of building leadership capacity in all students. When collaboration results in common expectations for student jobs, responsibilities, and leadership tasks, all students have access to the best supports for discovering the leadership within them.

Step 2: Classwide Supports

Every leader leads differently; therefore, teachers should consider how they will differentiate their support for their students. Some teachers might think student leadership consists of a uniform list of expectations, but that's not the case. Leadership presents a variety of challenges for students because of the different situations they encounter, their unique personalities, their communication styles, their patience or lack thereof, and their abilities to relate to others, especially students who are not easy to lead.

As a first step to provide classwide supports for student leadership, teachers should monitor student behaviors with respect to the jobs that students are assigned. Students should be able to accomplish these jobs with little to no support from their teachers. As teachers monitor each student's job effectiveness, they should look for knowledge of the job, work ethic, service and support to others, and communication skills. This observation will drive feedback.

Teachers can use figure 8.6 to help them pattern students' leadership tendencies. This tool is based on the work that William Ferriter (2013) has done in helping teachers pattern their leadership tendencies and build strong relationships so they can lead each other in accomplishing specific goals. While this tool is for adults, teachers can use it to coach students. Often, leaders fail not because they lack the effort or ability to get things done. They fail because they don't know how to influence and serve the personalities and tendencies of those they wish to lead.

Relationship Leadership

Relationship leaders:

- Trust everyone's intentions
- Give people the benefit of the doubt
- Believe in we instead of me

Vision Leadership

Vision leaders:

- Value ideas over individuals
- Define what the future looks like
- See a realistic future

Action Leadership

Action leaders:

- Define doable steps
- Focus on what needs to be done
- Make things happen

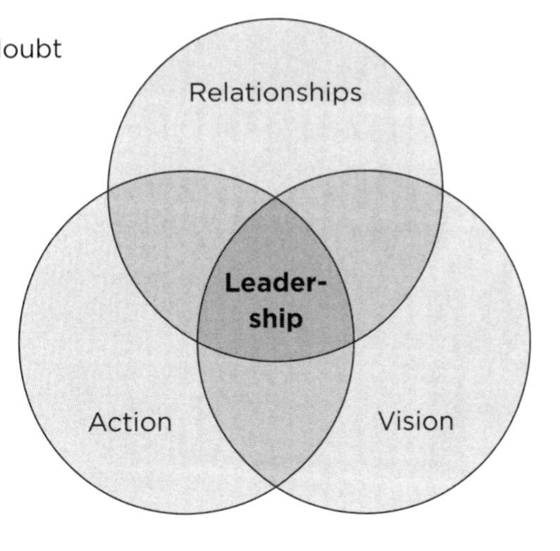

Source: Adapted from Ferriter, 2013.

Figure 8.6: The three leadership tendencies.

As shown in figure 8.6, relationship leaders are focused on building relationships as they lead, but that often results in relationships' inhibiting their ability to get things done. Vision leaders have powerful ideas and can define what the future could look like; however, they struggle with the ability to communicate their ideas to others who can't see the same vision. Finally, action leaders get things done and build strong plans of action, and as a result, they can steamroll people they work with who have different opinions. Every leadership strength is also a weakness, and great teachers find ways to help students learn more about those strengths and weaknesses in their own leadership.

Teachers can use their observations to pencil in where they believe students fall in the figure's Venn diagram. Next, teachers can provide a mini-lesson on the three leadership tendencies and then ask students to rate themselves. Teachers then compare their observations to students' perceptions and use those data to provide ongoing support for each tendency and coach students throughout the year. This framework is not an absolute tool to help students grow in leadership, but it does give teachers a great starting point to help students discover their leadership tendencies.

In addition to determining students' leadership tendencies, teachers might determine what kind of leadership influence students have in class and in school. In *Simplifying Response to Intervention*, authors Buffum et al. (2012) provide the tool in figure 8.7 to help principals select teacher leaders for campus leadership teams. While powerful for helping schools select teacher leaders, this tool is also effective for helping teachers identify the leadership strengths within their classroom and use that information as a starting point for building leadership capacity in students. Teachers can list each student's name in the category that they feel best matches the student's leadership style. From there, the teacher can use the information to help students see their leadership strengths and those of classmates, and make plans to develop their leadership style in the other categories.

Source: Adapted from Buffum et al., 2012, pp. 25–26.

Figure 8.7: Types of student leaders.

Power players are student leaders who lead the entire class to get back on track with a word or two. They have tremendous influence because they typically are the most liked or most popular. Teachers should know who the power players are in order to use those students' leadership skills to move activities and initiatives forward (Buffum et al., 2012).

Credibility leaders aren't loud in their leadership. They are respected because of their ability to work well with others. Sometimes, they lead more with their actions than with their words. *Expertise leaders* don't lead with their words or their actions, but their work speaks for itself. Their talents can inspire students to chase excellence in their own learning and abilities. Finally, some students are just *natural leaders*. They know how to organize students around a cause. They can rally the troops when difficulties or frustrations arise (Buffum et al., 2012). Similar to the information gained from figure 8.6 (page 215), teachers can use the information gained from figure 8.7 to provide specific leadership support for students. For example, if a teacher identifies a student as a power player, he or she would consider how to develop the student's abilities in expertise or credibility.

Finally, leadership instruction can come from others. Teachers can invite other leaders, such as campus principals, assistant principals, or even district leaders, to provide lessons on leadership or feedback to students. Sometimes, a different voice is the perfect classwide support to help students grow in their abilities as leaders.

Classwide supports for leadership work best as part of regular instruction. They should inspire students to become learning leaders and make the classroom environment a better place for all students.

Step 3: Individualized Student Supports

Just like with the other levels in the Hierarchy of Student Excellence, students will need individualized supports when teacher team and classwide supports prove unsuccessful. It is important to remember that we best support students when we identify their strengths first. From there, we identify their leadership tendencies (relational, vision, and action), and then determine what type of leader they are (power player, credibility leader, expertise leader, or natural leader).

Next, teachers can identify students' leadership weaknesses or areas in need of improvement. Perhaps the area for growth is communicating, working with like-minded peers, or working with diverse personalities. Based on narrowing the focus to the greatest area of need, the teacher can create a personalized plan of action to help each student grow in his or her leadership skills.

Teachers can use the problem-solving tool in figure 8.8 to evaluate student proficiency in leadership. As you work through the questions, ensure that any student difficulties are not due to a deficit in the lower levels of the Hierarchy of Student Excellence. Overlooking this step could cause you to create a plan for an issue that is not affecting the student's growth as a learner.

Individualized Student Support Problem-Solving Tool: Student Leadership	
Question 1: Has the teacher team created common expectations and supports for all students at this level? (Circle yes or no.) (If your answer is yes, continue. If your answer is no, stop and correct this area.)	Yes No
Question 2: Based on the team's work, has the teacher created his or her classwide structure for student leadership? (Circle yes or no.) (If your answer is yes, continue. If your answer is no, stop and correct this area.)	Yes No
Question 3: Is the student's failure due to deficiencies in the lower levels of the Hierarchy of Student Excellence? (Circle yes or no.) (If your answer is yes, stop this plan, and address the deficient level in the hierarchy. If your answer is no, proceed to question 4.)	Yes No

Figure 8.8: Individualized student support problem-solving tool—student leadership.

continued →

Individualized Student Support Problem-Solving Tool: Student Leadership

Question 4: Which student is struggling with leadership?

Student: ______________________________

List the student's strengths and difficulties with each component at this level.

Strengths:

Difficulties:

Question 5: What are the student's leadership tendencies and actions? (Check all that apply.)

Relational Leadership	Vision Leadership	Action Leadership
☐ Values students over ideas	☐ Values ideas over individuals	☐ Defines action steps for a plan
☐ Believes in teamwork	☐ Defines what the future looks like	☐ Focuses on what needs to be done
☐ Gives people the benefit of the doubt	☐ Sees a realistic future	☐ Makes things happen
☐ Has difficulty getting things done	☐ Makes people feel inferior or stupid	☐ Fails to involve others in the process
☐ Allows others to stall the team's work	☐ Makes the future difficult to understand	☐ Argues with others who have a different focus
☐ Lacks an ability to hold people accountable	☐ Dismisses ideas that are not part of his or her plan	☐ Frustrates people by making things happen

Notes:

Question 6: Based on responses from question 5, what kind of leader is the student, and why do you think this? (Check the most applicable answer.)

☐ Power player: Has relationships with students that can impact the class climate and makes things happen when he or she gets on board

☐ Credibility leader: Has the majority of students' respect and can influence students because of the respect they have for him or her

<table>
<tr><td colspan="2">

☐ Expertise leader: Is seen as the intellectual of the group and can use this intellect to influence the class

☐ Natural leader: Is a born leader and can unite students around a common goal and lead them to achieve it

Notes:

</td></tr>
<tr><td colspan="2">

Question 7: Based on the identified leadership struggles, tendencies, and style, in what specific leadership areas does the student need improvement?

☐ Communicating with peers
☐ Commitment to actions
☐ Motivating other students
☐ Trusting and respecting other students
☐ Modeling successful learning for others
☐ Organizing ideas
☐ Making a plan of action
☐ Building relationships
☐ Managing conflict
☐ Other

</td></tr>
<tr><td colspan="2">

Question 8: What are the goal and the deadline for the student to successfully embrace student leadership?

Goal:

Deadline:

</td></tr>
<tr><td>

Question 9: Did the student meet the goal by the deadline? (Circle yes or no.)

(If your answer is yes, continue the support. If your answer is no, return to question 4.)

</td><td>Yes No</td></tr>
<tr><td colspan="2">Notes:</td></tr>
</table>

Visit ***go.SolutionTree.com/instruction*** *for a free reproducible version of this figure.*

Conclusion

In this chapter, you learned that leading means much more than being in charge of students and bossing them around. Leadership is service, support, and influence, and our classrooms can serve as laboratories where students learn how to become transformational leaders. In order to help students discover the leader inside them, teachers need to equip themselves with a plan of action to teach students about leadership and support them when they struggle as leaders.

Every student can be a leader, and every student has a specific area of expertise to lead in the classroom. Good leaders model for others, communicate positively, and support their peers in reaching their goals. Students can work toward five different areas of leadership—(1) self-leadership, (2) group leadership, (3) class or club leadership, (4) interschool or civic leadership, and (5) global leadership—and we should give students opportunities to lead in all these areas. Additionally, we should teach leadership by providing students jobs in the classroom with structured supports that help them learn and understand how to accomplish the jobs. By providing a variety of leadership opportunities and monitoring student progress, teachers will help students find the leaders inside them.

This chapter concludes with a reflection tool (pages 221–222) that teachers can use to evaluate their understanding of the challenges they face when inspiring students to become confident, successful leaders. As you consider the questions and your responses to them, explore possibilities for improving those systems, including teacher team collaboration, classwide supports, and individualized student supports, based on the information and ideas in this chapter.

Reflection Tool: Student Leadership

Answer the following questions to help you create a more inspiring classroom where students have access to many leadership opportunities that they can apply both inside and outside the classroom.

Teacher Team Collaboration

- Has our team established plans to provide consistency with student leadership?
- How well do team members lead one another in deepening our knowledge of leadership?
- How well do we work together to develop expectations for student jobs and student leadership?
- How well do we work together to create grade-level leadership for our team?
- When a teacher experiences difficulty with any component of student leadership, what steps does he or she take to seek help from the team?

Classwide Supports

- How well do I model leadership for students?
- How well have I aligned my plans for student leadership with those developed by the team?
- How well do I monitor students to determine their leadership tendencies?
- How well can I determine what kind of leader each student is?
- How well have I created leadership initiatives for the class to undertake?
- How often do I seek campus or district leaders' leadership support for students?

Individualized Student Supports

- When a student struggles as a leader, how well do I consistently determine the root cause?

- Once I determine the potential root cause, how well do I verify that the failure is not due to my classroom supports or inconsistency from the team?
- How well do I ensure that the student's difficulty is not due to a deficit in a lower level of the Hierarchy of Student Excellence?
- How effective am I at identifying the student's strengths so I can leverage these strengths to address areas for growth?
- When I prescribe a personalized support for leadership, how committed am I to providing the intervention with frequency and consistency?
- How consistently do I gauge student growth in the target area to determine if my intervention was effective?
- When the student is still unsuccessful, how well do I reflect and refine the intervention to better help the student?
- When my efforts to help the student continue to fail, how well do I reach out to my team members to help me better respond to the student?

References and Resources

Adelabu, D. H. (2007). Time perspective and school membership as correlates to academic achievement among African American adolescents. *Adolescence, 42*(167), 525–538.

Adelman, H. S., Taylor, L. (2006). *The school leader's guide to student learning supports: New directions for addressing barriers to learning*. Thousand Oaks, CA: Corwin Press.

Armstrong, P. (n.d.). *Bloom's taxonomy*. Accessed at https://cft.vanderbilt.edu/guides-sub-pages/blooms-taxonomy on July 6, 2018.

Bass, B. M. (1985). *Leadership and performance beyond expectations*. New York: Free Press.

Bass, B. M. (1990). *Bass and Stogdill's handbook of leadership*. New York: Free Press.

Basye, D. (2018, January 24). *Personalized vs. differentiated vs. individualized learning*. Accessed at www.iste.org/explore/articledetail?articleid=124 on March 27, 2019.

Bloom, B. S. (Ed.). (1956). *Taxonomy of educational objectives: The classification of educational goals*. New York: Longmans.

Buffum, A., & Mattos, M. (Eds.). (2015). *It's about time: Planning interventions and extensions in elementary school*. Bloomington, IN: Solution Tree Press.

Buffum, A., Mattos, M., & Malone, J. (2018). *Taking action: A handbook for RTI at Work™*. Bloomington, IN: Solution Tree Press.

Buffum, A., Mattos, M., & Weber, C. (2009). *Pyramid response to intervention: RTI, professional learning communities, and how to respond when kids don't learn*. Bloomington, IN: Solution Tree Press.

Buffum, A., Mattos, M., & Weber, C. (2012). *Simplifying response to intervention: Four essential guiding principles*. Bloomington, IN: Solution Tree Press.

Carroll, T. (2009). The next generation of learning teams. *Phi Delta Kappan, 91*(2), 8–13.

Centers for Disease Control and Prevention. (2016). *Youth violence: Facts at a glance*. Accessed at https://www.cdc.gov/violenceprevention/pdf/yv-datasheet.pdf on March 27, 2019.

Centers for Disease Control and Prevention. (2019, April 2). *Adverse childhood experiences (ACEs)*. Accessed at www.cdc.gov/violenceprevention/childabuseandneglect/acestudy/index.html on June 10, 2019.

Childhelp. (2018). *Child abuse statistics and facts*. Accessed at www.childhelp.org/child-abuse-statistics on March 27, 2019.

Crisis Prevention Institute. (n.d.). *Nonviolent Crisis Intervention: Effective skills to safely manage and prevent difficult behavior.* Accessed at https://www.crisisprevention.com/What-We-Do/Nonviolent-Crisis-Intervention on March 27, 2019.

Daggett, W. R., & Gendron, S. A. (2015, June). *Rigorous learning: Bringing students from our classrooms to successful lives.* Rexford, NY: International Center for Leadership in Education. Accessed at www.leadered.com/pdf/2015MSC_BridgingStudentsFromOurClassroomstoSuccessfulLives.pdf on March 27, 2019.

Danielson, C. (2013). *The framework for teaching evaluation instrument.* Princeton, NJ: Danielson Group.

Day2Day Parenting. (2013). *Q&A: What is a normal attention span?* Accessed at https://day2dayparenting.com/qa-normal-attention-span on July 30, 2019.

Dictionary.com (n.d.). *Effective.* Accessed at www.dictionary.com/browse/effective on August 16, 2019.

Doppelt, Y., & Barak, M. (2002). Pupils identify key aspects and outcomes of a technological learning environment. *Journal of Technology Studies, 28*(1), 22–28.

Duckworth, A. L., Peterson, C., Matthews, M. D., & Kelly, D. R. (2007). Grit: Perseverance and passion for long-term goals. *Journal of Personality and Social Psychology, 92*(6), 1087–1101.

DuFour, R., DuFour, R., & Eaker, R. (2008). *Revisiting Professional Learning Communities at Work: New insights for improving schools.* Bloomington, IN: Solution Tree Press.

DuFour, R., DuFour, R., Eaker, R., & Karhanek, G. (2004). *Whatever it takes: How professional learning communities respond when kids don't learn.* Bloomington, IN: Solution Tree Press.

DuFour, R., DuFour, R., Eaker, R., Many, T. W., & Mattos, M. (2016). *Learning by doing: A handbook for Professional Learning Communities at Work* (3rd ed.). Bloomington, IN: Solution Tree Press.

DuFour, R., & Marzano, R. J. (2011). *Leaders of learning: How district, school, and classroom leaders improve student achievement.* Bloomington, IN: Solution Tree Press.

Dweck, C. S. (2000). *Self-theories: Their role in motivation, personality, and development.* New York: Psychology Press.

Ferriter, W. M. (2013, July 4). *What does leadership on professional learning teams look like?* [Blog post]. Accessed at http://blog.williamferriter.com/2013/07/04/what-does-leadership-on-professional-learning-teams-look-like on March 27, 2019.

Ferriter, W. M. (2015). *Creating purpose-driven learning experiences.* Bloomington, IN: Solution Tree Press.

Ferriter, W. M. (2017, April 2). "Once you know better, you have an obligation to do better." Rick DuFour [Tweet]. Accessed at https://twitter.com/plugusin/status/848621234292224005 on July 8, 2018.

Ferriter, W. M., & Cancellieri, P. J. (2017). *Creating a culture of feedback.* Bloomington, IN: Solution Tree Press.

Fisher, D., & Frey, N. (2008). *Better learning through structured teaching: A framework for the gradual release of responsibility*. Alexandria, VA: Association for Supervision and Curriculum Development.

Frey, N., Fisher, D. & Gonzalez, A. (2010). *Literacy 2.0: Reading and writing in 21st century classrooms*. Bloomington, IN: Solution Tree Press.

Gonzalez, S. (2018). *Note-taking: A research roundup* [Blog post]. Accessed at www.cultof pedagogy.com/note-taking on July 24, 2019.

Hansen, A. (2014, February 11). *Clarity precedes competence—applies to kids too!* [Blog post]. Accessed at www.allthingsplc.info/blog/view/246/clarity-precedes -competencemdashapplies-to-students-too on October 5, 2018.

Hanushek, E. A. (2005). The economics of school quality. *German Economic Review*, *6*(3), 269–286.

Hattie, J. (2009). *Visible learning: A synthesis of over 800 meta-analyses relating to achievement*. New York: Routledge.

Hattie, J. (2012). Feedback in schools. In R. M. Sutton, M. J. Hornsey, & K. M. Douglas (Eds.), *Feedback: The communication of praise, criticism, and advice* (pp. 265–278). New York: Lang.

Hattie, J. (2017) *Visible learning plus 250+ influences on student achievement*. Accessed at https://visible-learning.org/wp-content/uploads/2018/03/VLPLUS-252-Influences -Hattie-ranking-DEC-2017.pdf on August 16, 2019.

Haycock, K. (1998). Good teaching matters . . . a lot. *Thinking K–16*, *3*(2), 3–15.

Heathers, G. (1977). A working definition of individualized instruction. *Educational Leadership*, *34*(5), 342–345. Accessed at www.ascd.org/ASCD/pdf/journals/ed_lead /el_197702_heathers.pdf on March 27, 2019.

Himmele, P., & Himmele, W. (2011). *Total participation techniques: Making every student an active learner*. Alexandria, VA: Association for Supervision and Curriculum Development.

Jensen, E. (2014). *A descriptive study of differences between teachers at high and low performing Title I elementary schools*. Santa Barbara, CA: Fielding Graduate University.

Jensen, E. (2016). *Poor students, rich teaching: Mindsets for change*. Bloomington, IN: Solution Tree Press.

Johnson, B. (2014, August 14). *Deeper learning: Why cross-curricular teaching is essential* [Blog post]. Accessed at https://www.edutopia.org/blog/cross-curricular-teaching -deeper-learning-ben-johnson on March 17, 2016.

Killian, S. (2015). 8 strategies Robert Marzano and John Hattie agree on. *The Australian Society for Evidence Based Teaching*. Accessed at www.evidencebasedteaching.org.au /robert-marzano-vs-john-hattie on March 27, 2019.

Klem, A. M., & Connell, J. P. (2005). Engaging youth in school. In L. R. Sherrod, C. A. Flanagan, R. Kassimir, & A. K. Syvertsen (Eds.), *Youth activism: An international encyclopedia* (pp. 1–2). Westport, CT: Greenwood.

Kouzes, J., & Posner, B. (2018). *The student leadership challenge: Five practices for becoming an exemplary leader* (3rd ed.) [eBook]. San Francisco: Wiley.

Mangels, J. A., Good, C., Whiteman, R. C., Maniscalco, B., & Dweck, C. S. (2012). Emotion blocks the path to learning under stereotype threat. *Social Cognitive and Affective Neuroscience, 7*(2), 230–241.

Martin, D. J., & Loomis, K. S. (2007). *Building teachers: A constructivist approach to introducing education.* Belmont, CA: Wadsworth.

Martin, G. (2017). *Three surefire ways to develop student leaders for the future.* Accessed at https://aboutleaders.com/student-leaders/#gs.toe22a on August 4, 2019.

Marzano, R. J. (2003). *Classroom management that works: Research-based strategies for every teacher.* Alexandria, VA: Association for Supervision and Curriculum Development.

Marzano, R. J., Pickering, D. J., & Pollock, J. E. (2001). *Classroom instruction that works: Research-based strategies for increasing student achievement.* Alexandria, VA: Association for Supervision and Curriculum Development.

Marzano, R. J., Waters, T., & McNulty, B. A. (2005). *School leadership that works: From research to results.* Alexandria, VA: Association for Supervision and Curriculum Development.

Maslow, A. H. (1943). A theory of human motivation. *Psychological Review, 50*(4), 370–396.

Maslow, A. H. (1954). *Motivation and personality.* New York: Harper.

Maxwell, J. C. (2019). *Brainyquote: John C. Maxwell.* Accessed at www.brainyquote.com/quotes/john_c_maxwell_383606 on August 3, 2019.

McLeod, S. (2018). *Maslow's Hierarchy of Needs.* Accessed at https://www.simplypsychology.org/maslow.html on March 28, 2019.

Minero, E. (2017, October 4) *When students are traumatized, teachers are too.* Accessed at https://www.edutopia.org/article/when-students-are-traumatized-teachers-are-too on March 27, 2019.

Mitchell, A. (n.d.). *American presidents on education: 20 quotes throughout White House history* [Blog post]. Accessed at https://blog.4tests.com/american-presidents-on-education-20-quotes-throughout-white-house-history on March 28, 2019.

My Safe Harbor. (2019). *U.S. single parent households.* Accessed at http://lib.post.ca.gov/Publications/Building%20a%20Career%20Pipeline%20Documents/Safe_Harbor.pdf on July 28, 2019.

National Center for Education Statistics. (2016). *Table 204.10. Number and percentage of public school students eligible for free or reduced-price lunch, by state: Selected years, 2000–01 through 2014–15.* Accessed at https://nces.ed.gov/programs/digest/d16/tables/dt16_204.10.asp on July 2, 2018.

National Education Association. (2011, November 15). *NEA shares strategies for developing family-school-community partnerships* [Press release]. Accessed at www.nea.org/home/49666.htm on March 28, 2019.

National Research Council and Institute of Medicine. (2004). *Engaging schools: Fostering high school students' motivation to learn*. Washington, DC: National Academies Press.

Nye, P. A., Crooks, T. J., Powley, M., & Tripp, G. (1984) Student note-taking related to university examination performance. *Higher Education, 13*(1), 85–97.

Papert, S. (1998, June 2). *Child power: Keys to the new learning of the digital century. Speech delivered at the eleventh Colin Cherry Memorial Lecture on Communication at Imperial College London*. Accessed at www.papert.org/articles/Childpower.html on September 1, 2018.

Phillips, M. (2014, August 5). *A place for learning: The physical environment of classrooms* [Blog post]. Accessed at https://www.edutopia.org/blog/the-physical-environment-of-classrooms-mark-phillips on March 2, 2016.

Positive Behavioral Interventions & Supports. (n.d.). *Technical Assistance Center*. Accessed at www.pbis.org on September 26, 2018.

Pungello, E. P., Kainz, K., Burchinal, M., Wasik, B. H., Sparling, J. J., Ramey, C. T., et al. (2010). Early educational intervention, early cumulative risk, and the early home environment as predictors of young adult outcomes within a high-risk sample. *Child Development, 81*(1), 410–426.

Reeves, D. (2002). *The leader's guide to standards: A blueprint for educational equity and excellence*. San Francisco: Jossey-Bass.

Rivkin, S. G., Hanushek, E. A., & Kain, J. F. (2005). Teachers, schools, and academic achievement. *Econometrica, 73*(2), 417–458.

Rockoff, J. E. (2004). The impact of individual teachers on student achievement: Evidence from panel data. *American Economic Review, 94*(2), 247–252.

RTI Action Network (2019, July 20). *What is RTI?* Accessed at www.rtinetwork.org/learn/what/whatisrti on August 16, 2019.

Sanfelippo, J. (2018, November 24). *One-minute walk to work video #LeadershipChallenge* [Video file]. Accessed at www.instagram.com/p/BqkX3E5B9uZ/?utm_source=ig_share_sheet&igshid=87cm5eyhrf9f on March 27, 2019.

Schlechty, P. C. (1994, January). *Increasing student engagement*. Columbia: Missouri Leadership Academy.

Schlechty, P. C. (2011). *Engaging students: The next level of working on the work*. San Francisco: Jossey-Bass.

Schlechty Center. (n.d.). *Schlechty Center on engagement*. Accessed at https://studylib.net/doc/18233308/schlechty-center-on-engagement on March 27, 2019.

Sinek, S. (2009). *Start with why: How great leaders inspire everyone to take action*. New York: Penguin.

Sparks, S. (2016, August 11). Student mobility: How it affects learning. *Education Week*. Accessed at https://www.edweek.org/ew/issues/student-mobility/index.html on March 28, 2019.

Taylor, L., & Parsons, J. (2011). Improving student engagement. *Current Issues in Education, 14*(1). Accessed at http://cie.asu.edu/ojs/index.php/cieatasu/article/viewFile/745/162 on April 11, 2016.

Texas Education Agency. (n.d.). *Texas Essential Knowledge and Skills*. Accessed at https://tea.texas.gov/curriculum/teks on June 13, 2019.

Texas Education Agency. (2016). *Texas Teacher Evaluation and Support System (T-TESS) appraiser handbook*. Austin, TX: Author.

Webb, N. L. (2002, March 28). *Depth-of-knowledge levels for four content areas*. Accessed at http://facstaff.wcer.wisc.edu/normw/All%20content%20areas%20%20DOK%20levels%2032802.pdf on December 31, 2015.

Wiggins, G. (2014, January 1). *Final exams vs. projects: Nope, false dichotomy—A practical start to the blog year* [Blog post]. Accessed at https://grantwiggins.wordpress.com/2014/01/01/final-exams-vs-projects-nope-false-dichotomy-a-practical-start-to-the-blog-year on March 28, 2019.

Wiliam, D. (2018). *Embedded formative assessment* (2nd ed.). Bloomington, IN: Solution Tree Press.

Wink, J. R. (2017). *A leader's guide to excellence in every classroom: Creating support systems for teacher success*. Bloomington, IN: Solution Tree Press.

Wink, J. R. (2018, November 22). *Let's thank teachers for more than teaching kids*. Accessed at http://leadlearner2012.blogspot.com/2018/11/lets-thank-teachers-for-more-than.html on June 10, 2019.

Wolpert-Gawron, H. (2015, February 24). *Kids speak out on student engagement* [Blog post]. Accessed at https://www.edutopia.org/blog/student-engagement-stories-heather-wolpert-gawron on March 9, 2016.

Index

O

P

Q

R